THE CHURCH AND WOMEN

A COMPENDIUM

THE CHURCH AND WOMEN

A COMPENDIUM

Edited by Helmut Moll

IGNATIUS PRESS   SAN FRANCISCO

Cover by Riz Boncan Marsella

With ecclesiastical approval
© 1988 Ignatius Press, San Francisco
All rights reserved
ISBN 0-89870-164-3
Library of Congress catalogue number 88-81309
Printed in the United States of America

CONTENTS

CONTENTS

PREFACE

It is a pleasing task to write these words of introduction to the contributions which follow. I thank Father Joseph Fessio for his kind suggestion that I should do so. Father Fessio and I share a certain common heritage, so to speak, though he is from the United States and I am from Germany; for we both were students of Professor Joseph Ratzinger at the University of Regensburg. We met in the context of a reunion of Cardinal Ratzinger's former students and discovered, in conversation, that the Church in our two countries is facing similar challenges from an increasingly secularized society, challenges which have recently concentrated with particular force and criticism upon the identity and role of women in the Church. The idea for this compendium of articles, originally published in various German theological reviews, was born in the recognition that our common situations could be helped by some public exchange of the reflections of serious thinkers on the subject.

The various essays in this volume, then, represent approaches to the question of women in the Church by several contemporary theologians most of whom have written in German and whose contributions are now being made available for the first time to the English-speaking world in translation. These articles reflect the wide range of recent discussion, and include the issue of feminism, the possibilities of ministry in the diaconate, the theme of women's emancipation, and the repercussions of the question for other areas of concern as, for example, the role and importance of the family. These particular works have been chosen because all of them strive to defend and deepen Christian reflection on the role and identity of women today. They merit particular attention because their approach to clarifying the Christian task and mission of women is developed in a context which remains faithful to the data of Scripture, the witness of Catholic tradition, and the Magisterium of the Church.

While the discussion of these issues should and will continue to develop in the future, it is hoped that the publication of these essays for the first time in English will make a contribution which is enriching to present considerations in the English speaking world. At the same time, the opportunity for Americans to listen to German voices (and vice versa) is in itself a kind of Catholic experience which constitutes a hopeful sign of what the future may bring.

Helmut J. Moll

I

THE CHANGED
SELF-UNDERSTANDING OF THE
CHRISTIAN WOMAN

I

KARL LEHMANN

THE PLACE OF WOMEN AS A PROBLEM IN THEOLOGICAL ANTHROPOLOGY

Translated by Robert E. Wood

The place of women in the Church and in society belongs among the most important topics of our time. In 1963, Pope John XXIII, in his encyclical *Pacem in Terris,* said that this question belongs to the three most decisive "signs of the times", under which he named the economic and social improvement of the working classes and the development of a greater awareness of human rights.

> It is obvious to everyone that women are now taking a part in public life. This is happening more rapidly perhaps in nations with a Christian tradition, and more slowly, but broadly, among peoples who have inherited other traditions or cultures. Since women are becoming ever more conscious of their human dignity, they will not tolerate being treated as inanimate objects or mere instruments, but claim, both in domestic and in public life, the rights and duties that befit a human person.[1]

Meanwhile, this problem has become much more pressing in the Church and in society. Subsequent radical social changes have powerfully altered the self-understanding of women. Likewise here, the years 1968–1971 form a great divide. Many see the beginning of the end of a "patriarchal" order of society in which the man of the house had disposal, not only of possessions and servants, but also of his wife and children. The man alone appeared to be a human being fully capable of action and fully mature. For a hundred and fifty years the movement for the

---

[1] *Pacem in Terris, Peace on Earth* (America Press, 1963), I, 41, p. 14.

emancipation of women[2] systematically fought against this—real or alleged—tutelage through a world completely oriented toward the male, against so-called "androcentrism". While a first phase of this movement required a properly political majority and ultimately an economic, social and cultural equalization (equal rights as a citizen, active and passive freedom of choice, juridical equality in civil law and in criminal law, the right to education, the right to a profession), the present women's movement carries through the basic principle of equality radically and thus into all areas of life. The particular goals of the recent women's movement are well-known: equal pay for equal work, unrestricted opportunities for education and advancement, removal of discrimination in the allotment of positions and in the right to security or pension. The core demands of feminism are still more radical: control over one's own body, overthrow of sex-specific roles in child-rearing and in the place of employment, repeal of repressive laws, alternatives to the nuclear family and new methods of child-care, termination of male authority and possessive dominance over the wife, overthrow of every relation between people having the character of suppression. "Self-realization" is the goal of this revolution, desiring to free women from biological and physical "coercions" and to eliminate these coercions from social relations.

Revolt against "male society" should develop into the construction of a new human society. From this comes a "cultural revolution of the feminine". "We wish to destroy the patriarchate before it destroys the planet."[3]

Thus the contemporary women's movement, especially in its radical forms, approaches other movements in search of alternative forms of life. Less radical counter-movements to this basic tendency could scarcely make a difference. One must see the complete extent and context of these

[2] See H. Schroder, ed., *Die Frau ist frei geboren*, Texte zur Frauenemanzipation, Beck'sche Schwarze Series 201, 231, 2 vols. (Munich, 1979, 1981). A third volume is pending. Cf. E. Moltmann-Wendel, ed., *Menschenrechte für die Frau. Christliche Initiativen zur Frauenbefreiung* (Munich, 1974); G. Distel and N. Hasselmann, eds., *Kennzeichen. Studien und Problemberichte aus dem Projeckt "Frauen als Innovationsgruppen" des Deutschen Nationalkomitees des Lutherischen Weltbundes*, 3 vols. (Gelnhausen-Stein, 1977–1978).

[3] *Frauenjahrbuch* 1976 (Munich, 1976), p. 106.

movements if one wishes to assess them. The women's movement belongs to the contemporary tendencies toward emancipation which concern the self-liberation of man from political, social, cultural, and natural dependencies. Of course, women's liberation is also part of a process of individualization that has been around now for almost two hundred years. Yet the feminist challenge in the radical groups shows precisely where the ultimate decisions really fall. At base it is a question not only of strategies for obtaining equality, developing a new alternative subculture, fighting against male dominance, and realizing a change in sexual roles; it is also not only a matter of women's problems. It is a question of humanness as such. The recent women's movement has brought to light the fact that the decisive answers to our problem are directly or indirectly predetermined by global views of the meaning of human life and the order of human existence as such. Thus the battle over the place of women in the Church and in society is in essence a fight concerning anthropology. This holds no less for the theological dimension. Not infrequently the problems that arise are treated too shortsightedly as only questions of right regulations or are immediately linked to the highest theological norms and declarations. However, the norm is often an anthropological prejudice that rules in a hidden fashion.

This methodical approach is likewise important because the Old and New Testaments, in a great variety of important texts (see, above all, Gen 1–3; Rom 5:12; 1 Cor 7:1–16; 11:3–15; 2 Cor 11:2; Gal 3:28; Eph 5:22–33), present principles, impulses, and orientations of decisive import indeed for our present questions; yet it is also a question to what extent an "andro-centric worldview" that does not itself necessarily belong to the irremovable core of revelation governs them—at least in some places. The almost boundless literature shows that a considerable part of exegesis itself is, consciously or unconsciously, conditioned by an anthropological pre-understanding which governs it.[4] A formal hermeneutic of scriptural statements is not sufficient for this purpose.

---

[4] See Distel and Hasselmann, *Kennzeichen,* especially the detailed analyses by F. Crusemann, H. Thyen, K. Thraede, et al. For further literature, cf. notes 35–41, 56, 57, 62 below.

The following models represent only a sample.[5] They are consciously kept scanty and should be understood as basic types of possible answers. Still, they serve chiefly as the preparation of a systematic outline.

I. BASIC ANTHROPOLOGICAL MODELS FOR CLARIFYING SEXUAL DIFFERENCE: THE MODEL OF SIMULTANEOUS SUBORDINATION AND EQUALITY

Enough has already been written about the dominant belief in the subordination of women in classical theology. A. Mitterer, already in 1933, in his article, "Man and Woman according to the Biological World-View of St. Thomas and of the Present", had referred to the "three-fold inferiority of women and the superiority of the male".[6] The male is the complete, mature, superior representative of the species; the female is the imperfect, inferior representative. "There is inferiority of women in development (*biogenetic* inferiority), in being (*qualitative* inferiority) and in activity (*functional* inferiority)."[7] According to the Aristotelian view of generation held by Thomas, a girl comes into the world as a substitute product of nature because of the failure to produce a boy (*mas occasionatur*). The male is the normal product. This inferiority is the sexually determined difference and constitutes the essential distinction between man and woman. The woman relates to the man as the imperfect and defective to the perfect. In addition to corporeal inferiority there is also a spiritual inferiority. Woman is spiritually and morally weaker. She is related to the man as sensibility is related to reason or as *ratio inferior* to *ratio superior* in humankind as such. Moreover, Mitterer already speaks of

---

[5] Cf. the important and stimulating book by J. Burri, *"Als Mann und Frau schuf er sie"*. *Differenz der Geschlechter aus moral- und praktisch-theologischer Sicht* (Zurich, 1977), pp. 18ff., 23ff., 32ff., 40ff.

[6] "Mann und Weib nach dem biologischen Weltbild des heiligen Thomas und dem der Gegenwart", *Zeitschrift für katholische Theologie* 57 (1933): 491–556, especially pp. 514ff. *Die Zeugung der Organismen, insbesonders des Menschen nach dem Weltbild des hl. Thomas von Aquin und dem der Gegenwart* (Vienna, 1949); *Die Entwicklungslehre Augustins im Vergleich mit dem Weltbild des hl. Thomas von Aquin und dem der Gegenwart* (Vienna, 1956).

[7] Mitterer, "Mann und Weib", p. 514.

androcentrism and androcracy, which he attributes to a biologically untenable world view.[8]

Yet this form of triple-based subordination is balanced off in the order of redemption by a personal-religious equality between man and woman. Being made in the image of God (see Gen 1:27) is treated as a quality of the spiritual soul, through which the woman is equal to the man in this respect. In her concrete bodily-sexual constitution she is made from man and for man (see Gen 2:18ff.). Thus the complete equality of women as human beings will be first realized in the final resurrection. K. E. Borresen has indicated in his numerous works how, because of this anthropological disposition (subordination in the order of creation and equality in the order of redemption), there are irremovable conflicts in classical theology.[9] The consequences are familiar: a woman cannot represent the authority of Jesus Christ by reason of her essential subordination. Last but not least, because of this women are excluded from the priesthood. In emergencies, only if no man is present may a woman baptize. By virginity or widowhood a woman avoids her subordination better than in marriage. Yet it would be an erroneous conclusion to try to infer the evaluation of women in medieval theology from this basic anthropological position alone.[10]

Naturally, the hypothesis of subordination is no longer taken seriously in this form. Yet one must see that not a few proponents of an actual current devaluation of women hold a similar basic conception and draw from it radical consequences which Thomas, of course, had never deduced. Examples of such might be taken from the discussion in the nineteenth

---

[8] See the numerous examples in Mitterer, "Mann und Weib", p. 521, 525ff.

[9] *Subordination et Equivalence. Nature et Rôle de la Femme d'après Augustin et Thomas d'Aquin* (Oslo, 1968); *Die anthropologischen Grundlagen der Beziehungen zwischen Mann und Frau in der klassischen Theologie,* in *Concilium* 12 (1976): 10–17.

[10] See *La Femme dans les Civilisations des X–XIII Siècles. Actes du colloque tenu a Poitiers* (Sept. 23–25, 1976) (Poitiers, 1977); R. Thomas, ed., *Petrus Abaelardus* (Trier, 1980); A. Zimmerman, ed., *Soziale Ordnungen im Selbstverständnis des Mittelalters,* in *Miscellanea Mediaevalia* 12 (Berlin, 1979; D. Baker, ed., *Medieval Women* (Oxford, 1978); further literature and an informative overview is provided by E. Gossmann, *Die streitbaren Schwestern. Was will die Feministische Theologie?* (Freiburg: Herderbücherei 879, 1981), pp. 79ff., 134ff. S. Shahar, *Die Frau im Mittelalter* (Königstein, 1981), is informative on social history but less dependable theologically.

and twentieth centuries of A. Schopenhauer, P. J. Möbius and O.
Weininger.[11] There is no doubt that also in many moderate theories of a
so-called "natural hierarchy" between man and woman a questionable
aspect of feminine subordination is also present. Not seldom the element
of subordination can also appear in a still ultimately ambiguous glorifica-
tion of women, for example, in the praise of a woman's capacity for
devotion and her readiness to serve. Where a metaphysical or biological
inferiority of women is rejected, the subordination thesis is not entirely
overcome in its consequences, as E. Brunner has shown in the example of
the Reformation dogmaticians: the male is the free and creative spirit.[12]
The Christian inversion of all values must understand the subordination
of women given in creation as reciprocal service, which, to be sure, is
first realized in eternity where there is no longer sub-ordination and
super-ordination.

Thus it becomes clear that the basic anthropological position here
presented does not so easily exclude earlier biological views through the
admission of their being conditioned by the then-current world-picture.
Basically the conception of subordination still holds sway in many masculine minds. Masculine delusion—there is actually such a phenomenon—
and what the Latin Americans in the 1980 Synod of Bishops in Rome
called "machismo" cannot be thought without such an anthropological
presupposition, as vulgar as it may be. The women's movement in all of
its shades is extraordinarily sensitive to finding still such hidden and
unconscious residues of such a mentality.

The Model of Equality and Polarity

A broader and more important model is the cooperation of two equal
powers of operation, opposite or at least standing in tension with one
another, pictorially represented by two poles of an ellipse. This hypothe-

---

[11] A. Schopenhauer, *Parerga und Paralipomena*, 2 vols., ch. 27, pp. 362–371, and *Werke
in zwei Bänden*, ed. W. Brede, 2 vols. (Munich, 1977), pp. 709–723; P. J. Möbius, *Über
den physiologischen Schwachsinn des Weibes* (Halle an der Saale, 1900); O. Weininger,
Geschlecht und Charakter (Vienna-Leipzig, 1902; 1919: a much broader work!).

[12] See *Der Mensch im Widerspruch* (Zurich, 1965); *Die christliche Lehre von Schöpfung
und Erlosung. Dogmatik*, vol. 2 (Zurich, 1972).

sis of polarity arose at the end of the eighteenth century in Romanticism and in Idealism. Every qualitative inferiority of women falls away from the start: both sexes stand over against one another on the same level of relation. Male and female together first comprise the complete human being. Only in reciprocal fulfillment is humanness realized. The "natural" diversity of the sexes signifies no inferiority in the value of the person; rather, complete acceptance of the difference is the presupposition for true equality. Difference within essential equality is underscored. In the concrete, the world of the male seems to be marked by deed, battle, and reason; the world of the female by charm, domesticity, gentleness, and sensibility. Significantly, W. von Humboldt associated the masculine principle more with soul, straining energy, the capacity for conceptualization, decisive striving, a clarifying light, in short: *form;* while the feminine is spoken of in terms of persistent endurance, warmth, "bewitching charm and loving fullness", in short: *matter.*[13] If the thesis of polarity is developed still more strongly in the direction of a worldview, one views the relation of the sexes as one between nature and reason, charm and dignity, action and passion, love and magnanimity, form and matter. In their polarity, male and female become the primal example of a universal cosmic law. In anthropology the thesis of polarity attains a certain highpoint in F. J. J. Buytendijk and P. Lersch.[14]

Historically, the hypothesis of polarity has made an extraordinarily strong contribution to the equality of men and women. This is often overlooked in the heat of polemics. Still, there is the danger that polarity presents itself as a fixed metaphysical law. Then it can almost automatically naturalize the life-processes between the sexes. The life relation considered "as polarity becomes a process which automatically installs itself as a law in always equal ways and remains hopelessly enclosed in the circle of constant return. Thus it is overlooked not only that the relation of the sexes can likewise be a mis-relation, but generally that it is a

[13] Cf. the exposition and examples in J. Burri, *Als Mann und Frau erschuf er sie,* pp. 25ff. In the Romantic era there are many examples of this model. See K. Behrens, ed., *Frauenbriefe der Romantik,* Insel-Taschenbuch 545, (Frankfurt, 1981).

[14] F. J. J. Buytendijk, *Die Frau. Natur-Erscheinung-Dasein* (Cologne, 1953); P. Lersch, *Vom Wesen der Geschlechter* (Munich, 1947); cf. J. Burri, *Als Mann und Frau,* pp. 34ff.

relation of a personal sort."[15] There is the threat of a loss of the personal, and also of the ethical, dimension.

> In the relation of polarity, if it is not to be emptied of its entire sense, there is no personal fulfillment and failure, no expectation and disappointment; nothing happens that would not already be known; there is no room for hope and despair, rejoicing and doubting; there is no personal maturing and no life history. However, the relation of man and woman lives precisely from out of these personal and historical experiences.[16]

Outside of this, there remains, in all the positive results of the model of polarity, the ever-lurking danger that the otherness of the female is constantly apprehended in subtle forms as inferiority and subordination. Finally one often gets the impression that this metaphysics of the sexes operates in an ahistorical, mystical realm (the eternal timeless female, the eternal feminine) which comes to stand outside the concrete, conflict-laden encounter of man and woman.

It is no accident that this interpretation of femininity has gained favor, above all in the twentieth century, also in the religious-ecclesiastical and theological area. By including the discussion of femininity in the basic features of creation-theology, dialogic and ethics, one could thereby avoid the dangers indicated, or at least hold them in check. A model example of this reception and re-creation is G. von le Fort, *Die ewige Frau. Die Frau in der Zeit. Die zeitlose Frau.*[17] Woman is the receptive; to her belongs the mystery of devotion (submission). Passivity is not—as in ancient philosophy—something purely negative, but in the light of Christian grace, the most positive. To woman belongs adoration, compassion, self-forgetfulness and willingness to serve. The picture of woman thus becomes a symbol of the eternal woman which is completed in the mystery of Mary. In a theological respect, L. Bouyer has reinforced these features.[18] The male "represents what essentially transcends him,

[15] E. Metzke, "Anthropologie der Geschlechter", *Theologische Rundschau,* Neue Folge 22 (1954), pp. 211–241, especially p. 238.

[16] Ibid., p. 238.

[17] Munich, 1934.

[18] *Frau und Kirche* (Einsiedeln, 1977) (with an important epilogue by Hans Urs von Balthasar).

what he by himself and through himself is unable to be", but the female "is herself . . . potentially, in her maidenhood, everything that she represents, and in her motherhood she becomes it actually in that she realizes it in herself."[19] Only for the male is a quite transitory fatherhood possible, while the female contains in herself, in her interior, the highest fruitfulness. Teilhard de Chardin, in his "Hymn to the Eternally Feminine", praises the basic principle of femininity in creation (cf. Spr. 8, 22) which, in ever-new essential transformations, reaches from the lowest bit of matter through all the regions of living forms even to the divine-human.[20] The completion of the feminine Teilhard sees in the virgin and mother Mary.[21] The reflections of Hans Urs von Balthasar, who more than all his predecessors knows that no metaphysical polarity can simply clarify the difference between the human sexes, tower far over all the attempts indicated.[22] The pre-Christian "natural man" had no solution on his own. It can only be gathered from the indestructible difference between Jesus Christ and the Church. Owing to the essential harmony between the orders of creation and redemption, this mystery still also operates in the "natural" difference of the sexes.[23]

It is apparent that these very different sketches can scarcely be subsumed under a single model and basically even already begin to sublate the paradigmatic "polarity".

[19] Ibid., p. 38.

[20] Einsiedeln, 1968 (Kriterien 11). Teilhard de Chardin's text is on pp. 5–14, the extraordinarily rich and indispensable commentary by H. de Lubac on pp. 17–161.

[21] Cf. H. de Lubac's commentary, in ibid., pp. 147–160.

[22] See the epilogue, by von Balthasar, to L. Bouyer, *Frau und Kirche,* pp. 87ff., and the now different contributions in *Theodramatik* II/1 (Einsiedeln, 1976), pp. 334–350; II/2 (Einsiedeln, 1978), pp. 260–330. For a deeper look into mariology, see J. Ratzinger and von Balthasar, *Maria-Kirche im Ursprung* (Freiburg, 1980); on the application of the whole discussion to the problems of ministry, see the contributions in *Die Sendung der Frau in der Kirche,* published in the German edition of *Osservatore Romano* (Kevelaer, 1978).

[23] See the detailed treatment in von Balthasar, "Die Wurde der Frau", *Internationale Katholische Zeitschrift: Communio,* no. 4 (July 1982), p. 346.

The Model of Abstract Equality of the Sexes

One can understand the third model only against the background of the two hypotheses of interpretation developed thus far. On the one hand, one turns against every hierarchical notion of order between male and female and rejects all emphasis on the differences between the sexes if in speaking of "otherness" one already sees the beginning of a lesser ranking for the female. Thus the third model, over against the diversity of the sexes emphasized in the thesis of polarity, stresses the equality of the sexes above all. The subordination of the female is traced back to historical and social development. The so-called "differences" are only secondary developments on the basis of historical and social givens. Thus there is no pregiven "nature" of man and woman. A formula such as the *essence* of the female is especially suspect, since in every exposition of a specifically feminine mode of behavior or a "natural tendency" of the female one smells the ideologically tinged kernel of devaluation or even suppression. On the basis of this basic position the solution of the feminine question is ultimately only possible in an alternation of the constitution of society. It is understandable that in this connection women are considered above all in terms of differences owing to the reproductive function. Women want to free themselves—this appears to be the result—from the "apparently 'natural' compulsions of their biological reproductive function". The "realm of reproduction itself... has separated itself progressively from the compulsion of the realm of production. Thus it has changed its character; while merely biological and physical reproduction would always be important, the social relations have become ends in themselves."[24] From this basic postulate follow significant new conceptions of sexual morality, the number of children, divorce and abortion. Thus the new women's movement turns against its own beginnings: "motherhood" would be positively considered, above all as a counter-move to the egoistically individualist masculine world. The establishment of something like a feminine principle—it is now explained—has generally first led to the defense of "manliness".

[24] H. Schenk, *Die feministische Herausforderung. 150 Jahre Frauenbewegung in Deutschland,* Beck'sche Schwarze series 213 (Munich, 1980), pp. 222f.

Her (woman's) emotionality, her warmth, her spontaneity loosened, dissipated, and relaxed him (the man) when he returned from the professional battlefield which demands from him harshness and discipline, external tension, if he does not wish to fall behind. Her dependency, helplessness, anxiousness and naiveté afford him the feeling of his own strength, circumspection, invulnerability. The "femininity" of women first makes the "masculinity" of man possible as such; only if women take over the emotionally compensating role would that caricature of masculinity be possible which today governs the society of work.[25]

Thus the feminist attack directs itself to the difference of sex roles as such. Thus it also frees the male from norms of behavior which ultimately ruin him as well. Feminism also frees the man; it first creates the free human being as such.[26] The women's movement is thus the most radical political movement for the liberation of human beings.

Before we assess this model, we must still take note of a key aspect whose importance is not seldom overlooked. The model just sketched no longer allows from its very beginning such a question as to the "essence", the "nature", the "peculiarity", the "otherness", the "differentness" of woman. This consequence is expressed in its clearest form in a standard work of the recent women's movement by Simone de Beauvoir.[27] Especially important are the concluding results in "Toward Liberation".[28] "One is not born, but rather becomes, a woman. No biological, psychological, or economic fate determines the figure that the human female presents in society; it is civilization as a whole that produces this creature, intermediate between male and eunuch, which is described as feminine."[29] Marriage and motherhood are a trap of which one must be wary.[30]

[25] Ibid., p. 196.

[26] See also K. Böhme, *Ansätze zu einer Theorie von Partnerschaft* (Monographien zur Philos) (Forschung: Königstein, 1979).

[27] *The Second Sex* (New York, 1952); *Das andere Geschlecht. Sitte und Sexus der Frau* (Hamburg, 1951); *Le Deuxieme Sexe* (Paris, 1949).

[28] Cf. de Beauvoir, *The Second Sex,* pp. 796ff.

[29] Ibid., p. 301.

[30] See the interview with A. Schwarzer, "Das Ewig Weibliche ist eine Luge", in *Der Spiegel* 15 (1976): 195.

The fact that we are human beings is infinitely more important than all
the peculiarities that distinguish human beings from one another. . . . In
both sexes is played out the same drama of the flesh and spirit, of
finitude and transcendence; both are gnawed away by time and laid in
wait for by death, they have the same essential need for one another.[31]

De Beauvoir does not deny that there can be "differences in equality".[32]
She is concerned with something else: "To emancipate woman is to
refuse to confine her to the relations she bears to man, not to deny them
to her."[33] Words such as gift, conquest, compatibility do not thereby
lose their meaning. It is that "by and through their natural differentiation
men and women unequivocally affirm their brotherhood."[34]

It cannot be our task to investigate the very diverse tendencies of the
women's movement in their individual theoretical foundations. This
holds likewise for the exceptionally manifold branches of "feminist
theology".[35] The greatest part of feminist theology has the various
struggles for emancipation (from inferiority of a personal-political,
economic, social, and bodily sort) as presupposition[36] and understands
itself as a radical variation on the various liberation movements.[37]
Women count as the first and oldest of the suppressed. In this matter the
Bible plays an ambivalent role. On the one hand, in radical movements,
the androcentric world-picture of Scripture is placed in question up to its
very last utterances: the talk about God as "Father" and "Son" drives
women out of the Church (*Beyond God the Father*). One must free God

[31] de Beauvoir, *The Second Sex*, p. 810.

[32] See ibid., p. 813.

[33] Ibid., p. 813.

[34] Ibid., p. 814. Cf. Chr. Zehl Romero, *Simone de Beauvoir* (Hamburg: Reinbek, 1978),
pp. 120ff.

[35] See the informative overview by H. Pissarek-Hudelist, "Feministische Theologie
—eine Herausforderung?" *Zeitschrift für katholische Theologie* 103 (1981): 289–308,
400–425; also E. Gossmann, *Die streitbaren Schwestern*, pp. 79ff., 134ff.

[36] See E. Moltmann-Wendel, *Freiheit-Gleichheit-Schwesterlichkeit. Zur Emanzipation
der Frau in Kirche und Gesellschaft*, Kaisertraktate 25 (Munich, 1977), pp. 33ff.

[37] See C. J. M. Halkes, *Gott hat nicht nur starke Söhne. Grundzüge einer feministischen
Theologie*, Gütersloher Taschenbucher Siebenstern 371 (Gütersloh, 1980), especially pp.
158–174; B. Brooten and N. Greinacher, eds., *Frauen in der Männerkirche*, Gesellschaft
und Theologie, Division on Praxis der Kirche 40 (Munich-Mainz, 1982).

from a masculine hermeneutic. Finally, everything reaches a peak in the scandal of Incarnation: Jesus was a male. But in this way the fate of Jesus becomes that of the male: "God has come off badly in the male."[38] Other tendencies will simply not abandon the Bible with its incontestably patriarchal tendencies but will read it with new eyes (e.g., the Magnificat of Mary in Luke 1 as a song of protest), interpret it anew (e.g., feminine features in God's mercy), indeed re-write it.[39] Ultimately biblical women (Miriam, Deborah) and especially the women around Jesus (Mary, Mary Magdalen, Martha) become symbols of a misconcerned revolution.[40] The "official" picture of Mary subjected to pure readiness to suffer and serve should be radically altered, for Mary is ultimately a symbol of the prophetic power for liberation and sisterhood. To discover new images of Mary is a contribution to the humanization of women.[41]

Many studies in Church history and exegesis on the suppression and liberation of women reflect little on their own anthropological point of departure. In general they begin with radically emancipatory–egalitarian positions as discussed above. Within feminist theology different voices are heard only hesitantly drawing a multi-leveled picture—in the first instance also of Church history.[42]

[38] Thus the title of the book by I. Wenck, in Gütersloher Taschenbucher Siebenstern 1046 (Gütersloh, 1982). For a confrontation on this matter, see A. Roper, *Ist Gott ein Mann? Ein Gesprach mit Karl Rahner* (Düsseldorf, 1979).

[39] See C. J. M. Halkes, *Gott hat nicht nur starke Sohne,* pp. 97–118; R. Radford Ruether, *Maria—Kirche in weiblicher Gestalt,* Kaisertraktate 48 (Munich, 1980).

[40] Besides the literature already mentioned, see B. H. Langer, H. Leistner, E. Moltmann-Wendel, *Mit Mirjam durch das Schilfmeer. Frauen bewegen die Kirche* (Stuttgart, 1982); and the special issue, "Zur feministischen Theologie", of the journal *Evangelische Theologie* 42 (1982), no. 1.

[41] See E. Moltmann-Wendel, *Ein eigener Mensch werden. Frauen um Jesus,* Gütersloher Taschenbucher Siebenstern 1006 (Gütersloh, 1981); W. Schottroff and W. Stegemann, eds., *Traditionen der Befreiung. Sozialgeschichtliche Bibelauslegungen,* vol. 2, *Frauen in der Bibel* (Munich, 1980).

[42] See some of the first movements in this direction: E. Gossman, *Die streitbaren Schwestern,* pp. 13ff., 19ff., 67ff., 99ff.

2. BASIC LINES OF A
CHRISTIAN ANTHROPOLOGICAL REPLY

A reply from the viewpoint of Christian anthropology can only be sketched here by a consideration of the foundation. It is impossible to treat the exegetical, historical, and social problems connected with the question. The foundation is, of course, not the complete building. A complete anthropological development in the context of christology and ecclesiology must be postponed here. We do not hereby deny its importance. With respect to the basic anthropological problematic referred to in the determination of sexual difference there is still no immediate leap possible into the doubtless deep investigations of the foundations in christology, ecclesiology and mariology. The first step should not be taken before the second. This holds at the same time for the necessary comparison with the theoretical position of the women's movement and feminist theology. Is the "role" of sex really only socially dictated? Why does talk of "biological compulsion" forbid us to inquire about such a thing as the "nature" of the female? Is the woman really only an artificial product of civilization? Are there basically not even two sexes? How can one prevent possible differences between the sexes serving to bring about inequalities or to let them exist? How can respect for differences be brought into agreement with striving toward equality?

These questions are a challenge for anthropology which has remarkably little reaction to them. The Christian view of man must, in any case, seek an answer.

Sketch of the Direction for a Solution

A Christian answer in the specific sense is not possible on the basis of the models of "subordination" and "egalitarian equality". Whoever as a theologian does not conclusively renounce the category of "subordination" with all its consequences can be no credible advocate of another answer. Only if it is apparent from the very beginning that equal dignity and unlimited equality for male and female are held fast is there a chance to make clear that egalitarian equality of the sexes must not be the only way to attain a true equality of rank. It is a question of how one views a possible "difference". In case a difference really exists, in no case should it lead—and especially not indirectly and secretly—to a hidden devaluation. Many forms of the model of "polarity" are not entirely free of this, as was demonstrated earlier. They must position themselves on the inner ambivalence shown above. Thus a clarification and deepening of the anthropological basis is required. This formula can serve as a first indication of the direction for a solution proposed in what follows: *equal rank and equal dignity for women and men in the recognition of a human existence stamped by diversity.*

The Question of the Vocation and "Nature" of Women

If one insists on a diversity of the sexes and thus on a "characteristic" of female and male, then the question arises as to how one grounds such a view. The biological differences ought not to be over-valued. The socially determined differences (e.g., upbringing) are indeed greater than one formerly thought. If one emphasizes a specific feature or a special vocation for the female, one is very quickly entangled in problems that are difficult to untangle. In the declaration, "On Questions of the Place of Women in the Church and in Society", produced by the German Bishops' Conference and opening new paths on many issues, the essential vocation of women is seen in "responsibility for life and for the humane conditions of life".[43] Is the male, therefore, less responsible for this? And whoever prefers to see the characteristic of women in their relation to the sheltered realm of home and house must first become clear on how diverse are the life-spaces of a lady in antiquity, a farmer's wife on a large farm and a contemporary wife in her narrow flat. Here one cannot simply bracket out a social-historical treatment of the change in meaning of the term "house". It remains the concept behind (*Rückgriff*) the "nature" of male and female. Here it is immediately clear that there is no "nature" without historically developed culture, no Bios without social organization,

---

[43] The German Bishops, no. 30, published by the Secretariat of the German Bishops' Conference (Bonn, 1981), 14. A few lines further it says, characteristically: "Indeed, for biological reasons, (the male) is less immediately tied to the life of offspring; but that gives him the possibility of attending *from a greater distance* to the ability of this life to develop so that it can become independent and responsible" (emphasis added).

and no essence without a determinate situation. Outside of this, the human sciences inform us that the variable range of the possibilities of cultural forms is considerably greater than had for the most part been hitherto thought. For many, the social separation of the sexes in this respect has thus something "arbitrary" about it. The concrete "division of labor" between male and female has—as ethnology shows—often only little to do with the basic biological differences.[44] Much that appears to us as "natural" and inevitable in role differences goes back to historical determinants and social inventions. In any case, one would do well to place the radius of the malleability of "nature" as wide as possible.

Testing in the Empirical Dimension

The development of the social sciences has only recently reached a position on the variables in the anthropological position of women. "The" human sciences to which one often appeals are still ultimately not agreed on the evaluation of the phenomena of sexual differences. The differentiated situation should at least be briefly sketched out in what follows, without thereby intending to present an ultimate and definitive statement.

Contemporary biology and anthropology hold fast to a proper character for each of the sexes—and this in contradiction to the radical liberation movements. A few references must suffice: from outer appearance, only "raw physical power" should be "the sole criterion which allows a certain measure of distinction between the strong and the weak sex".[45] Very different are the so-called biorhythms in men and women.[46] In earliest times they referred above all to a series of perceptual differences between men and women:

> Women have a finer sense of taste than men; they detect small traces of a flavor more easily than men. Presumably with men the sense of smell

[44] Cf. the examples from cultural anthropology in M. Mead, *Male and Female* (New York: Morrow, 1949).

[45] J. Zander, "Das Andere in unserem Geschlecht", in E. Weinzierl, ed., *Emanzipation der Frau. Zwischen Biologie und Ideologie,* Schriften der Katholischen Akademie in Bayern 100 (Düsseldorf, 1980), pp. 57–66, especially p. 62.

[46] Ibid., pp. 62ff.

is more finely developed. Women have, especially in the fingers and hands, a more sensitive sense of touch than men. The adjustment of the eyes to darkness . . . occurs more quickly in the case of women than in the case of men. . . . Women therefore see better in the dark. Men react more strongly to intensive light.[47]

In intelligence studies it is demonstrated that no sex is superior to the other, so that entire swarms of speculation for hundreds of years on the "inborn weak sense" of women dissolve into nothing.

There are also indications of a cognitive specialization of the sexes. This, for example, can lead to distinct representative proportions in the professions. Men appear to have a differentiated spatial understanding, while women possess a greater gift for communication.

> There may be fewer women architects, engineers and pictorial artists, since these professions especially require more capacities of spatial representation. Similar factors explain perhaps also the lesser number of women composers. On the other hand, women musicians (singers as well as instrumentalists) are less rare. This could lie in the fact that these talents depend on functions in which women are good—on linguistic capacity and refined motor coordination. Thus the distinct representation of the sexes in several professions has a biological basis.[48]

Of course, this does not justify excluding anyone from any profession. "Women are distinguished from men perhaps in the number of those gifted for particular regions, not yet in the level attainable by those most highly gifted."[49]

These references, which could easily be multiplied, show that, beyond sexual characteristics and functions, there is biological-psychological

---

[47] D. E. Zimmer, *Der Mythos der Gleichheit* (Munich, 1980), p. 52.

[48] Zimmer, *Der Mythos der Gleichheit,* p. 57, a citation of the Canadian brain-physiologist, S. F. Witelson (cf. his "Geschlechtsspezifische Unterschiede in der Neurologie der kognitiven Funktionen und ihre psychologischen, sozialen, edukativen und klinischen Implikationen", in *Centre Royaumont. Pour une Science de l'Homme. Die Wirklichkeit der Frau* [Munich, 1979], pp. 341–368, a collective work under the direction of E. Sullerot with the aid of O. Thibault, henceforth referred to as *Die Wirklichkeit der Frau*).

[49] Zimmer, *Der Mythos der Gleichheit,* p. 57 (with a comprehensive bibliography).

evidence for a substantial difference between the sexes which cannot reduce to socially enforced or historico-culturally developed "roles".[50] The appeal to biology must not thereby mean the fixation of an inalterable fate. But if one ignores this in its significance, then women themselves must pay the price. "That thereby a service to reproduction is indicated for women is clear enough. Managing conflict through denying reality has always shown itself as dysfunctional in the long run."[51] If the potentiality of "nature" is completely denied, it will take its toll. In the differentiation of the sex-roles very much can be reduced to circumstance and history, but not everything. Nature is not so deterministic as was often presupposed, and every culture remains secretly "natural" in the end, unharmed by all human interference.

On the basis of these insights the formula of H. Meyer appears as a happy synthesis of our present state of knowledge when he speaks of a "social stylization of genetic dispositions".[52] There are, along with all the indeterminateness of humanness, still definite genetic dispositions which receive a social stamp. Without these two elements no comprehension of human existence is possible. At the same time one has to note that the student of things human has to be very careful in determining the relation between the influence of genetic-hormonal factors and culturally determined circumstances and must, in keeping with the contemporary state of inquiry, leave open very much.[53]

It is clear, then, that a simple overlooking of, or an unexamined compensation for, biologically and physically important differences between male and female can cause great harm and only impoverish the sexes.

[50] See the numerous inquiries in Sullerot and Thibault, *Die Wirklichkeit der Frau;* A. Degenhardt and H. M. Trautner, eds., *Geschlechtstypisches Verhalten. Mann und Frau in psychologischer Sicht,* Beck'sche Schwarze Series 205 (Munich 1979); N. Bischof and H. Preuschoft, eds., *Geschlechtsunterschiede. Entstehung und Entwicklung. Mann und Frau in biologischer Sicht,* Beck'sche Schwarze Series 207 (Munich, 1980); F. Wesley and C. Wesley, *Die Psychologie der Geschlechter,* Fischer Taschenbuch 6728 (Frankfurt, 1981).

[51] N. Bischof, "Biologie als Schicksal?" in Weinzierl, ed., *Emanzipation der Frau,* pp. 43–56, especially p. 56.

[52] *Frau-Sein, Genetische Disposition und gesellschaftliche Prägung* (Opladen, 1980), p. 259.

[53] Cf. the diverse exposition in the literature mentioned in notes 45, 48, 50, and 52 above.

The Sexual as a Totalistic Determination of Humanness

The human being is thus not a unisexual being, as many feminist conceptions suggest. Sexually specific distinctions are not indifferent to the
essence of the person.[54] The bodily region is not a distinct region that is
ultimately unimportant. The human exists only in the "double issue"
(*Doppelausgabe*) of male and female. It is likewise not only a matter of
"roles" that stands in the way of total human plasticity. Sexuality is not a
mere condition of humanness without which a person could also exist or
a reality of which he or she is arbitrarily capable of disposing.[55] The
female is a person in the specific mode of being female. She is no less a
person than the male, but she is a person in her own mode. This thesis has
considerable consequences for the evaluation of the bodily and the sexual
as such.

Persons in Completely Equal Modes

Of course, these reflections, while not denying the diversity of the sexes,
decisively presuppose as the highest principle that male and female have
equal personal dignity. The female is no diminished male, but an original
creative idea of God. The female is not simply created for the male but
for God. Likewise the female is pregiven (*vorgegeben*) to the male and
thus outside his disposal. The Yahwist's creation account is indeed imbedded
in an androcentric world picture, but as a more exact exposition would
show, counter tendencies are clearly demonstrable.[56] The female owes
her dignity, not to the male, but to God. As a human being she is born
equal to the male. This basic biblical feature will develop through Jesus'
relation to women (see Mark 10:2–9) on to St. Paul: "There are not Jews

---

[54] In this connection we must forego discussion of the manifold problems of the
androgyn (dual sexuality in a single life-form) or of a unisexual primordial human that
does not basically involve a new solution.

[55] See K. Barth, *Die kirchliche Dogmatik,* III/4 (Zurich, 1951, 1969), pp. 179ff.; also
J. Splett, *Der Mensch ist Person. Zur christlichen Rechtfertigung des Menschseins* (Frankfurt,
1978), pp. 110–137.

[56] See O. H. Steck, *Die Paradieserzählung. Eine Auslegung von Genesis 2, 4b-3, 24,*
Biblische Studien 60 (Neukirchen, 1970), pp. 89ff; C. Westermann, *Genesis,* Biblischer
Kommentar I/1 (Neukirchen, 1971), pp. 312ff.; cf. note 57, which follows.

or Greeks or slaves or free or male or female, for all would be one in Christ Jesus" (Gal 3:28).[57] Before God and in Jesus Christ there is no devaluation of the female. Of course, already from the time of the New Testament through the entire history of the Church there has been a struggle between the recognition of equality and the acceptance of the historical situation of suppression and subordination.

Person transcends all "roles", likewise that of spouse, mother, friend, partner, rival. There is no value that depends upon whether she fits into a pregiven role. She ought never become a means to an end. The dignity of the person requires an ultimate immediacy of human beings before God and an inviolable freedom and dignity. Only God guarantees this dignity which is to be respected in every case and unconditionally.

> Thus the female is not ultimately there for the sake of the male and also not for the sake of the family. She is absorbed neither in her role as faithful companion and mother nor in the one task of completing the main work of the male and working together with him. She has value, dignity, import, rank not through her husband. She has value and dignity in herself.[58]

Today this equality must be realized economically, socially, and legally. Insofar as the requirement of "self-realization" signifies *this* equal dignity of person for the female, it deserves the complete support of Christians and of the Church.[59]

---

[57] Cf. the inquiry undertaken by H. Thyen, " . . . nicht mehr männlich und weiblich . . . ", in *Kennzeichen* 2, pp. 107–203 (on the Old Testament, cf. F. Crusemann, also in *Kennzeichen* 2, pp. 13–106).

[58] W. Kasper, "Die Stellung der Frau als Problem der theologischen Anthropologie", in *Lebendiges Zeugnis* 35 (1980): 5–16, especially p. 10.

[59] See the official ecclesiastical pronouncements of Vatican II in *Gaudium et Spes* (arts. 9, 29, 52, 60); Pope John Paul II's writing on the tasks of the Christian family in the contemporary world, *Familiaris Consortio* (Nov. 22, 1981), nos. 22–24; the document, already noted, of the German Bishops' Conference; *Zu Fragen der Stellung der Frau in Kirche und Gesellschaft. Eine Studie zum gemeinsamen Leben von Frau und Mann,* sponsored by a committee of the Evangelical Church of Germany, published by the Church Chancery under mandate of the assembly of the ECG (Gütersloh, 1979).

Primordial Mutual Reference

The female cannot be exclusively defined as the complementary opposite to the male, be it in the sense of subordination (which conditions evangelical theology in other respects from Luther to Bonhoeffer) or in the manner of an ordination to the male that remains ambivalent (K. Barth).[60] Women see behind such determinations the attempt to conceive of the female only in terms of the male who is the "authentic" human. Thus the unrestricted dignity of the female person is of such an eminent significance: she is one proper Self, which she ought entirely to be. Her essence does not consist solely in adapting herself to Church and society, in helping out and assuming a stand-by role. Only if the female is granted her proper personal dignity can one also speak of the devotion and the task of her proper Self. "Only one who is totally something can likewise totally give something."[61]

However, with the same discrimination, the newly attained Self must not close itself in absolutely, arbitrarily, and narcissistically. It is a basic mistake ever to consider male and female as centers closed in upon themselves. Then almost the only equality is one of competitive or even inimical juxtaposition and opposition. The recognition of personal dignity is something completely other than consenting to an individualistically understood autonomy. With all his or her distinctive value, ordination to society and its tasks is still part of the essence of the person. Male and female together realize the complete human being. "And God created human being as his image: as the image of God he created it, (thus) man and woman he created them" (Gen 1:27, following the translation of O. H. Steck). From this it follows that, according to this conception, an "essence of being human", a determination of the human being, cannot be given apart from its existence in two sexes.[62] This mutual reference is a personal otherness (*Gegenüber*) and relatedness (*Zueinander*). Precisely

---

[60] Cf. E. and J. Moltmann, "Menschweden in einer neuen Gemeinschaft von Frauen und Mannern", in *Evangelische Theologie* 42 (1982): 80–92.

[61] Moltmann-Wendel, *Freiheit-Gleichheit-Schwesterlichkeit*, p. 70.

[62] Westermann, *Genesis*, p. 221; W. H. Schmidt, *Die Schöpfungsgeschichte der Priester-schrift*, Wissenschaftliche Monographien zum Alten und Neuen Testament 17 (Neukirchen, 1973³), pp. 132ff., 199ff., 214ff.; E. S. Gerstenberger and W. Schrage, *Frau und Mann*, Biblische Konfrontationen 1013 (Stuttgart, 1980).

in being other, both are indispensably linked to one another. This relation is not simple to describe. The usual notion of partnership is almost too formal to be able to capture the peculiarity of the personal and bodily encounter. The concept of "completion" especially has its difficulties, since it could give the impression that the other only serves one's own self-improvement. As such it is not a matter of two components completing themselves. "In truth, the relation between male and female begins precisely in that they push against one another in their relatedness and experience their foreignness and nonsimilarity, but in such a way that, in the acceptance of the other in his/her personal existence, the responsible life-history of two human beings begins."[63]

This reference to one another (not: ordination of the female to the male!) is not limited to male and female alone. Likewise, attention is not first or exclusively directed to the freeing of still suppressed peoples and classes, as is usually the case in the texts of the women's movement. The mutual reference of male and female in marriage testifies to its fruitfulness in a greater We, namely that of the child and the family. In this way, it is bound to many forms of community and does not only serve "self-realization", which could also occur in two isolated individuals. Of course, it is also not possible radically and in principle to uncouple sexuality and love, sexuality and motherhood, reproduction and family from one another. In their equal personal dignity male and female realize *one* life-community, that is, they are "one flesh", as the Scripture says (see Gen 2:24; Mark 10:1ff.; 1 Cor 6:16; Eph 5:31).[64]

An important text by Margaret Mead from 1949 shows the continuous dialogue of life in common companionship arising out of the acceptance of the diversity of the sexes:

> Our tendency at present is to minimize all these differences ... or at most to try to obliterate particular differences that are seen as handicaps on one sex.... But every adjustment that minimizes a difference, a vulnerability, in one sex, a differential strength in the other, diminishes

[63] Metzke, "Anthropologie der Geschlechter", p. 239.

[64] Cf. Steck, *Die Paradieserzählung,* especially on Gen 2:24; on the notion of "one flesh", see M. Gilbert, "Une seule chair" (Gen 2:24), in *Nouvelle Revue Theologique* 110 (1978): 66–89.

their possibility of complementing each other, and corresponds—
symbolically—to sealing off the constructive receptivity of the female
and the vigorous outgoing constructive activity of the male, muting
them both in the end to a duller version of human life in which each is
denied the fullness of humanity that each might have had. Guard each
sex in its vulnerable moments we must, protect and cherish it through
the crises that at some times are so much harder for one than for the
other. But as we guard, we may also keep the differences. . . . Yet both
are necessary, and the skill of one sex gives only a partial answer. We
can build a whole society only by using both the gifts special to each
sex and those shared by both sexes—by using the gifts of the whole of
humanity.[65]

Thus it also becomes clear how the beginning we have attempted here
is able to assimilate individual elements of the "polarity" model. This can
happen, but we need not treat of it here.[66] A still further line of
reflection is required beforehand. Everything turns on the question
whether the Christian can say Yes to the creation of God. Of course,
creation does not shine in its pristine light. It is darkened in many ways;
wherefore, according to the witness of the Yahwist creation account (see
Gen 2–3), the relation of the sexes and the situation of women are
likewise found to be full of suffering. Still this is not the ultimate word of
Scripture. To Adam corresponds Jesus Christ; to Eve, Mary. In this way
the new chapter of a further theological reflection must begin. Nonetheless,
we ought to stop, for such continuation becomes credible only if the
insights thus far attained are not thereby lost.

[65] Mead, *Male and Female*, pp. 371–2, 384.
[66] See the reflections, mentioned in note 22 above, by von Balthasar, which lead us
reliably in the broadest direction, yet are still much too little heeded.

2

BARBARA ALBRECHT

IS THERE AN OBJECTIVE TYPE "WOMAN"?

Translated by Maria Shrady

We are dealing here with a subject in question form. I shall attempt to outline the various answers as far as this is possible within the scope of a single essay.

THE DENIAL OF AN OBJECTIVE TYPE "WOMAN"

The question mark in our title clearly indicates that woman as an objective type, bestowed beforehand and rooted in the order of being or creation, has become questionable. Many people, most of them women, no longer accept such an order of being and the type "woman" rooted in it. Indeed, they violently object to the mere assumption that such a question should be asked.

A similar point of view was recently expressed in a section of a resolution concerning pastoral service in the community, published by the Joint Synod of the German Bishops. The text reads: "In the parishes, by means of catechesis, homilies, and adult education programs, one should strive to abandon outdated concepts and conventions regarding the nature and role of woman."[1] But what concepts and conventions are these? The Synod is silent on the matter. Not so the women. For those who belong to the feminist or women's liberation movement in Central Europe and in the United States the answer is unequivocal. They

---

This speech was delivered in 1982 at the Educational Conference in Haus Marie-land, Schönstatt.

[1] *The Pastoral Service in the Community,* III, 3.2.3.

have freed themselves long ago from the antiquated myth of the "Eternal Woman" (Gertrud von Le Fort), and from the strait-jacket of an archaic ideology based on the idea of "The" woman as prefigured in Mary: virgin, handmaid, and mother. Feminists and their sympathizers are about to enlighten women in the world and in the Church about their true situation by means of a world-wide social, psychological, economic, and, above all, cultural revolution. They call for an uprising against the oppression of women by men, now thousands of years old, and they call for the construction of a "counter-culture" (C. Halkes).

The immediate objective is the liberation of women from domination by men. Instead of male domination, there will be self-determination and autonomy. "Only we ourselves can free ourselves from our misery!"

The road to this objective is marked by an elemental struggle. Feminists are by no means content with equality in a patriarchal society and in a male Church. Their goal is revolution, a radical change of society and Church, abolishing the old patriarchal order. The first step is a very concrete one, consisting in the abolition of the acquired gender roles,[2] which had been forced upon women by men, elevating the "type of the female beast of burden" to an ideal.[3]

When, for example, the Church in its papal addresses and pastoral letters speaks of "the ideology of motherhood" (C. Halkes), and uses such outworn clichés for women as "heart, soul, and love", "it reveals its total loss of reality" (M. Albus). It is precisely from this prison of stereotyping, from the acquired Christian sacrificial role, that women wish to break away.

In a speech, delivered at the Congress for German-speaking Pastoral theologians in Vienna (Jan. 2–5, 1982) entitled "How Do Women See Themselves?", the Protestant feminist E. Moltmann referred to the factors which favor women's breaking out of their roles. These are: (1) growing democratization; (2) minority movements throughout the world; (3) feminism (the awareness of lack of power being a unifying factor); (4)

---

[2] Cf. M. Daly, *Jenseits von Gottvater, Sohn & Co. Aufbruch zu einer Philosophie der Frauenbefreiung* (Munich, 1980), 145. English edition: *Beyond God the Father: A Radical Beginning for a Philosophy of Women's Liberation,* 2nd ed. (Boston: Beacon Press, 1985.

[3] Moltmann-Wendel, ed., *Frauenbefreiung, Biblische und theologische Argumente* [Women's liberation: biblical and theological arguments] (Munich and Mainz, 1978), 59.

medical-technical developments where, thanks to the pill, women may at last decide over their own bodies.

K. Børrensen refers to this when he remarks that women can now free themselves from patriarchal structures because of the "biological revolution".

If the almost total control of the infant death rate can go hand in hand with artificial birth control, the physical and psychological potentialities of woman will no longer be exhausted by her reproductive function. As a result, an excess of energy will become available for extrafamilial functions. . . . Every struggle for liberation presupposes an excess of energy, creatively put to use.[4]

To those factors which favor woman's breaking out of her role belongs no doubt her increasing participation in professional life, which makes her economically independent of men, permitting her to discard the role of a "domestic in the family". Furthermore, the growing divorce rate contributes to an enhanced self-confidence and autonomy.

One could add to these factors "the marriages without certificate", and the phenomenon of the "singles" who refuse any type of permanent tie and thus come closest to the feminist image of the ideal woman. (They have not renounced such an image.)

The *new ideal* is the completely autonomous woman who no longer finds her identity in "partnership" or "complementarity" with man. She is neither subordinated to man nor attached to him.[5] The "new woman" achieves her identity in and with herself, in a new and "autonomous culture", in a liberated self-esteem, and in an "explosion of creative fantasy of a sex hitherto powerless".[6]

Because "partnership"—so the feminists maintain—is the "sleeping pill of emancipation", theologians should finally stop writing and talking about such things as "partnership", "equal but distinct roles", and complementarity. Such talk, according to C. Halkes, cements anew the old so-called distinctions between the sexes. It would be better

[4] K. E. Børresen, "Women and Men in the Creation Narrative and in the Church", in *Concilium* 6–7, 1981, 497f.

[5] Cf. E. Moltmann-Wendel, *Freiheit, Gleichheit, Schwesterlichkeit* [Freedom, Egality, Sisterhood] (Munich, 1977), 70.

[6] M. Daly, op. cit., 37

for theologians to listen to women over a long period of time and write nothing, so as not to develop an anthropology all over again. This was demanded by C. Halkes in her Viennese lecture: "How Do Women Experience the Church?"

The long-range objective of women's liberation is, in Halkes' words, the autonomous "androgynous person" freed from any reference to the opposite sex. This, incidentally, is equally applicable to men, although the liberation of men is still unattained. Through by-passing the female and male, one (woman) attains what is fully human.[7]

For this successful striving for autonomy, feminists have arrived at a symbol: the virgin. A virgin, says Halkes, is not primarily a woman who abstains from sexual intercourse, but one who does not lead a "derivative" life, be it as mother of a daughter, or wife of. . . . " A woman is virgin if she "matures to wholeness within herself, and if she is intact as a person",[8] in short, a totally autonomous person.

All signs indicate that feminism (and feminist theology in particular) has rejected the image of woman which has been valid for thousands of years, and—despite protestations to the contrary—not to free itself from an image, but to exchange it for a new objective one, self-fabricated and not rooted in the order of being—or creation, owing nothing to God the Creator. "We are the final cause" of this new image, shouts M. Daly from the United States, clad in her radical-feminist spacesuit, in which she freed herself as former religious and theologian from the Catholic Church and has traveled into space "beyond God, the Father".[9]

PERSONAL POSITION

After having given an outline of the new woman as an autonomous, androgynous person as envisaged by radical feminism, I should like to express my own view. I consider the entire enterprise simply presumptuous—in various ways.

[7] C. Halkes, *Gott hat nicht nur starke Söhne* [God Does Not Only Have Strong Sons], GTB Siebenstern 371 (Gütersloh, 1980), 49.

[8] C. Halkes, " 'Another' Mary", in *Una Sancta* 4 (1977) : 332.

[9] M. Daly, op. cit., 5.

In my opinion, these feminists are blind to the reality of being, and therefore they seek self-realization without accepting this reality, without accepting themselves as women. They insist on their right to become what they wish, forgetting that there are pre-existing conditions outside of one's choice and design.

What Bishop K. Hemmerle calls the "secret dogmas" of the majority of our youth can, if I am not mistaken, be also detected in the basic assumptions of feminism.

It is part of feminism's "secret dogma" that anything objectively given or pre-assigned, not determined by the individual, is a priori an obstacle to self-fulfillment and must therefore be rejected. I wish to determine all the conditions of my life myself! (Even the possibility is utopian!) This "dogma" results in the belief that change alone (down to an ontological revolution and to the creation of a counterculture) is a worthwhile goal. Stability, on the other hand, measuring against an objective norm which is contained in the creative order, submitting to the fundamental givens of life, is in itself regarded as alienation. The rage against Rome and all it entails is so violent because the radical feminists feel instinctively that the Catholic Church is the strongest bastion, the last institution which fervently defends marriage, family, and a concept of man and woman which corresponds to the order of creation.

Nowadays, many women succumb to the error of presumption which, in its striving for autonomy, barely conceals a defective self-esteem. This desire for autonomy entails the danger "that tomorrow there will be neither man nor woman", merely a neuter. "He made war upon the 'woman' " (Rev 12:37). "We understand that the devil when he wishes to wield power over an entire civilization and over all humanity, first persecutes woman."[10]

A depressing result of his successful influence is presented by the rejection of woman as a pre-ordained type. Let us address ourselves to the consequences.

---

[10] *Bloss Konvention? Pater Kentenich über das Ideal der Frau* [Mere convention? Father Kentenich about the ideal of woman]. Compiled by M. A. Klaiber, ed. by the Secretariat of the League of Women, Marienland, Vallendar, no date; no. 28, 33, p. 26ff.

THE CONSEQUENCES OF REJECTION

Feminist philosophy and theology call for a revolution against a patriarchal society and Church. These manifestoes are published in Germany by the women's magazines *Emma* and *Courage* as well as by the publications of "Frauenoffensive" [Women's Offensive]. C. Halkes estimates that in the Federal Republic of Germany alone at least half a million women are regularly exposed to feminist ideology, and that as a result an enormous reservoir of sympathizers has been created which is still expanding.

One of the catastrophic effects can be observed in the growing number of abortions and the rising divorce rate, for which women claim responsibility. In 1976 approximately 100,000 women left their husbands and families, citing feminist arguments as their reason.[11]

The reverse side of these findings, or the "alternative solution", is cohabitation without a marriage license. The sociologist G. Schmidtchen has accumulated some statistics on the subject and has concluded that in 1967, 43 percent of men and 65 percent of women below the age of thirty believed that things had gone too far. In 1973, however, only 5 percent of young men and 2 percent of young women shared this view. 87 percent of the young men and 92 percent of the young women saw nothing wrong. Prof. Schmidtchen continues:

> There are changes taking place within the life of the sexes, the results of which on family and society cannot even be foreseen. . . . One can form an adequate impression of the virulence of the political and sociological potential for change inherent in the feminist movement by examining young women. What emerges is too progressive for young men to understand.[12]

In every case it is the children who suffer first of all, and whose plight goes largely unnoticed. Let society and the state take care of them! What

[11] C. Koepcke, *Frauenbewegung zwischen 1800 und 2000* [Women's movement between 1800 and 2000], Heroldsberg, (Nürnberg, 1979), 168.

[12] G. Schmidtchen, "Information about Women. Gender Role Differentiation from a Sociological Viewpoint", in E. Weinzierl, ed.: *Emancipation of Woman, between Biology and Ideology,* Publications of the Catholic Academy in Bavaria, no. 90 (Düsseldorf, 1980), 33f.

feminists desire is liberation of such binding ties as marriage and the "disadvantage" of bearing children. For as long as this "disadvantage" remains, freedom from male domination is illusory.[13]

To recapitulate: the effects of the struggle for autonomy and the liberation from an objective type "woman", which had led to the ideology of motherhood and hence to the "hostile image of woman", weigh heavily on the children and the young. Never has the number of suicides been higher among them than today. This is not merely caused by pressures in school, but predominantly by the loss of a mother and a secure home. Today every tenth child is emotionally disturbed. There is a rising rate of alcoholism and drug abuse among school children and criminal behavior, including vandalism, among students. Juvenile robberies have tripled within the last fifteen years,[14] not only due to "rebellion against a fixed world", but largely to the absence of an experienced and devoted mother, as well as to the lack of specific education suited to the needs of each sex.

And the women themselves? The prophetess of our time, C. Meves, demonstrates in her profoundly disturbing book *Anima: The Soul of Young Girls Violated*[15] the devastating results of "the disobedience to creation"[16] that leads to the loss of what is central.

C. Meves points out how the feminist battle-cry "From male domination to self-determination" has proven to be an illusion. The over-evaluation of the intellect and the mechanization of thinking has led to a loss of creativity, of empathy, and of a rounded perspective of the world; woman has been deprived of her instinctive self-assurance, her antennae, as it were, of being. This loss of the central also manifests itself in a general masculinization of her appearance and in such symptoms as

[13] A. Röper, *Ist Gott ein Mann? Ein Gespräch mit K. Rahner* [Is God a Man? A conversation with K. Rahner] (Düsseldorf, 1979), 51.

[14] H. D. Schwind, "Rebellion against a Ready-Made World", in FAZ of November 25, 1981, p. 10.

[15] C. Meves, *Anima: Verletzte Mädchenseele—Die Frau zwischen Entfremdung und Entfaltung* [Anima: The soul of young girls violated—woman between alienation and development] (Kassel, 1979).

[16] C. Meves, "Against Nature. False Ideals Render Women Unhappy", in *Rheinischer Merkur*, no. 8, 1978, p. 10.

anorexia nervosa and absence of menstruation with resulting infertility. The medical statistics show a growing rate of psychosomatic disturbances, stress symptoms, depression, alcoholism and increasing suicide in women. All this seems to indicate that the feminist path to liberation is a dangerous one, leading to a new bondage, a deviation, marked by a fall from the creative order. Such a fall inevitably ends up in a disintegration (J. Kentenich) which surfaces in such symptoms as we have described above. The emancipation of woman thus turns into an emancipation from "being a woman"[17] and ends in disaster.

THE AFFIRMATIVE RESPONSE TO
AN OBJECTIVE TYPE "WOMAN"

Is there such a thing as woman as an objective type? I would like to answer in the affirmative. This does not exclude the opinion which I share with C. Bamberg "that any attempt to separate neatly the female from the male or to define each sex exactly is doomed to failure".[18] Nevertheless, woman with more or less defined feminine characteristics exists and is based upon a preordained, objective type. (The same applies to man.)

"God created man in his image. Male and female he created them" (Gen 1:27). According to this biblical statement, man exists in no other way but in this "double edition of man and woman".[19] Neither of them is autonomous. Both refer to each other and are capable and in need of complementarity, not to struggle against, but to attract and complete each other. They have been created to be partners, "opposite poles, not opposites".[20] The creative order in its human-personal aspect is elliptical

[17] W. Kasper, "The Position of Woman as Problem for Theological Anthropology", in *Lebendiges Zeugnis* [Living witness], Special Pamphlet "Woman in Church and Society" (October 1980), 7.

[18] C. Bamberg, "Challenge by the Woman's Issue in the Church", in *Lebendiges Zeugnis,* loc. cit., 56.

[19] W. Kasper, loc. cit., 8.

[20] J. Illies, "Man and Woman—Opposite Poles?" in *Die andere Seite der Biologie.* HB, 677 (Freiburg, 1978), 100.

in character. We are dealing here with primal realities, given to men and women beforehand. Any attempt to undermine them is absurd and will finally prove to be counter-productive.

Within these fundamental realities everything essential is contained as in a grain of seed. What is common to both is their having been created by God. It was not Adam who created women but the Lord God. God cast a deep sleep upon Adam while doing this, as we are told in the creation narrative (Gen 2:21). This emphasizes by means of poetic imagery that woman is "an original creative thought of God",[21] from him and toward him, and, being his image, equal in dignity and worth with man. As God-created image, woman (this is likewise true of man) contains her being within herself and thus does not lead an existence derivative of man. She exists in a state of immediacy to God, independent and responsible for her actions and hence equal to man in misery and addiction to sin.[22]

Finally, woman is equal in regards to salvation history, in all that God has done and still does for sinful humanity by giving his beloved Son, in the Incarnation, Crucifixion, and Resurrection of Jesus Christ. Before God and in Jesus Christ there is no subordination or underevaluation of woman. All sex differentiations have in the true sense of the word become "indifferent".[23] Where salvation is concerned, "there is neither Jew nor Greek; there is neither slave nor free man; there is neither male nor female" (Gal 3:28). They are all "one", united in Jesus Christ, equally loved and redeemed by him.

Equality of personhood in the order of creation and redemption, however, does not mean equality and uniformity in one's human existence. Quite the contrary, God, in his limitless imagination, created two models, two archetypes of man, distinct in every cell—"to the roots of the hair"[24]—distinct in anatomy and in the number of blood corpuscles as well as in psychological and mental constitution. Although men and women are equal in their immediacy toward God, they are distinct and

---

[21] W. Kasper, loc. cit., 7.

[22] Cf. The German Bishops, *Zu Fragen der Stellung der Frau in Kirche und Gesellschaft* [Concerning the role of woman in Church and society] (1981), II, 1.

[23] W. Kasper, loc. cit., 9.

[24] Cf. J. Illies, loc. cit., 98.

not interchangeable on the plane of their human nature. Being different here does not constitute "less", but rather "more". For only that way can two equal persons become fruitful in their relations and communications to and for each other, so that there may be life on this earth.

This distinct manner of being human by no means denotes inferiority. Neither is it a product of cultural or social conditioning. In confronting feminist theories it should always be emphasized that man and woman's distinct manner of being human is rooted and prefigured in the objective order of being and creation. The Swiss scientist N. Bischof comes closest to my point of view. During a conference of the Catholic Academy in Bavaria entitled "Emancipation of Woman: Between Biology and Ideology" (1978), he drew attention to the sexual differentiation on the plane of the gamete. "The selection of sperm cells by mobility" (to travel the longer distance) and the egg cell by vitality at the price of immobility . . . determines that the egg-producing organism becomes the receiving one. This, in all likelihood, is the most momentous factor in the genesis of sex differentiation",[25] the determining clue to all differentiation within that which men and women possess in common.

Notwithstanding that both have counter-sexual tendencies as well, we shall now examine the original distinctness within the psychological and mental sphere.

Contrary to all ideas about autonomy and other such utopian desires, there exists an antecedent condition according to which man and woman (not only woman, as C. Bamberg seems to hold)[26] find themselves "in relation" to God, to each other, and to the world. This being-in-relation, however, manifests itself in different ways. Being-in-relation for woman is real, earthbound, directed toward persons, above all, toward children. For she was created as "the mother of all the living" (Gen 3:20) to be a physical as well as a psychological and spiritual mother, not an autonomous virgin, as C. Halkes wishes us to believe. This quality endows woman with a particular intensity vis-à-vis life and human beings; it makes her "intact" as a person and able "to participate constructively in

[25] N. Bischof, "Is Biology Destiny? Concerning the Natural History of Gender Role Differentiation", in E. Weinzierl, ed., op. cit., 48.
[26] C. Bamberg, loc. cit., 54.

providing a future."[27] She goes about this not so much by aggressively shaping things, discovery, by research and control of the world, not by constant mobility, often at the price of flexibility. For women are as a rule more tied to a home, to a permanent place to which they belong—be it family, school, a hospital, a firm, a parish, or a convent. On the whole it can be said that women, particularly, suffer from any form of relocation.

The constructive participation in the future does not happen exclusively in an abstract, speculative, intellectual manner which is situated in the realm of ideas; more often it expresses itself in intuitive empathy with others and their surroundings. Generally it is demonstrated by sustaining and supporting, by nurturing and caring for people here and now, in the concrete sphere of human living. P. Kentenich frequently uses the symbol of the circle in regards to women, the arrow in regards to men.

This "being in relation" within the circle obtains its realization in circling around a person—be it God or man; inversely, it is realized by imparting color to each thing, by investing one's work-place and also one's dress with a personal style. "Just as everything I perform as a woman has a personal touch, so I seek the person in everything."[28]

The orientation of the circle to its center corresponds to the heart in woman's life and work, which influences the substance and style of her actions. Her soul is at work in them, her subconscious, her unconscious ground of being. Her thoughts are the thoughts of the heart, her plans are good or evil plans of the heart, her emotions are tremors of the heart caused by love or hatred. This special quality may, of course, veer into the terrifying possibility of the negative as happens in the case of concentration camp guards and terrorists. It witnesses to the fact that woman wants to completely possess what she does and desires; completely embrace, love, live, and hate. P. Kentenich called this characteristic "the claim for totality", which generates an awesome gift for self-surrender. This again may deviate into a loss of self, involving the loss of the order of being or creation. "Loss of the order of being is invariably followed by

---

[27] C. Meves, "Emancipation: Against Woman and Family?" in *Katholische Bildung* 9 (1979): 457.

[28] J. Kentenich, in *Bloss Konvention?*, loc. cit., no. 53, p. 40.

deterioration."[29] Not revolution of being, but fidelity to being must be our goal.[30]

As men and women we should be aware of the meaning of fidelity to being and to all it involves. I am quite concretely in agreement with C. Meves when she says: "The true psychological-spiritual emancipation has not yet begun; for it would presuppose that women develop a consciousness of their own specific attributes; that they would recognize that assimilation to men, in whatever form, will never liberate them from "slavery", whereas a concept which will help develop their potentialities will. Only in this way, by becoming increasingly aware of their self-worth, and by realizing that there exists no future for humanity without their psychological and spiritual contribution, could ways to their emancipation be discovered. It would then clearly emerge that women have to take different educational paths than men, and that their realization should be sought in special education institutions."[31]

MARY

All we have said so far can be demonstrated in the person of Mary, the most important woman in the history of the world. Totally surrendered, she remains a "person in relation" to God, to her child, to men, be it in Nazareth or in Bethlehem, in Cana, at the foot of the Cross, or in the cenacle. And since her Assumption, body and soul, into Heaven, she is the transfigured and perfected being in relation to the triune God and to us men. She is our advocate with the Lord, comforter of the afflicted, help of Christians, Mother of Good Counsel, Queen of Peace.

The New Testament shows that all subsequent events were based on her response to God's call by the angel. It actively involved her, a woman, in the greatest event of human history: the Incarnation of God's eternal Son within her, for the salvation of the world and all times.

---

[29] J. Kentenich, *Outline of a Contemporary Pedagogy for the Catholic Educator,* Education Meeting, 1950 (Vallendar-Schönstatt, 1971), 87 among others.

[30] J. Kentenich, in *Bloss Konvention?,* loc. cit., 82.

[31] C. Meves, "Suffering from Emancipation: Reflections of a Woman", in *Liberty Must Be Learned,* HB, 517 (Freiburg, 1975), I, 3.

Without coercion she speaks her *fiat* in personal freedom as a woman: "I am the handmaid of the Lord; be it done to me according to thy word" (Lk 1:38). It sums up her entire being: "I am . . . "; as it expresses her entire surrender as a woman: "I am—the handmaid of the Lord!" Mary does not give something, she gives herself. Let us listen once more to the metaphysician P. Kentenich: "Complete surrender! I make a distinction here between *ratione objecti* and *ratione subjecti*. When woman surrenders completely (*ratione objecti*), the surrender to the person is of primary concern, while surrender to the idea and work is secondary. That is significant . . . Total surrender, *ratione subjecti*, means that *everything* is surrendered to the person. All faculties of body and soul, everything."[32] This personal surrender is epitomized by the surrender of the "heart" to the personal "Thou" of the triune God: Thou, Thou forever! Thou, all in all! Thou, and Thy will! In this triad (also disclosed in the evangelical counsels) Mary's consent is encompassed.

"Be it done to me." Mary's self-surrender is embodied in the active-passive virginal conception. She conceives in the Holy Spirit the seed of God, the Eternal Word. When the Litany of Loreto invokes her as "spiritual vessel", "singular vessel of devotion", "house of gold", "ark of the covenant", it stresses the totality of her conceiving through visual imagery. Her readiness to conceive as handmaid of the Lord (not as handmaid of man!)[33] is the most profound form of her service; it requires all her powers of body, soul, and spirit. This is the way her love is spent: the virginal mother loves with her whole heart.

The movement of circling around the center—for Mary there is but one center, he himself—is often alluded to in Scripture. She ponders (fully understood or not) every word and every event in her heart, in contemplative wonder (Lk 2:19, 51).

Thus Mary is the feminine "reflection of the eternally circling love, joined by her womb to the triune God".[34] "She is the image and instrument of the Holy Spirit."[35] The *Holy Spirit,* within the inner-

[32] J. Kentenich, in *Bloss Konvention?*, loc. cit., no. 90f., p. 59.

[33] J. Kentenich, "Ethos and Ideal in Education, Paths to Personality Formation", Education Meeting, 1931 (Vallendar-Schönstatt, 1972), 143.

[34] Ibid., 145f.

[35] J. Kentenich, in *Bloss Konvention?*, loc. cit., no. 3, p. 9.

trinitarian life, is love: love spending itself within the Divine Persons, joining them in personal love, love personified. He, the Spirit (in Hebrew he is spoken of in the feminine gender), links and unites persons in Heaven as on earth, from Heaven to earth, and back to Heaven. He is that divine person who mediates, unites, and joins together.

Father Kentenich, decades before the current debate and theological argumentation, perceived in the Holy Spirit the deepest mysteries of Heaven and earth, and of God and woman in each other. The Holy Spirit (not Mary)[36] is the "feminine dimension of God",[37] if one may use such language in a hypothesis not yet sufficiently refined. Mary is, in her graced femininity, the instrument of the Holy Spirit silently serving the loving union of God with man, man with God, and men with each other.

We have been inquiring whether there was such a thing as an objective type "woman". After having listened to those who deny it, and having examined the consequences, we have occupied ourselves with the affirmative answer to the question. "We are grateful for the privilege of being women."[38]

What seems most significant is P. Kentenich's view of the closeness of the Holy Spirit to Mary—and in her to every woman who is willing to receive him. To the degree in which the Holy Spirit of God becomes

[36] A. Greeley, *Maria: Über die weibliche Dimension Gottes* (Graz, 1979); English edition: *The Mary Myth: On the Feminity of God* (New York: Harper & Row, 1977).

[37] God is all in all, uncreated, beyond gender, the plenitude of what he has created in his image, and for that reason he reveals himself in some texts of the Old Testament "like a mother" (e.g., Jer 42:14, 49:14f.; 66:13). Similar texts also appear in the New Testament Apparently Pope John Paul I referred to them when he spoke of God being "both Father and Mother".

In the great spiritual literature of the Middle Ages one encounters (in reflection and simile) astonishing statements of similar nature. Hildegard of Bingen speaks of God's "embracing maternal love", which descended through the "Word, which is the fount of Life itself" (*Know the Ways* [Salzburg, 1963], 157). Catherine of Siena, a Doctor of the Church, has handed down what God revealed to her in the *Gespräch von Gottes Vorsehung* [Discourse on God's Providence] (Einsiedeln, 1964, 196f). "My joy, the Holy Spirit, submits to be her [the Soul's] servant to whom he ministers. The Holy Spirit is mother to her and nurses her at the breast of my divine Love."

[38] J. Kentenich, in *Bloss Konvention?*, loc. cit., no. 3, p. 9.

effective in Mary and in us women, the war-torn world has a chance to become whole again. For it is fundamentally the Spirit of God who links Heaven and earth through us women, creating the atmosphere

> which mediates, which is just "there", and yet achieves what is really decisive: joining and interlacing. . . . Our primary function is therefore receptiveness to the Spirit as exemplified by Mary, the ability to be led and to be taken into service, without making ourselves the center of attention. In short, it is that attitude which simply is there, gathering and binding together.

The instrumental "betwixt", "being with", and "for" is "the role of the Spirit: we are 'in between', and this is our mission, so that the Father may speak and the Son may answer and that their unity may become strong."[39]

Being with and for each other in unity should increasingly become our passionate concern, our service to life in the Church and in the world. It may be said about this feminine-marian "spirit-role" that there cannot be a single moment, a single task or situation, in which anything else would be demanded of us than living this part.

---

[39] H. Heinz, "On Earth as It Is in Heaven. The Triune God as Measure of Our Pastoral", in H. Heinz, ed., *Gemeinde der Zukunft—nicht erst morgen* [Parish of the future—Not just tomorrow] (Munich, 1975), 73.

3

WALTER KASPER

THE POSITION OF WOMAN AS A PROBLEM OF THEOLOGICAL ANTHROPOLOGY

Translated by John Saward

i. THE CHALLENGE OF THE EMANCIPATION OF WOMEN

The position of woman in society and the Church is one of the most important subjects under discussion in the world today. Pope John XXIII had a strong sense of its importance, as he did of so many other questions. In his encyclical *Pacem in Terris* (1963) he included women's participation in public life and their increasing awareness of their human dignity among the signs of our times. Clearly, this issue presents a special kind of challenge to the life and teaching of the Church today.

This clear insight of the good and wise Pope John does not mean that a full or even partial awareness of the problem facing us has dawned throughout the Church. In practice, the three famous "C's" are still the rule for women—Children, Church, Chores. Many sermons, much pastoral exhortation, and a good deal of other Church talk are out of touch with the concrete situation. They represent a nowadays largely unrealistic and romantic view of women, in which younger women especially cannot recognize themselves. In addition, in the ecclesiastical sphere, women are subjected even today to numerous legal restrictions which seem anachronistic, if not absurd. One reason among numerous others for the silent departure of many women from the Church is the fact that often the women no longer identify with the Church, because they have the impression that the Church is not in solidarity with them and their problems.

Yet however important the question of the position of women in the Church may be, the problem goes deeper. Ultimately, behind the problems of ecclesiology, which are at their most intense in the question of the ordination of women, lie problems of anthropology: a crisis and a radical change in women's self-understanding, or rather in the self-understanding of man and woman.

This is easily confirmed by glancing at social developments. At present we are experiencing the end of the patriarchal order of society, in which the head of the household has dominion over not only his property and servants but his wife and children as well. Only the male is the fully competent and mature human being. The male is the ideal and primary representation of the human. Things have reached the stage where many languages use one and the same word for "male" and "human" (English *man;* French *homme;* in German the impersonal *man*). Only in our century has this view, which has persisted for thousands of years, been radically changed, and the change is due to women becoming conscious of their full and equal dignity as human beings and their equal rights to participation in public life. It is perhaps the most significant cultural revolution of our time.

The emancipation of women has a history going back over a century. In the first phase it was taken up with the demand for legal and political enfranchisement, then for economic, social, and cultural equality. Today the women's movement has entered a second phase. It is no longer a matter of women's rights to an equal place in the world of men, but of a critical rebellion against male society in general and the construction of a new, more human society. This is why the women's movement is numbered among those modern movements of emancipation which are concerned with humanity's self-liberation from cultural and national dependency, with making people aware of their dignity as human beings and with its practical realization.

True, there are differences of opinion, both inside and outside the women's movement, about what this new human society should look like and how women's emancipation is to be understood: is it bound up, as Marxists think, with the proletarian, national, and racial liberation movements, or is it a sexual revolution independent of them? But whatever direction the women's movement takes, the issues concern not just women but the human race as a whole, the order of human society and the values underpinning it. That is why the women's movement no longer reaches its real and concrete culmination in questions of equal rights, but in the ethical issues of divorce, birth control, abortion, extramarital relations, and so on.

Thus analysis of the social situation leads to the conclusion that the problem of woman is primarily a problem of human existence, a problem of anthropology. Asserting this does not take the edge off the problem, but rather sharpens it, because now we are dealing not just with the reversal or redistribution of social and ecclesiastical roles, but with developing our awareness of what we are as human beings, what we are as men and as women, what a human society might be. Only when we pose the problem in this way does it become clear to us why this question touches human beings and human society at the very deepest level and provokes such powerful emotions.

Since the days of John XXIII the Church has certainly recognized the challenge, but she has not by any means responded adequately to it. Today she is faced with totally new questions about the Christian image of man. Starting from the Christian understanding of man as a person, she must give a creative answer to the challenge of the philosophy of emancipation. The thesis to be expounded in what follows is this: the Christian view of woman as a person can incorporate the legitimate demands of the philosophy of emancipation. However, it also can and must reflect critically on it and deepen it, thus preventing the emancipation of woman becoming her emancipation from being a woman. It must encourage women in creative fidelity to their own vocation. This thesis will be developed below in three subordinate propositions.

2. THE EQUAL PERSONAL DIGNITY OF MAN AND WOMAN

The first and most fundamental affirmation of Christian theology is this: man and woman are both, in a fully equal way, persons.

Nowadays this affirmation seems self-evident to us. It is not self-evident, however, when one considers the long tradition that regarded women as failed men and second-class human beings. Jewish and Greek philosophical influence led the Fathers of the Church to dubious outpourings debasing women. Many passages in the New Testament seem to support such discrimination against women. However, when one looks at the general tendency of the biblical message about creation and redemption, a different picture emerges which can provide the foundation for a renewed theological anthropology of woman, or rather of the relationship of man and woman.

According to the more ancient of the two accounts of creation (Gen 2:4–25), the one which comes in second place in the Bible, God created the man first and appointed him to be lord of creation. Only later is the woman created, because it is not good for the man to be alone, and because none of the other creatures is fit for him. Thus, according to this account, woman is seen as the helpmate assigned to man. In its vivid imagery the Bible even says that woman was created out of the rib of man, which is, of course, to be understood symbolically rather than realistically. What it might mean is that woman is created, according to the measure of man, as his completion. There are thus still traces in this narrative of an androcentric view, i.e., one referring to man. But we also find tendencies in the opposite direction in this ancient text. Woman is created by God—again in symbolic language—while man is fast asleep. In biblical terminology that means that woman's existence, as far as man is concerned, is an inaccessible mystery, with its explanation and answer in God alone. Woman is not a frustrated and inferior man, but an original creative thought of God. Ultimately she is not from and toward man, but from and toward God. She owes her being and her dignity, not to man, but to God. That is why, in the final analysis, she is not at man's disposal: no, she is his equal. Both man and woman come from God and belong together; they form one flesh; they are one person.

What the more ancient creation account clearly asserts in its general tendency, even though its details remain ambiguous, is expressed with complete clarity in the later account, which is put into first place (Gen 1:1–2, 4). There it says: "God created man in his own image, in the image of God he created him; male and female he created them" (Gen 1:27). There are widely differing answers to the question what this divine image in human beings concretely consists in. By and large it is generally agreed today that it consists in neither the human being's spiritual soul alone nor in his external, upright shape alone. What is meant is the whole human person in body and soul, the whole person in relation to God, the human being as a responsive covenant partner for God. The concept of the image of God thus describes human beings as creatures made for dialogue, created by God and for God. This structure of dialogue and partnership in human beings is reflected in their relationships to one another. Humanity only exists in the "dual version" of man and woman, who are both mutually dependent on one another. The image of God and the differentiation of the sexes thus belong together. Man and woman are both God's image; they are both directly in relationship to God and in that respect are completely equal. But in the equality of this dignity of theirs they are ordered toward one another in partnership. So it is understandable that the covenant between man and woman in marriage can become the image and likeness for God's covenant with his people.

The reason why not only man but woman too is in the fullest sense God's image is that the God of the Bible can be given female and maternal attributes as well as male and paternal ones. This is evident, for example, in the prophet Isaiah: "As one whom his mother comforts, so I will comfort you" (Is 66:13). Nevertheless, if, especially in the New Testament, there is a predominance, at least terminologically, of the idea of God as Father and God is addressed as "our Father", this does not mean, as many feminists fear, that the Jewish and Christian traditions are hopelessly and one-sidedly sexist. Rather, both the idea of God as Father and the idea of God as mother, in the meaning they have in the Bible and Christian tradition, must be understood analogically. This means that (1) both ideas are used as images; (2) they must be understood and interpreted in terms of religious, not sexual, language; (3) in their application to God, every kind of finite limitation including, therefore, sexual limitation, is excluded; and (4) in any likeness, the ever greater unlikeness of God and man is emphasized. Ultimately God is neither male nor female; he founds neither a patriarchal nor a matriarchal order, but rather a human order, in which the equal dignity of men and women is respected and given practical expression.

Against this background we can begin to understand why, in the history of the covenant, not only men but women too become Israel's representatives and can speak and act in the name of the whole people: Deborah, Miriam, Huldah, Ruth, Esther, Judith, and all the other great female figures of the Old Testament. In the New Testament it is again a woman—Mary—who, in the name of all humanity, says Yes to God's new covenant with man and thus becomes the gateway through which salvation enters the world. Thus, in salvation history, woman is in no sense purely passive, in no sense just an object, but a completely self-determining, active subject. Man and woman, in their relationships with and toward each other, are actively involved in God's history with mankind.

This becomes fully clear in Jesus. Not only is his personal relationship to women completely natural, he also includes women among his closest followers. At the same time, in following Jesus, women are not simply relegated to the kitchen and confined to caring for people's physical well-being. As the story of Martha and Mary vividly demonstrates, women are not just lowly maidservants, working away in obscurity, but, like men, attentive listeners, who are taken into service with all their intellectual capacities and at Easter become the first witnesses of the Resurrection.

Jesus' most important statement about the position of woman is what he says about the indissolubility of marriage (Mk 10:2–9). Jesus makes reference to the Jewish practice according to which a man can unilaterally dismiss his wife. In contrast, Jesus goes back to the original order: "At the beginning of creation it was not so." By doing this, Jesus abolishes the double-standard morality; he makes woman the equal companion of man. Man cannot have her at his disposal, because the two of them together are at God's disposal. "What God has joined together, let not man put asunder." With these words Jesus protests, for the sake of God, against inequality and injustice with regard to women. According to the original order of creation, Jesus wants to say, man and woman have the same rights and the same duties before God and one another.

Like the Old Testament (cf. Gen 3), in saying this, of course, Jesus knows that human hardheartedness, sin, has spoiled the relationship of man and woman. The Bible is aware of the profound ambivalence of the relationship between the sexes. The Kingdom of God which Jesus proclaims is meant to restore the original intention of the created order and to put it into effect in an unsurpassable way. This new creation becomes a reality in the Cross and Resurrection of Jesus Christ. For those who share through baptism in the new creation, "there is neither Jew nor Greek, there is neither slave nor free, there is neither male nor female, for you are all one in Christ Jesus" (Gal 3:28). Before God and in Christ there is no subordination or undervaluing of woman. Before God and in Christ all the differences specific to the sexes are immaterial.

Such new and revolutionary assertions need time for their consequences to be assessed both theoretically and, above all, practically. In the New Testament we have a real struggle between assertions of woman's subordination to man and the affirmation of her equality. This struggle has left its mark on the entire history of the Church. We must honestly admit that there are pressures and movements today, largely outside of Christianity, which are causing us Christians to become fully conscious again of the central and fundamental points of the New Testament texts. If, therefore, in the language of the Christian tradition, we formulate our thesis and say that "man and woman are both, in a fully equal way, persons", this is not, unfortunately, a self-evident truth, but a highly critical proposition with many practical consequences.

"Person", in the sense in which the Christian tradition understands it, means the unique being who exists "in himself" and "for himself", a value and an end in himself, never a means to an end, an inviolable dignity with an absolute right to respect. The foundation of this dignity, from the Christian point of view, is that every human being has a direct relationship to God as his image, so that man is ultimately beyond the ken of man. On the face of every human being shines something of the glory of God.

If our starting-point is this dignity of the person, it is clear that thinking about women in terms of roles misses the mark. A woman cannot be defined by her role as wife nor by her role as mother, friend, partner, colleague, competitor, or even as cheap labor. As an autonomous person a woman is more than all this. She transcends all these roles. Her value does not depend on whether she fits into one or several of these roles and does justice to them. Her value is determined by the God from whom she comes and for whom she exists. That is why a woman does not exist in the end for the sake of man, nor even for the sake of the family. She finds her meaning neither in her role as devoted companion and mother nor as the worker who supplements and collaborates with the main work performed by man. She does not receive value, dignity, prestige, or position through man. In herself she has value and dignity.

This personal autonomy would remain abstract, were it not expressed in the legal and economic autonomy and equality of man and woman. If women are to become aware of themselves as persons and to make that dignity a concrete reality, it is most important that they share in contemporary education; here, irrespective of economic profitability, the same opportunities must be open to both girls and boys. So the Christian-inspired view of woman as an autonomous person has far-reaching consequences in the socio-political and educational spheres, consequences which, especially in ecclesiastical circles, are far from having been fully appreciated, let alone put into practice. If the slogan of "woman's self-fulfillment" means "woman's fulfillment of her personal dignity", it deserves the emphatic support of the Church.

3. THE DIFFERENTIATION OF MEN AND WOMEN

The second affirmation of Christian anthropology about the relationship of man and woman is this: there is no such thing as *the* human being and *the* human person. The human person exists only in the "dual version" of man and woman. A woman is thus a person in her own specific way—by being a woman. She is no less a person than a man is, but she is a person in her own way.

This thesis too has its foundation in the biblical doctrine of creation, which sees the whole human being in soul and body as the creature of God. The doctrine of creation justifies neither a materialistic nor an idealist view of human beings; with its integral understanding of the human person, it is realistic through and through. Christian anthropology sees the human body as a real symbol, as the "excarnation" of the human spirit, the spirit being the form and life principle of the body. With this view Christianity by its very nature—unfortunately not always in its concrete historical realizations—is incompatible with every form of Gnosticism, which in its hostility to the body and sexuality regards the real human being, the self, as an inner personal core indifferent to the body and sexuality. If the body is the real symbol of the human spirit, then bodily, sexually specific differences cannot be irrelevant to the constitution of the person. So we cannot say that there is just a minor biological difference between man and woman with admittedly great sociological consequences; the sexual is not a specialized zone or sector but a determination of the human being which affects the whole person, all that is human. The equality and equal value of man and woman, on the Christian view, are something very different from an abstract identity. Man and woman are two equally valuable but different expressions of the one nature of humanity.

Gnosticism's contempt for the body and sexuality is, of course, not just a thing of the past, a historical phenomenon; in changing forms it recurs again and again throughout history and is powerfully present in many forms of modern emancipation philosophy. The devaluation of the sexual expresses itself not only in a falsely understood asceticism, but also in a libertinism, which regards sexuality as ultimately trivial and inconsequential for the person, and not least in the attempt to emancipate human beings from their natural preconditions. The ideological character of this attempt can be seen in the fact that it has to suppress those important insights of modern biology and medicine which indicate the deep-seated differences of bodily constitution between men and women.

Of course, at this point in the present discussion, the question is posed: What constitutes the specifically feminine? Romanticism gave rise to a polarized definition of the sexes. The male characteristics were held to include activity, the power to achieve, world-mastery, creative enthusiasm, abstract thought, and so on. Woman was defined by receptivity, protectiveness, solicitude, care, intuition, down-to-earth thinking. This polarized picture of the man/woman relationship had a particularly marked effect on the Catholic world. Consider, for example, what is in its own way a splendid book, *Die ewige Frau* by Gertrud von le Fort: in hymnic language this book contains a whole metaphysic of the feminine. This vision fits into a broad stream of human tradition, for which male and female represent cosmic metaphysical principles.

More recently this kind of metaphysical interpretation of the difference between the sexes has had a guarded and critical reception. The American ethnologist Margaret Mead has popularized the discovery that many of what in our culture are considered to be typically female qualities and activities are characteristic of the male in some other cultures. Contemporary anthropology emphasizes that the human being is not just a natural being but a cultural being as well. Human nature includes, therefore, diverse cultural expressions and considerable historical variation.

This is the point of departure for the feminist movement. The fundamental work is Simone de Beauvoir's classic, *The Second Sex* (1949), which is based on the existentialist philosophy of Jean-Paul Sartre. In Existentialism, human beings do not have a preconditioned nature; they project themselves by virtue of their freedom. Nowadays the point is made differently: the differences between the sexes are conditioned by socialization processes; they are instilled, they arise through role expectations and role patterns. The reaction to this trend in feminism is represented in the German-speaking world by, for example, Ursula Erler in her book, *Zerstörung and Selbstzerstörung der Frau*. Following Hannah Arendt, she develops the thesis that man and woman are differentiated by the fact that only the woman can be a mother. Now being a mother is not just a biological phenomenon: it affects the whole being of a woman. Motherhood, says Ursula Erler, is not a biological destiny but a way of arranging one's life. The issue here is not role but being. This, if anything, is what the self-fulfillment of woman is about.

It is once again from the idea of creation that the Christian proceeds to state his position in this conflict of opinions. According to the Christian view of creation, the Creator has given his creature its nature and has given it differently to the two sexes. God made man and woman equal in dignity, but not simply the same. Now God did not just give human beings their nature, he also gave them the task of cultivating it. So human beings are not merely biological beings but cultural beings of extreme historical diversity. Being male or being female is something they have to cultivate. This begins with the culture of the body and extends to the personal arrangement of one's life. Yet culture does not mean an emancipation from nature, but the creative realization of its possibilities.

Woman's vocation, in accordance with creation, is the vocation to the service of life. She is Eve, that is to say, the mother of all the living (Gen 3:20). This vocation to motherhood can be fulfilled in different ways: in marriage and the family, but also in celibacy, which frees people to devote themselves in another way to the service of the coming generation. In both cases this much is true: an emancipation of woman at the expense of children and the coming generation would be an emancipation from being a woman. Responsibility for life and for humane conditions of life constitute the vocation of woman; this is what must give her esteem and dignity. That is why it is irresponsible that this vocation to be a mother has been so disparaged in its public reputation during the last two centuries. In particular, talking about the "right to abortion" as an expression of woman's self-fulfillment represents a misjudgment and reversal of the true dignity of woman.

Everyone knows that, in the circumstances of life today, problems result from this affirmation. These problems do not have to mean just a burden for women; no, they imply tasks for women and men. A new appreciation of motherhood ought to lead, for example, to a revision of our tax and social security system. The proposition that women are different must not be interpreted to the disadvantage of women—as many, not just feminists, fear—and not without reason. What it does entail is the task of creating conditions, in society and the Church, in which women can fulfill their being and their vocation in the best possible way.

This demand means ultimately the renunciation of a one-sided orientation toward the so-called male ideals. In the past these have led not only to the exploitation of women but also to the overexploitation of nature and the destruction of the environment as a humane world in which to live. Women and men must liberate themselves today from this ideal and develop instead a plan of life and a model of society in which sensitivity, empathy, feeling, and heart receive a new status. This would mean the end of a society influenced one-sidedly by so-called male values and norms, a shift and break in cultural history of the greatest proportions. The Church too ought to abandon what sometimes seems like a one-sidedly masculine appearance and disclose the feminine dimension more. Prayer, hymnody, and liturgy must become receptive to concrete experiences of happiness and pain, joy, and sorrow. Theological formulas and dogmas must be complemented by images and symbols reflecting concrete life. It is a question of the whole human being, of man and woman. If this succeeds, then the women's movement, in terms not only of cultural and intellectual history but of Church history as well, is one of the most significant revolutions of our age.

4. THE PARTNERSHIP OF WOMEN AND MEN

What we have just said leads to the third and final thesis of Christian anthropology about the relationship of man and woman: the autonomous personal fulfillment of woman can only be accomplished in the partnership of men and women. Man and woman can be fulfilled only with one another, not in opposition to one another. They have their common future and their common hope in their children. The slogans of class struggle cannot be applied to the relationship of the sexes. Their relationship can only be described and become a reality as a partnership.

This thesis follows by logical necessity from the two previous propositions. The difference between those who have the same nature and the same value leads necessarily to the idea that they are mutually complementary, the one pointing beyond itself to the other. That is why man and woman find themselves by finding one another and by becoming one flesh, that is to say, a "We person". Thus being a person—being in and for oneself—becomes a reality in being with and for the other: self-fulfillment is not achieved by means of egotistical self-assertion and self-aggrandizement, but only in self-giving, self-surrendering love. A person is fulfilled in relationship and communication. The unconditional character of the person becomes a reality in the relationship of man and woman, and so that relationship attains its ultimate realization only when it is willed unconditionally and therefore definitively. Indissoluble marriage is, therefore, the only place where the full and final communion of man and woman can be achieved in a way that is humanly worthy. Only when a woman is unconditionally and therefore definitively accepted, affirmed, and loved is she accepted in sexual partnership as a personal subject and not degraded as an object and means. However, women's emancipation in the sense of emancipation from the "yoke" of marriage is possible only on the basis of a misunderstanding of human and thus of womanly dignity, of a misunderstanding of what persons are, persons who realize their unconditional character in irrevocable fidelity.

This thesis is not in any way directed against an authentic understanding or practice of freely chosen Christian celibacy. On the contrary, in the New Testament, celibacy chosen freely for the sake of the Kingdom of Heaven is a decisive form of a rightly understood emancipation of woman, because it sets a woman free from the compulsion and obligation of marriage and from her destined role as wife, mother, and housewife. In the New Testament, the unmarried woman, wholly taken up with the affairs of the Lord, concerned, not with how she pleases her husband, but with how she pleases the Lord (1 Cor 7:32), is the woman who is really free of man. Even without a husband she is "someone" in the community. She has a "status" of her own; even without a husband she enjoys esteem and respect. This does not imply any disdain of sexuality and marriage. For if freely chosen celibacy becomes a real alternative to marriage, marriage in turn becomes a really free decision. Thus Christian celibacy does not devalue marriage, it revalues it, making it one freely chosen possibility along side another. That is the reason why the dignity of Christian marriage and Christian celibacy can never be played off against one another. They stand or fall together!

If, with the Christian tradition, one makes statements like this about marriage and celibacy, one must also, of course, be aware of the great problems facing their practical realization today. The two most important problems can be mentioned only in passing here: so-called "marriage" without a certificate and breakdown in marriage and in celibacy. Both problems affect the position and the pain of many women in today's society and Church to such an extent that the discussion could easily concentrate on them. Therefore, we shall discuss here a third problem, one closely connected with our modern civilization. Modern industrial society is characterized, among other things, by the separation of the private, family sphere from the public, professional sphere. It was precisely because of this separation that women for a long time were confined to the private, family sphere. Nowadays many women feel this to be stifling, though when they try to free themselves from it, they are pushed into a stressful, indeed murderous, dual role. What is more, progress in science and civilization has considerably increased the life expectancy of women. For many women the maternal role is now no longer a lifetime task, but just a chronologically limited phase of their life. At the same time, due to the same progress, eroticism and sex can be disconnected from their reproductive function. Because of all this, a new situation has arisen containing many opportunities, above all the opportunity of an increase in concrete autonomy and freedom, though it also involves considerable burdens and disadvantages for women. In this new situation and the dual role it brings about, many women feel uncertain of themselves; indeed, for many it leads to a profound identity crisis.

Women cannot bear, all on their own, the brunt of the crisis in marriage and the family triggered by modern developments. There must be a general restoration of friendship and family relationships. There must be new forms of the married partnership of men and women and more flexible relationships in the world of the professions and the economy. The redistribution of roles would give new possibilities of self-fulfillment not only to women but also to men. They could and should liberate themselves from a role that alienates them from being fully human. The Church has no reason for clinging to unrealistic, one-sided, and outmoded models. She ought rather to give her energetic support to the new possibilities. In her own sphere she should try to promote models of this new kind of partnership in which women and men can make their full and specific contribution to the life of the Church. By so doing, on this issue, the Church would be able to be more clearly what she defined herself to be at the last Council—a sacrament, that is to say, a sign and instrument of unity with God and among men.

One can only hope that Christian women and men will recognize their task at this time, not to pursue uncritically the slogans of emancipation, but, on the basis of the Christian understanding of the personal dignity of man and woman, to give a genuinely Christian response to the challenge of the women's movement. It must be a response that points forward. Now it is our Christian conviction that you can point forward only by pointing upward and by being fed by faith in God's order in creation and redemption. For the mystery of God is the real answer to the question of the mystery of man, the answer too to the question of the mystery of woman. One can only wish that the churches recognize the signs of the times and not just the dangers, but above all that they recognize the opportunities that lie, for themselves and their cause, within this movement.

II

THE CHURCH'S TEACHING ON MARY AND THE MISSION OF WOMAN IN THE CHURCH TODAY

4

JOSEPH CARDINAL RATZINGER

ON THE POSITION OF MARIOLOGY AND MARIAN SPIRITUALITY WITHIN THE TOTALITY OF FAITH AND THEOLOGY

Translated by Graham Harrison

I. THE BACKGROUND AND SIGNIFICANCE OF THE MARIOLOGICAL TEACHING OF VATICAN II

The question as to the significance of mariology and marian spirituality cannot be divorced from the historical situation of the Church which gives rise to it. We shall be in a position to understand and give a proper reply to the profound crisis which has overtaken our thinking and speaking about Mary, and with Mary, only if we see it in the context of the larger development to which it belongs. In the period beginning with the end of the First World War and lasting until Vatican II, the internal life of the Church was influenced by two great spiritual movements, both of which—though in very different ways—to some extent bore "charismatic" features. Thus, since the marian apparitions in the middle of the nineteenth century, a marian movement had gone from strength to strength, finding its charismatic roots in La Salette, Lourdes, and Fatima, and culminating, throughout the whole Church, in the pontificate of Pius XII. On the other hand, the period between the World Wars, particularly in Germany, saw the development of the liturgical movement, which had its origin in the renewal of Benedictine monasticism that began in Solesmes, but also in the eucharistic teaching of Pius X. Against the background of the youth movement, increasingly, its influence spread to the broad mass of church people, at least in Central Europe. The ecumenical movement and the biblical movement joined forces with it to become one mighty river. Its basic aim, which was to renew the Church by going back to the scriptural sources and the primitive form of ecclesial prayer, likewise found an initial official ratification by Pius XII in the encyclicals on the Church and the liturgy.[1]

The more these movements achieved significance in the whole Church, the more tangibly problematical became their relationship with each other. In many ways, because of their fundamental attitudes and their theological orientations, they seemed to be mutually opposed. The liturgical movement itself liked to refer to its spirituality as "objectively" sacramental; by contrast, the marian movement clearly emphasized the subjective and personal side. The liturgical movement stressed the theocentric character of Christian prayer, which goes "through Christ to the Father"; the marian movement, with its watchword *per Mariam ad Jesum,* seemed to be characterized by a different idea of mediatorship; it seemed to linger with Jesus and Mary, pushing the classical trinitarian relationship into the background. The liturgical movement looked for a spirituality which took its bearings strictly by the Bible or at all events by the ancient Church; marian spirituality, which at this time was greatly influenced by the apparitions of the Mother of God, was much more indebted to the tradition of the middles ages and of modern times. It pursued a different style of thought and feeling.[2] There were dangers here, of course, threatening the healthy core and even causing zealous protagonists of the other side to throw doubt on it.[3]

---

[1] Cf. J. Frings, *Das Konzil und die moderne Gedankenwelt* (Cologne, 1962), p. 31–37.

[2] Characteristic of the difference between these two attitudes—a difference that goes far beyond the realm of mariology—is the approach in J. A. Jungmann's book *Die Frohbotschaft und die Glaubensverkündigung* (Regensburg, 1936); the vehement reaction to this work, which had to be withdrawn from bookshops at the time, illustrates the situation very clearly. Cf. Jungmann's own observations on this, written in 1961 in B. Fischer and H. B. Meyer (eds.), *J. A. Jungmann, Ein Leben für Liturgie und Kerygma* (Innsbruck, 1975), p. 12–18.

[3] Cf. R. Laurentin's study *La question mariale* (Paris, 1963) with its generous amount of material. Noteworthy, for instance, is the warning of Pope John XXIII, quoted on page 19, against certain practices or excessive forms of spirituality and even of the veneration of the Madonna, forms "which also give a very poor impression of the spirituality of our good people". In the concluding address at the Roman Synod the Pope repeated his warning against this kind of spirituality which lets the imagination

In any case it had to be part of the task of a Council, held at a time such as this, to work out the correct relationship between these two divergent movements and lead them toward a fruitful unity—but not by simply eliminating the tension. And it is a fact that one cannot properly understand the wrestling of the first half of the Council—the dispute about the Constitution on the Liturgy, the doctrine of the Church and the correct place of mariology, about revelation, Scripture, tradition, and the ecumenical dimension—except against the background of tension between these two forces. What was at stake in these debates, though it was by no means at the forefront of people's awareness, was a striving for a proper relationship between the two charismatic currents which constituted, as it were, internal "signs of the times" for the Church. Subsequent work on the Pastoral Constitution would involve getting to grips with the "signs of the times" coming from outside. In this drama the celebrated vote of October 29, 1963 acquires the significance of a spiritual watershed. The question was whether mariology should be presented in a document of its own or should be part of the Constitution on the Church. This would establish the importance and mutual relationship of the two streams of spirituality and thus give a decisive answer to the Church's existing internal condition. Both sides commissioned men of the highest caliber in the attempt to win the Plenum over. Cardinal König spoke in favor of integrating the texts, which in fact meant giving priority to liturgico-biblical spirituality and theology. Cardinal Rufino Santos of Manila pleaded for the marian element to be allowed to stand on its own feet. The vote of 1,114 to 1,074 showed an assembly divided, for the first time, into two almost equal groups. All the same the Council Fathers, indebted to the liturgical and biblical movements, won a victory (albeit narrow), leading to a decision whose importance could hardly be overestimated.

From a theological point of view the majority, led by Cardinal König, were doubtless right. If the two charismatic movements were not to be seen as opposed but as complementary, an integration of the texts was indicated, in which neither would be absorbed into the other. The work

run riot and contributes little to the soul's concentration. "We would invite you to hold to more venerable and simpler things in the Church's practice."

of Hugo Rahner,[4] A. Müller,[5] K. Delahaye,[6] R. Laurentin,[7] and O. Semmelroth[8] had shown convincingly, in the years following the Second World War, that the liturgical, biblical and patristic spirituality and theology had an inner openness to the marian dimension. These studies had rooted both approaches more profoundly in that center which united them; on this basis they could maintain their distinctiveness and further develop its fruitfulness. In point of fact, the attempt to do this convincingly and vigorously in the marian chapter of the Constitution on the Church was only a partial success. Moreover the postconciliar development was largely marked by a misunderstanding of the Council's teaching on tradition, a misunderstanding that was significantly promoted by the oversimplified accounts of the Council debate in the media. The whole debate was reduced to Geiselmann's question concerning the "sufficiency" of the content of Scripture,[9] and this in turn was interpreted according to a biblicism that condemned the entire patristic inheritance to insignificance—which also undermined the former thrust of the liturgical movement. Biblicism itself, however, in the context of the modern academic situation, turned into historicism; admittedly, the liturgical movement had never been wholly free from this tendency. Rereading their writings today, one is aware that they are too dependent on an archaeological approach that assumes a process of decline: anything that makes its appearance after a particular point of time is automatically regarded as inferior, as if the Church were not equally alive and

---

[4] H. Rahner, *Maria und die Kirche* (Innsbruck, 1951); H. Rahner, *Mater Ecclesia. Lobpreis der Kirche aus dem ersten Jahrtausend* (Einsiedeln, Cologne, 1944).

[5] A. Müller, *Ecclesia-Maria. Die Einheit Marias und der Kirche* (Fribourg, 1955).

[6] K. Delahaye, *Erneuerungen der Seelsorgsformen aus der Sicht der frühen Patristik* (Freiburg, 1958).

[7] R. Laurentin, *Court traité de théologie mariale* (Paris, 1953); R. Laurentin, *Structure et théologie de Luc 1–2* (Paris, 1957).

[8] O. Semmelroth, *Urbild der Kirche. Organischer Aufbau des Mariengeheimnisses* (Würzburg, 1950); cf. also M. Schmaus, "Mariologie": *Katholische Dogmatik V* (Munich, 1955).

[9] I have attempted to show that Geiselmann's approach in fact misses the kernel of the problem: K. Rahner and J. Ratzinger, *Offenbarung und Überlieferung* (Freiburg, 1965, 25–69); cf. also my commentary on chapter 2 of the Constitution on Revelation in *LThK Supplement II*, 515–28.

capable of development at all times. All this led the liturgical approach to become narrowed down to a biblicist-positivist line which was sealed off in its backward gaze and had no room for the dynamism of a faith that is continually unfolding. On the other side, historicism's distanced attitude necessarily led to "Modernism"; since what is merely of the past is no longer alive, the present is on its own; this leads to home-made experimenting. In addition, the new, Church-centered mariology was (and largely remained) alien to those Council Fathers who had advocated marian spirituality. Nor could the resultant vacuum be filled by introducing the title "Mother of the Church", which Paul VI used at the conclusion of the Council as a deliberate response to the clearly brewing crisis. In practice the triumph of Church-centered mariology initially resulted in the collapse of all mariology whatsoever. It seems to me that the altered face of the Church in Latin America after the Council, the concentration of religious affectivity, at times, on political change, is also to be understood against this background.

2. MARIOLOGY'S POSITIVE FUNCTION IN THEOLOGY

The new approach was primarily initiated by the Apostolic Letter of Paul VI (February 2, 1974) on the proper form of marian devotion.[10] As we have seen, in practice the resolution of 1963 led to the absorption of mariology by ecclesiology. A reexamination of the document must start from the premise that this historical effect contradicts its actual intention. For the marian chapter 8 had been written deliberately as an inner parallel to chapters 1–4 on the structure of the Church; the aim was to balance the energies of the biblical, ecumenical, and liturgical movements and those of the marian movement so that they could relate fruitfully to each other. Let us put it in positive terms: properly understood, mariology exercises a twofold clarifying and deepening influence on the concept of the Church.

1. As against the masculine, activist, and sociological approach of the "People of God" there is the fact that Church—*Ecclesia*—is feminine.

[10] Apostolic Letter "Marialis Cultus" (February 2, 1974).

This brings out a dimension of the mystery that points beyond the sociological aspect; only here can we see the real basis and unifying power that ground the Church. Church is more than "people", more than structure and action: in her lives the mystery of motherhood and of that spousal love which makes motherhood possible. Church spirituality, love for the Church, is possible only on the basis of this mystery. Where the Church is seen only in masculine, structural, and institutional terms, it has lost the really distinctive aspect of *Ecclesia*, that central core of which the Bible and the Fathers speak when referring to the Church.[11]

2. Paul expressed the specific difference of the New Testament Church vis-à-vis the "wandering people of God" of the Old Covenant in the term "Body of Christ": Church is not the organization, but the organism of Christ. Only as mediated by christology does it become a "people" at all, and this mediation takes place in the sacrament, in the Eucharist, which, for its part, presupposes Cross and Resurrection. Consequently whenever we speak of the Church as "People of God" we always add, at least mentally, the concept "Body of Christ".[12] However, even "Body of Christ" requires clarification in the modern context of discussion if it is not to be misunderstood, for it could easily be interpreted according to a Christo-monism, i.e., an absorption of the Church, and hence of man, the believing creature, into the utter uniqueness of christology. In Paul's usage, however, the "Body of Christ" (which we are) is always to be understood against the background of Genesis 2:24: "The two become one flesh" (cf. 1 Cor 6:17). The Church is the body, the flesh of Christ, in the spiritual tension of love in which the conjugal mystery of Adam and Eve is fulfilled, in the dynamism of a unity which does not eliminate reciprocity. This means that the very eucharistic-christological mystery of the Church which is proclaimed in the term "Body of Christ" can only keep its proper proportions if it includes the marian mystery, namely, that of the Virgin who hears the word and—having been liberated

[11] Cf. H. U. von Balthasar's authoritative presentation "Wer ist die Kirche?" in *Sponsa Verbi* (Einsiedeln, 1960), 148–202.

[12] Cf. J. Ratzinger "Kirche als Heilssakrament" in J. Reikerstorfer (ed.) *Zeit des Geistes* (Vienna, 1977), 59–70; cf. also my *Das neue Volk Gottes* (Düsseldorf, 1969), 75–89.

by grace—utters her "Fiat" and thus becomes Bride and hence Body.[13]

This being so, mariology can never be simply dissolved into the terms of ecclesiology. It is a fundamental misreading of the typology of the Fathers to see it as reducing Mary to a mere exemplification—and hence replaceable—of theological concepts. Typology is meaningful only if the Church is recognizable in her personal form through the irreplaceable personal figure of Mary. In theology, the person is not traced back to some state of affairs: on the contrary, this state of affairs is traced back to the person. A purely structuralist ecclesiology must denature the Church into a mere program of action. The marian dimension is essential if the area of the emotions, too, is to be fully anchored in faith; only thus can there be a complete human response to the reality of the incarnate Logos. At this point I can see the relevance of speaking of "Mary conquering all heresies": where man's affective side is rooted in this way, he is bound *ex toto corde*—from the bottom of his heart—to the *personal* God and his Christ; then it becomes impossible to melt christology down into a Jesus-ism that can be atheistic and purely material. The experience of recent years gives astonishing verification of the truth of these ancient maxims.

3. THE PLACE OF MARIOLOGY IN THE TOTALITY OF THEOLOGY

The foregoing has also clarified the place of mariology in theology. G. Söll, in his impressive book on the history of mariological doctrine, comes to the conclusion, at the end of his historical analysis, that marian teaching should be seen in the context of christology and soteriology rather than that of ecclesiology.[14] Without wishing to diminish the extraordinary achievement of this book or the significance of its historical conclusions, however, I regard the contrary decision of the Fathers of Vatican II as correct, both from the systematic point of view and within a

[13] Cf. H. U. von Balthasar (note II above); cf. also the beautiful interpretation of the Annunciation in K. Wojtyla, *Zeichen des Widerspruchs* (Zurich, Freiburg, 1979), 5of.

[14] G. Söll *Mariologie* (= *Handbuch der Dogmengeschichte* ed. Schmaus, Grillmeier, Scheffczyk, and Seybold, vol III/4 [Freiburg, 1978]).

total historical perspective. True, the history of doctrine shows incontrovertibly that the teachings on Mary initially arose out of christological necessity and developed within christology's framework. But it must be added that everything that was said in this context did not form a distinct mariology, nor could it; it remained an explication of christology. By contrast, however, we find in the ecclesiology of the period of the Fathers a preliminary adumbration of the whole of mariology, albeit without naming the name of the Mother of the Lord: the *Virgo Ecclesia,* the *Mater Ecclesia,* the *Ecclesia immaculata,* the *Ecclesia assumpta* — everything that will one day be mariology is present here as ecclesiology. Of course, ecclesiology cannot be isolated from christology, yet the Church does have a relative independence vis-à-vis Christ, as we have already seen: it has the independence of his Bride who, though one Spirit with him in love, yet remains his partner in reciprocity. There was no mariology as a distinct area in theology until this ecclesiology, which was initially nameless but envisaged in personal terms, fused with the teaching on Mary found in christology. This process began with Bernard of Clairvaux. Thus Mary cannot be assigned exclusively to christology or ecclesiology, let alone be dissolved into a more or less superfluous example. Rather, to speak of Mary is to touch on the *nexus mysteriorum* — the inner interwovenness of the mysteries, which are manifold, in relation, and yet one. Christ and the Church, for instance, are grasped in the paired concepts Bridegroom/Bride and Head/Body, but this relationship is surpassed in Mary, since in the first instance she is not Christ's Bride, but his Mother. Here we can glimpse the function of the title "Mother of the Church"; it expresses the fact that the doctrine of Mary both expands the ecclesiological framework and is related to it.[15] One cannot simply argue, therefore, that Mary is the image of the Church only because she was first the Mother of the Lord. This would be a crude oversimplification of the relationship between the order of being and the order of knowing. Such an approach could rightly be countered by referring to passages like Mark 3:33–35 or Luke 11:27f and asking whether physical motherhood is theologically significant at all. It is only possible to prevent Mary's

---

[15] On the title "Mother of the Church" cf. W. Dürig, *Maria—Mutter der Kirche* (St. Ottilien, 1979).

motherhood being confined to the biological sphere if the reading of holy scripture is permitted to proceed on the basis of a hermeneutics which excludes this dichotomy and recognizes the relationship between Christ and his Mother as a theological reality from the very outset of understanding. Such a hermeneutics has been developed in patristic ecclesiology (which, as we have mentioned, does not refer to Mary by name but is couched in personal terms) on the basis of scripture itself and the Church's inner experience of faith. In a nutshell, this hermeneutics affirms that the salvation worked in history by the Triune God, the true center of all history, is called "Christ and his Church" — Church signifying the union of the creature with its Lord in spousal love, thus fulfilling, along the path of faith, the creature's hope of divinization.

Accordingly, if Christ and *Ecclesia* are the hermeneutic center of Scripture, representing God's saving involvement with mankind, then (and only then) we have a locus where Mary's motherhood becomes theologically significant as the ultimate, personal concretization of what is meant by "Church": the moment she utters her Yes, Mary is Israel in person, she is the Church in person and as a person. Doubtless, she is this personal concretization of the Church by physically becoming the Mother of the Lord through her *Fiat*. But this biological fact is theological reality in that it realizes the most profound spiritual content of the Covenant which God wished to make with Israel. Luke indicates this marvellously by relating 1:45 ("Blessed is she who believed") and 11:27 ("Blessed are those who hear the word of God and keep it"). So we can say that the teaching on Mary's motherhood and the teaching on her embodying of the Church are related to one another as *factum* and *mysterium facti,* as fact and its meaning. Both are inseparable: the fact without the meaning would be blind, and without the fact, the meaning would be empty. Mariology cannot be developed out of the mere fact, only out of a fact understood in the hermeneutics of faith. Consequently, mariology can never be merely mariological: it is part of the whole fundamental edifice of Christ and Church and is the most concrete expression of its interconnection.[16]

[16] Cf. the impressive study by I. de la Potterie, "La Mère de Jésus et la conception virginale du Fils de Dieu. Étude de théologie johannique" in *Marianum* 40 *(1978):* 41–90, esp. 45 and 89f.

4. MARIOLOGY—ANTHROPOLOGY—
FAITH IN CREATION

If this line of thought is followed through, it becomes clear that mariology expresses the very core of what is meant by "salvation history", while at the same time going beyond the categories of pure salvation history. If mariology is recognized to be an essential part of a hermeneutics of salvation history, a misunderstood *solus Christus* is confronted by the true greatness of christology, which must speak of a Christ who is "Head *and* Body", i.e., who embraces redeemed creation in its relative autonomy. Straight away this expands the horizon beyond salvation history in that it complements the mistaken view, according to which God is the sole agent, with the reality of creation, a creation which has been summoned and equipped by God to respond to him in freedom. In mariology we come to see that the doctrine of grace does not erode creation but is the definitive Yes to creation. Thus mariology guarantees the proper autonomy of creation; it is a pledge of faith in creation and sets its seal on an authentic doctrine of creation. At this point we encounter questions and tasks that, as yet, have hardly been tackled.

1. In her believing response to the call of God, Mary appears as the prototype of a creation which is likewise called to respond; she manifests the freedom of the creature, a freedom which is not dissolved, but comes to its fulfillment, in love. But it is precisely as a woman that she exemplifies saved and liberated mankind, that is, in the physical specificity which is inseparable from the human being: "male and female he created them" (Gen 1:27). The "biological" is inseparable from the human, just as the human is inseparable from the "theological". On the one hand all this is intimately connected with the dominant trends of our time, and on the other hand it contradicts them head-on. For today's anthropological program circles around the issue of "emancipation" with a radicalism that was hitherto unknown, seeking a freedom to "be like God" (Gen 3:5). This idea of "being like God", however, involves cutting man loose from his biological conditioning, from the "male and female he created them." This difference between the sexes which is an inalienable part of man as a biological being and is deeply written into his nature, is regarded as an utter irrelevance, as a historically invented "role enforcement", and is

relegated to the "merely biological" realm which does not concern man as such. Hence the "merely biological" is a thing to be manipulated by man, something external to what is human and spiritual. (Ultimately this results in the freedom to dispose of unborn life.) Treating the "biological" as a thing is felt to be a liberation; man leaves the *bios* below him, he uses it as he will and is a human being—not a man or woman—independently of it. In reality, however, he wounds himself thereby at his deepest level and abhors himself, because, in truth, it is only as a body, only as man or woman that he is a human being at all. In treating this fundamental condition of his own self as a contemptible triviality, as a thing to be manipulated, he himself becomes trivial and a thing; "liberation" then only serves to degrade and subject him. Where the biological aspect of humanity is eliminated, humanity itself is obliterated. So we have the issue of whether men are allowed to be men and women to be women—the issue of the creature as such. Since human specificity can be avoided least in the question of motherhood, any emancipation that denies the *bios* attacks woman in particular, rejects her right to be a woman. Conversely the preservation of creation is particularly connected with the question of woman. She in whom the "biological" is "theological", namely, in being the Mother of God, is the point at which the paths diverge.

2. Like her motherhood, Mary's virginity is a ratification of the humanity of the "biological", of human totality before God, guaranteeing that the human being, as man and woman, is involved in faith's eschatological hope and claim. It is no accident that virginity, while it is designed and possible for the man too, was first formulated with regard to the woman, the "keeper of the seal" of creation, and attains its normative form in her, which the man only imitates, as it were.[17]

---

[17] On the unity of the biological, human, and the theological aspects cf. I. de la Potterie, 897. On this whole issue cf. L. Bouyer, *Frau und Kirche* (Einsiedeln, 1977), English translation: *Woman and the Church* (San Francisco, 1979). Here one might mention the lovely episode in A. Luciani, *Ihr ergebener* (Munich, 1978), 126; he tells of his encounter with a class of schoolgirls who were complaining about alleged discrimination against women in the Church. He countered this by showing that Christ had a human mother but did not have an earthly father, nor could he have: the perfection of the creature, as creature, is found in woman, not in man.

5. MARIAN SPIRITUALITY

The foregoing considerations finally allow us to explain the structure of marian spirituality. Its traditional place in the Church's liturgy is Advent and the feasts associated with Christmas—Candlemas, the Annunciation.[18]

So far we have seen that it is the characteristic of the marian element that it personalizes (revealing the Church not as a structure but as and in a person) and incarnates (the unity of *bios,* person and the relationship to God, creation's relative autonomy as God's partner, the relative autonomy of the "Body" of Christ vis-à-vis its Head); and that these two functions together involve the realm of the heart, the affective realm, and thus root faith in the deepest levels of human nature. They point to Advent as the liturgical locus of the marian element; in turn, Advent sheds further light on its significance. Marian spirituality has an Advent quality, filled with the joy of imminent expectation; it looks to the incarnational reality of the Lord's nearness, which is both gift and self-giving. Ulrich Wickert puts it very well when he says that Luke shows Mary to have a twofold Advent aspect: at the beginning of the Gospel, when she expects the birth of her Son, and at the beginning of the Acts of the Apostles, when she awaits the birth of the Church.[19]

In the course of development, however, a second factor acquired more and more influence. True, marian spirituality is first of all incarnational, turned toward the Lord who has come; together with Mary, it endeavors to learn how to abide with him. But the feast of Mary's Assumption into Heaven, which acquired new importance in the definition of 1950, also brings out the eschatological transcendence of the Incarnation. Mary's path is also marked by the experience of being turned away (Mk 3:31–35; Jn 2:4); in being given away beneath the cross (Jn 19:26) she shares in the abandonment which Jesus himself had to experience on the Mount of Olives (Mk 14:34) and on the Cross (Mk 15:34). Only through this turning away can what is new come about; only by going away can the real coming take place (Jn 16:7). Thus marian spirituality is also, of

---

[18] Both feasts, in accord with ancient tradition, are feasts of the Lord in the new missal. This in no way diminishes their marian significance.

[19] U. Wickert, "Maria und die Kirche" in *Theologie und Glaube* 68 (1978): 384–407; quotation, 402.

necessity, a spirituality of the Passion; in old Simeon's prophecy of the heart pierced by a sword (Lk 2:35) Luke, from the outset, has woven together Incarnation and Passion, the joyful and the sorrowful mysteries. In the Church's spirituality Mary appears, as it were, as the living image of Veronica, as the icon of Christ, bringing him into and making him present in the human heart, translating his image into the heart's beholding and thus enabling us to grasp him. As we look at the *Mater assumpta,* the Virgin Mother assumed into heaven, Advent expands into the *eschaton;* incarnation becomes the way whereby God's taking of flesh, far from being revoked in the cross, is made ultimate. Thus the medieval expansion of marian spirituality beyond the limits of Advent and into the totality of saving mysteries corresponds most definitely to the logic of biblical faith.

In conclusion we can indicate, on the basis of the foregoing, a three-fold task for marian spirituality:

1. The way to maintain what is distinctive in the marian element is always to see it in its strict relation to the christological; in this way both can attain their proper dimensions.

2. Marian spirituality may not withdraw to partial aspects of the Christian totality, let alone reduce the latter to partial aspects of itself; it must open itself to the whole panorama of the mystery and become a path, enabling others to open themselves to it.

3. Marian spirituality will always be in tension between theological rationality and faith's affectivity. This tension is of its very essence; neither pole must be allowed to fade. Where the emotions are involved, we must not forget the sober mean of reason, but on the other hand the sobriety of a faith which seeks understanding must not stifle the heart, which often sees more than mere reason. It is not for nothing that the Fathers took Mt 5:8 as the kernel of their theological epistemology: "Blessed are the pure in heart, for they shall see God"—the organ for seeing God is the purified heart. It could be the task of marian spirituality to awaken the heart and purify it for, through, and in faith. If it is modern man's distressful fate increasingly to fall apart into mere *bios* and mere rationality, marian spirituality could counteract this "decomposition" of the human being by helping him to rediscover unity in the center, by attending to his heart.

5

LEO SCHEFFCZYK

MARY AS A MODEL OF CATHOLIC FAITH

Translated by Dr. Gordon Seely

I. THE SYMBOLIZATION OF MARY

The focus of the reality of Catholic faith on Christ and on the Church gives rise to the question, to what position can Mary and the marian mystery still lay claim in such a concentrated whole. To the modern conception of faith, which above all is concerned with the fundamental, the simple, and the essential, marian Catholic thought may appear as incidental or merely decorative, something which is not only unessential, but which even distracts from what is essential or replaces it.

Until the present time, non-Catholic thinkers have regarded marian truth as a subsidiary outgrowth of that syncretism which could be explained by the origin of the Church in the religious melting pot of the classical world, and which, as far as Mary is concerned, cannot deny its descent from the classical mother deities. As a matter of fact, the religious history of the ancient world reflects the tendency to make room for the feminine and the material principle in the divine reality. The appearance of such explanations, in view of the status of research in the history of dogma is, on the one hand, somewhat astonishing, but on the other hand, is explained by an unchecked penchant to adopt contemporary opinions. Sometimes even a "Farewell to Mary"[1] is demanded in the name of a good intention—progress in ecumenical dialogue, which Catholic marian teaching and piety could hinder.

To be sure, in this dialogue too little attention is paid to the Protestant partner, who is not as completely alienated from marian thought as is often believed. As a result of the desired focus on the essence of Catholic

[1] Cf. G. Söll, *Abschied von Maria?* [Farewell to Mary?] (Donauwörth, 1974).

belief, which should convince through its rigor and rationality, the marian mystery appears in any case to many Christians to be in need of limitation. Under the influence of such tendencies, it is not astonishing that a certain shrinking and atrophying of marian devotion and piety has entered the Church. In the already-mentioned efforts to focus teaching of the faith on the christological center, the question is scarcely raised whether in any such legitimate concentration (about the nature and extent of which one must certainly on the whole be clearer, so that concentration does not result in "reduction") the marian mystery, so connected to this center, should be abandoned or diminished. Both the place of Mary in Scripture[2] and also her connection with the mystery of Christ in tradition make it, in any case, unlikely that such a separation could legitimately be permitted.

In addition, from the standpoint of the practice of the faith and of Catholic piety, it is to be feared that the weakening of marian devotion would take from Catholicism much of its religious feeling, its warmth, and its radiance, which even Protestant critics, judging from the purely religious-psychological aspect, grant to it on the basis of its marian orientation.

The religious-psychological aspect cannot, of course, provide a theological foundation for Catholic marian devotion. One could, using psychological arguments, as easily recommend marian devotion as reject it. In addition to the reasons for rejection already mentioned, there are others which are repeatedly advanced: the alleged meager interest of the New Testament in the figure of Mary, the relatively late appearance of the marian dogmas in tradition, and, related to these, difficulties in dogmatic historical foundation. To that, in the case of such mysteries as the "Virgin Birth" and the "Assumption of Mary", add the fact that secular, natural scientific counterarguments are advanced with special vehemence. It is then understandable that fidelity to marian faith will be harder, even though the Second Vatican Council has certainly given it a deeper theological foundation,[3] from which, however, the expected impulses for faith and life have not flowed.

---

[2] Compare *Heilige Schrift und Maria* (ed. by the Deutschen Arbeitsgemeinschaft für Mariologie) [*Scripture and Mary* (published by the German Study group for mariology)], (Essen, 1963).

[3] *Lumen gentium*, 52–68.

Although in considering marian devotion today certain deficiencies are evident, one should not on the other hand overlook the fact that counter currents are stirring which, in view of the rootedness of this faith in theology and in the Catholic sense of life, one can expect. The question remains, however, if in every case those deep arteries can again be opened which alone can preserve the vitality and the freshness of marian devotion. It is sometimes observed that the faith, which has become somewhat weakened, ought to be revived by methods which place it in the realm of idealization or existentialization, which have lately again become dominant, and which are identical with a pure symbolization of its character.

This clearly happens when little is said about the real, historical person of Mary and about her objective place in the events of salvation, when her character is viewed only as a sign and is understood, for example, as the realization of a more essential humanity in the presence of God in the world. Mary should be understood as a model of humanity before God, from which essential fundamental spiritual attitudes and ways of behaving can be learned by the believing person. Mariology then becomes instruction in Christian self-understanding, in pardon, and in salvation for every person.

By necessity, the attention of the believer will be diverted from the particular features and from the individual, the concrete, and the unique in the figure of Mary and this attention will be directed to the general, the ideal, and the timeless. This is made clear in a sharply defined, single example, namely, in the interpretation of the virginal conception of the *virginitas ante partum.* Interest is no longer directed to the occurrence as such, or to the fact, which as so-called purely biological fact, was disparaged from the beginning. What alone interests us is the meaning, the idea, the timeless sense which, as is said, has shown itself in the story of the Virgin Birth. This idea is that of the power of God over men and of the complete openness of man to God. No one who seriously considers this interpretation of the character of Mary and of marian teaching will be able to assert that something completely false, inaccessible, or erroneous is intended. But such an assertion does not legitimize or prove this new interpretation of Catholic marian teaching, because something radically and absolutely false is rare. As the proverb says, in every false attempt there lies a grain of truth. For example, in the Catholic world it has always been understood that heresy is not born from a complete distortion of the truth, but rather from partial selection, from over-emphasis of the particular, and neglect of the whole.

So in the symbolizing of the figure of Mary, the only reproach is to its limitation and exclusivity. That is, this interpretation of marian truths is inappropriate and becomes plainly false for human self-understanding, if one denies the fundamental facts of salvation or if one abandons the undergirding, incarnate historical reality.

Therefore in recovering marian truth in the present situation it is insufficient to elevate the symbolic or spiritual meaning of the statements about Mary and to extract from that existential impulses. That is legitimate only when these impulses emerge from the facts of history and can be deduced from these facts. Otherwise, one has no criterion for knowing that one is dealing with salvation which comes from God instead of following his own casual impressions or imaginings, which certainly cannot obligate all men and which also, as such, cannot be perceived by the person concerned to be obligatory.

2. THE MARIAN MYSTERY AS AN UNFOLDING OF THE TRUTH OF CHRIST

As important as the reference to the deep, life-sustaining rootedness of marian truth is in the life of Catholic faith, it certainly provides no theological foundation for the marian faith of the Catholic Church. This foundation is doubly necessary in view of the strength of marian veneration, because it alone can defend against and curtail unwelcome exaggerations. Theological foundation alone can secure for marian devotion and piety its anchoring in the whole of the Catholic world of faith, and thereby guarantee its legitimacy.

Without this theological anchoring, particularly today, marian truth would be in danger. One can, of course, easily make the objection that the concern here is with only a peripheral truth, which in the *hierarchia veritatum* occupies only a marginal position. From there it is not a long step to sever completely that which lies on the periphery from the total context, especially when the hope of being able to remove a difficulty in ecumenical discourse is joined with the setting aside of what is marian.

Such an action is impossible in Catholic theology exactly because of the connectedness of this truth with the whole universe of belief. More penetrating Protestant theologians have always seen and stressed this coherence, so that, at least to them, a recantation of marian truth must appear as a dubious service in the reunion of the separated churches. And so Karl Barth maintains, if only in dismissing it critically, that "Catholic mariology is connected separately with all the rest of theology".[4] The comment of a more recent Protestant theologian points in the same direction. He expresses the conviction that marian truth cannot be separated from total Catholic dogma and that, as a result, "the Protestants can appropriate neither the Catholic way of thinking nor Catholic mariological statements."[5]

If one inquires more closely into the coherence of marian dogma with the totality of the Catholic confession of faith, one can come to the realization that marian teaching is virtually a model, an outstanding conception of the Catholic faith. In tradition this realization received concrete expression, for example, in the designation of Mary as "scepter of the true faith". Why could the concensus of faith bestow such a designation on Mary?

This is grounded in the fact that Mary possesses a unique relation to the event of the Incarnation and to the God-Man Jesus Christ. As virginal Mother of Jesus Christ her character and her deeds signify an ultimate extension and anchoring of the mystery of the divine–human mystery in the natural life of men and the world. That this central mystery of Christendom was, so to speak, planted in the womb of a woman, the Mother of God, has given it a connection to all human values and realities beyond anything one could have imagined. But since her relation to the mystery of Christ was not only biological, but one determined by the grace of God and by free will, still other important

[4] *Kirchliche Dogmatik,* I, 2, 157.
[5] W. Borowsky, "Die evangelischen Christen und die Mariologie", in: *Ökumenische Information* ["Protestant Christians and mariology"], KNA 22/1974, 9f.

mysteries of faith illuminate the character of Mary: the mystery of the shared responsibility of men in the redemption, the mystery of the Church conceived in virginal maternity, the mystery of redemption and grace, the mystery of intercession in the communion of saints, the mystery of perfection, which also embraces the body. So, in fact, in the marian mystery an unfolding of the truths and reality of faith is clearly visible, which in the person of Mary finally again flow together as in a living pinnacle.

It is not, however, only the elements of faith which in Mary appear in an especially illuminating way, it is also something of structure, form, and style, which for Christian faith is to be observed in the figure of Mary. Once again, and definitively in Mary, support and motivation will be given to the fundamental assumptions of Catholic faith after salvation became incarnate.

The fact of God becoming man in Jesus Christ is, to be sure, according to Catholic understanding of the faith, the central argument in favor of salvation taking flesh and the argument against all spiritualizing tendencies to dilute it. All efforts to spiritualize or idealize that which is Christian really had to ricochet off the *concretissimum Christianum.* The marian mystery, however, is frankly the innermost security and defense against such tendencies, because Mary, as the virgin Mother of God, represents the ultimate concretization of the mystery of the God-Man in the human world, in material creation, and in all of its earthly realities.

She is the strongest, ultimate guarantee for the divine becoming concrete in the created, of the supernatural becoming concrete in the natural. Of course one cannot prove that God had to use such means, and that he had no possibility other than this for a deeper rooting of the divine in the human. One should, however, reflect that it is not men who are allowed to construct the economy of salvation, or even only to reconstruct it. When one acknowledges this, then he can also appreciate that this conception of the economy of salvation is highly suitable for men, because of the special way in which it embraces and takes account of them and of the human. This suitability finds its apex in Mary its highest development. The woman who was the Mother of Christ is intended like *no other divine creation* to guarantee the reality of divine activity in the world, to strengthen its rootedness in the human and natural, to ensure its concretization in the secular order, and thereby to guarantee God's appeal in the redemption to all that is human.

If Catholicism is the most uncompromising representative of faith in God becoming man, then Mary is the most sublime vessel and the finest means for the rooting and extension in humanity of the Incarnation of God through Christ. One cannot be surprised that the specifically Catholic faith regresses and atrophies precisely where the understanding of Mary as the highest witness to the Incarnation of God dwindles. No truth other than the marian would more closely approach the mystery of the trinitarian life and activity of God, the supernatural complexity of trinitarian God, redemption, and grace. Therefore it is understandable that her place in theology as in piety cannot be compared with the position of any apostle or saint, because no apostle or saint, as individual and as person, possesses a corresponding meaning and place in the economy of salvation. Mary holds such position precisely because of her unique relation to Christ and to the mystery of the redemptive Incarnation which she, from the human side, helped to expand and grow deeper and to integrate in the world. Because her existence and activity above all should help the human side of the redemptive work of God to express itself and should strengthen the human side of this divine-human mystery, it is also understandable, that she can be in a special way a model, a mediating strength, and a helper for men seeking salvation.

With the inclusion of Mary in the economy of salvation there occurs a fundamental option for a mariology whose orientation is grounded in salvation history as opposed to a marian teaching which, above all, views the individual figure and her privileges, and possibly persists in this view.

The approach of using the privileges of Mary can easily give rise to the misunderstanding that God, in this case, has endowed a person with the fullness of his graces and gifts, only to produce for mankind a miracle of his generosity and to create in Mary a pinnacle of holiness in the world. In this way of looking at things the figure of Mary would run the risk of being isolated and made only into an object of human admiration. In such a way Mary could be honored as "Queen of Saints" and as "Queen of the Angels", but this gradual inflation would yield no new meaning beyond that of the veneration of the saints. On the other hand, this element of inflation could be viewed as unsupported and eccentric.

The marian mystery will be spared from the danger of being viewed from such an isolated perspective if Mary is integrated into the economy of salvation which includes her more precisely "in the mystery of Christ and the Church".[6] In relation to Christ, Mary will be recognizable in her virginal divine maternity as handmaid and servant conveying to mankind the event of redemption, in relation to the Church as premier representative of the redeemed community, whose being and activity is imprinted on the Church indelibly and permanently.

Only when Mary is integrated in this manner into the event of salvation as "handmaid of the Lord" and as the leading member of the Church, who always remains a member (Augustine: *excellens membrum*) do her privileges, which in Catholic faith can never rightly be overlooked, receive their deeper meaning.

Then it will be understood that her fullness of grace (compare Luke 1, 34), her radical freedom from sin (Immaculate Conception), her complete transfiguration at the end of her earthly life (the Assumption) do not signify arbitrarily bestowed ornaments, but rather constitute correspondences to her mission and service, which she as mediatrix of the saving christological events must fulfill.

In order to perform this service in a way that is in concert with the Savior, she became the Virgin Mother of God, the first one saved and totally saved, at the summit of the community of the saved, to which potentially all men belong.

In the time following the end of the actual historical presence of Christ, when Christ entered the Church sacramentally, the relation of Mary to the Church, that is, the ecclesiological view of the marian mysteries, then naturally attains its special importance. Only from the aspect of her being a type of the Church, does the marian mystery yield its riches, which today can stimulate the desire for ecumenism, which at first appears to be hampered by marian devotion. For in the marian typology of the Church, we are no longer concerned with a single person, but rather with the one common Church. Viewed from this perspective, the divine maternity of Mary appears as the exemplary cause of the maternity of the Church.

---

[6] *Lumen gentium,* 52.

The Church as the Mother of Christ expresses a full reality and a genuine event which, of course, after the birth of Jesus Christ from Mary can no longer be a physical one. It can only be concerned with a lasting, supernatural, grace-filled presentation of Christ. More precisely stated, it is the process in which the Church continually receives Christ, bears him in herself, and brings him new members. The mystical-spiritual Body of Christ grows through this process of receiving and presenting, the *Christus totus* will be continually brought to life in the world, above all he generates new life in baptism, the sacrament which is the source of life. Because in this way the Church conceives and bestows Christ, she is, like Mary, the Mother of Christ but also the Mother of the faithful, who for their part comprise the Body of Christ.

The deep theological meaning of the Mary-Church typology can be more clearly shown in contemporary polarity. Today a view of the Church is advanced which understands church as a human clustering around the work or the message of Jesus. According to that, the Church is the community of those who, out of free human initiative, gather around an idea which is derived from Jesus. The Church takes on the character of a human, rational construction, which arises from the desire and the effort of men. Such a church lacks any grace-filled, mystical basis. It is no longer the maternal womb, from which, in a grace-filled mystical way, supernatural life arises and which in itself carries the mystery of divine fullness. This sociological-humanistic misunderstanding of the Church goes hand in hand with faith in the divine maternity of Mary becoming ineffective. The statement that we today can no longer love the Church as "mother"[7] has as its background the foꞏfeiture of the mystery of the divine maternity of Mary, because where Mary is no longer in a salvific way acknowledged as Mother, the Church then loses its maternal, salvific characteristics and becomes an organization of human interests and rational purposefulness.

In this way the meaning appropriate to the Church of every single marian mystery can be revealed: "the Immaculate Conception" as a tangible illustration of the essential holiness of the Church (which also cannot be tainted by the sinfulness of the members); "the Assumption

---

[7] H. Küng, *Christ sein* [To be a Christian], 513.

into Heaven" as the participation of the Church in the state of fulfillment, which it has already attained in Mary at its summit.

However, the virginity of Mary, understood by the Church as being "everlasting", provides a special touchstone for the meaning (as well as for the present critique) of marian faith.

3. VIRGINITY THE TOUCHSTONE

A decisive criterion for a full marian faith lies in the recognition of the virginity of Mary, which the Church, in the undisputed awareness of the biblical source of this truth, in the formula *dei genetrix sancta virgo* (DS 252) relatively early made binding in faith. Even though marian truth is not centered in this statement of faith, and although being the Mother of God represents the more important definition of the identifying character of Mary, her virginity, as the unique form of the materialization of this maternity is, in addition, part of the identifying character of the Mother of Jesus. Seen from the point of view of the history of faith and of dogma, it is known, that without the virginity of the Mother of Jesus, the development of a marian mystery would never have occurred. It would have stopped with a recognition and veneration of a "holy family", which truth Catholic belief also acknowledges, without being able to ascribe to that belief the importance of marian faith. That must have its basis in the inner relationships which were familiar to Christian tradition, but which today are not so often evident.

Concerning the meaning in tradition which the virginity of Mary had, the Protestant theologian H. Asmussen states

> whoever reads the old Church fathers stops short when he hears them praise the virginity of Mary. This praise has its roots in the New Testament. Later one did not pay special attention to the virginity of Mary. That contradicts the message of the New Testament.[8]

---

[8] H. Asmussen, *Maria, die Mutter Gottes* [Mary, the Mother of God] (Stuttgart, 1960), 18.

Today admittedly it is almost the opposite, so that even the anchoring of this mystery in the New Testament is doubted. Without being able in this connection to take up and answer all questions of the critique of the biblical authenticity of belief in Mary's virginity, one must seriously consider the fact that historical-critical research since M. Dibelius[9] to a large extent rejects the conformity to revelation of faith in the virginity of Mary, which above all would be established in the Lucan infancy narrative.

Placing this account in the literary genre of legend or of edifying folk tale also encounters decisive opposition. So, for example, the concern in the case of the "crib motif" is not with the emphasis on the poverty of the child, but rather with the paradox between the lowly, human birth and the call to be *Soter* and *Kyrios,* Savior and Lord. There is no social poverty motif here although there is no need to be upset with the popular sensibilities that find such an interpretation. What is involved here is the paradox in salvation history between human origins and divine purpose or promise.[10]

As far as the legendary is concerned, for the question at hand this means that even on this point the genre of the legend is not completely apropos. What genuine legends accomplish regarding the birth of Jesus Christ is seen in clear contrast in the post-canonical literature, even in the *protoevangelium Jacobi* and in other infancy narratives, which are completely drawn from fantasy and from a thirst for details. Such features are lacking in the Lucan infancy narrative, which fundamentally presents the prelude for the entire Gospel and which strives to be a confession of Christ, and is concerned with the unique origin of the *Kyrios* and *Soter.*

Once clearly aware that little is accomplished by recourse to the genre of legend, in more recent times, especially on the Catholic side, one sought to establish another explanation. These accounts are attributed to the well-known *Midrashim,* which come from exegesis of the Old Testament. These are edifying explanations of scriptural texts by rabbis,

---

[9] M. Dibelius, *Jungfrauensohn und Krippenkind. Untersuchungen zur Geburtsgeschichte im Lukasevangelium* [Son of the Virgin and Cradle Child. Investigations in the birth narrative in the Gospel of Luke], 1932: Botschaft und Geschichte I, (Tübingen, 1953), 1–78.

[10] H. Schürmann, *Das Lukasevangelium I* (*Herders theol. Kommentar zum Neuen Testatment,* ed. by A. Wilkenhauser, A. Vögtle, R. Schnackenburg) [The Gospel of Luke I (Herder's Theological Commentary to the New Testament)] (Freiburg, 1969), 104f.

with practical applications to daily life, taught in Jewish synagogues and schools, although typically only since the second century after Christ. In this regard it is important to mention the fact that in the infancy narrative there is clearly no exegesis, no commentary on Scripture and, what is more, no practical ethical application suggested. The whole seeks to be, in connection with the introductory words of Luke 1:1–4, in fact, a narrative of a salvific event that is appropriate to a confession of faith. If one wants in this connection to employ an Old Testament genre, then he should, according to H. Schürmann, suggest the narrative form of the *Haggadáh*.[11] The *Haggadáh* is a kerygmatic and theologizing explanation of traditions of faith. It stands clearly in contrast to unhistorical allegorical interpretations and has a clear historic, though theologically motivated interest. It seeks to interpret and penetrate certain subjects and traditions theologically and in terms of salvation history. Thus the *Haggadáh* stands in a positive relation to history, even when this relation in the individual case is difficult to pinpoint.

That is the final result of all attempts to seek the exact literary form of the infancy narrative. One joins H. Schürmann in saying: "Clearly, the literary style of Luke 1–2 cannot be classed in a pre-existing genre."[12] It is much more the category of "Gospel", of historical writing that is confessional and homiletic, that thoroughly seeks to express what has occurred, not however in the manner of profane, critical historical writing, but rather in the form of a believing confession of a history wrought by God.

If in this framework one wants to approach more accurately the truth of the Immaculate Conception, there is no reason in exegesis to pass it off as a later invention or to deny its claim to truth. One can't fail in this case to recognize that the denial of the virginity of Mary, expressed in the infancy narratives, does not result in most cases from exegetical reasons, but, in the successors of Bultmann, from presuppositions inherent in a world view.

For them, from the beginning, as a result of their unified world view and monistic conception of reality, there can be nothing unique or

[11] Ibid., 22.
[12] Ibid., 24.

without analogy in the world. Such a position, however, contradicts the profession and fundamental orientation of the historian because the historian as historian can neither affirm nor refute in a text an exceptional salvific fact.[13] He can only consider the credibility or authenticity of the source or, as the case may be, of the author. In this respect no historian can question the credibility of these accounts or, as the case may be, of these witnesses. If he nevertheless wanted to doubt the fact of the Virgin Birth, he would have to introduce evidence that such a fact is impossible. One can surely occupy himself with such a proof, not as a historian, but only as a philosopher or theologian.

So it is not historical science that is behind the challenge to the Virgin Birth, but rather a particular philosophy and theology, which is not the theology at the foundation of the Church.

The more recent stance of the Protestant systematic thinker W. Künneth regarding this question, which in the realm of Protestant faith is certainly not settled, shows that Catholic confessional thinking about this interpretation is not unique. In disputing the proffered objections from the history of religion, from historical criticism, and from modern thought about the nature of the world, he points out "that in biblical narrative we do not find ourselves in the sphere of mythological ideas, but rather on the ground of real history and concrete reality".[14]

So historical criticism can neither deny nor confirm the mystery of faith of the virginity of Mary. Thus emphasis must rest on the theological sense of this mystery. When one recognizes in this case a mystery it is also implied that attention should not be hastily directed to the biological fact clearly contained in it. A mystery of faith is always something much more inclusive and unfathomable than a tangible miracle. It expresses something of God's life, activity, and designs for men, which they are not fully able to grasp, but which most intimately concerns them and, in

---

[13] Compare H. Staudinger, *Gott. Fehlanzeige? Überlegungen eines Historikers zu Grenzfragen seiner Wissenschaft* (Trier, 1968), 148; idem, *Die historische Glaubwürdigkeit der Evangelien* [Reflections of an historian regarding the scope of his science] (Würzburg, 1974), 37f.

[14] W. Künneth, *Fundamente des Glaubens. Biblische Lehre im Horizont des Zeitgeistes* [Fundamentals of belief. Biblical teaching on the horizon of the Zeitgeist] (Wuppertal, 1975), 119.

view of their nature and end, can uncommonly fascinate them. There are mysteries of faith like the Trinity, the creation, Providence, and the sacraments, which do not belong to the order of miracles, but which portray deep mysteries. One cannot therefore dwell exclusively on the biological element in the case of the mystery of the Virgin Birth and the virginity of Mary.

At this point it must be immediately added: as this mystery appears in revelation and as the Church conceives it, the so-called biological fact cannot be eliminated from the whole. Otherwise this mystery, which takes place in history, would collapse. Only in observing both factors, the theological and the natural-historical, can the meaning of the mystery unfold in its total fullness. Remarkably, Karl Barth, among modern theologians, has demonstrated that most forcefully when he asserted, that the *natus ex virgine* and the *concepit de Spiritu Sancto* belong together and in their unity announce the mystery of a new creation.

> What in any case is meant by these statements is a self-generating event in the realm of the natural world understood in the fullness of this conception, therefore in the unity of the spiritual with the physical, in time, and in space, in noetic and ontological reality, which as such can neither be understood from the connectedness with other events in this world, nor arises from this connectedness, but whose extraordinariness can, to be sure, be misunderstood subjectively as error, deception, invention, symbol making, or, objectively as a temporarily unexplained but essentially explainable natural mystery. It can really only be understood as a directly worked sign coming from God himself, and from God himself alone, of independence and immediacy, of the mystery of his action, and as a precursive sign of his kingdom to come.[15]

For Barth, the Virgin Birth is, more specifically, the sign that God's incarnation does not lie in continuity with possibilities contained with the world. Therefore the Virgin Birth is also no natural possibility within the human world or in the whole operation of the world. It is instead a reality-filled symbol of pure grace and a sign of the absolute sovereignty of God, which must ever more so be all the more suited to

---

[15] *Kirchliche Dogmatik* [Church Dogmatics] I, 2,198.

the second, higher creation, as the first creation itself took place fully independent of the possibilities of the created.

The Virgin Birth is the highest sign of the absolutely free, given, totally unearned grace of God, which is and must be anchored in the Christ event, if man does not wish to suffer the illusion of self-redemption. This conception is found again in similar fashion in H. Asmussen, who proceeds from the tragic history of the world and then points out that the desire for salvation of all peoples was always connected to a new birth, to a completely new, independent origin. To that he joins the realization, found among all men of every age, "that from a natural birth, no condition can result, which one really could call salvation".[16]

> From that he draws the conclusion: because our birth is always unrelated to salvation, a new birth must snatch us out of the circle of misery. And this new birth is the birth from the Virgin. Therefore, it is necessary to praise virginity to promote our salvation. Without the virginity of Mary there is no salvation.

Fundamentally, that says in modern language what Tertullian's formulation already expressed: *"Nove nasci debebat, novae nativitatis dedicator"*, that is, "The author of a new birth must be born in a new way."[17] Here also the factor of the new budding of grace is the decisive motif for the interpretation of the Virgin Birth. For Mary herself, her virginity signifies, going far beyond biological fact, the posture of exclusive devotion to God in Jesus Christ, which ought not be compromised by a second, similar attachment to a person. Mary's virginity is the sign of that total attitude of receptivity, which every member of humanity should demonstrate and exhibit toward God's grace.

In Mary this attitude, which among men is always full of doubt, broken, threatened, and changeable, is brought to absolute certainty. In her it is directed to completeness, stability, and definitive certainty, to eschatological, ultimate perfection. In Mary the total openness and devotion of the creature corresponds to the absolute sovereignty of God. Something fundamental from the structure of the working of grace is reflected here.

In addition, access is opened to the significance of the virginity of

---

[16] H. Asmussen, loc. cit., 20.
[17] *De carne Christi*, 17.

Mary which is ecclesiastical and a model for the Church. It has been emphatically depicted in the patristic age, which saw in Mary chiefly the "model of the Church". The virginity of Mary was always treated and witnessed forcefully in its archetypical (and that means always in its effective) orientation toward the Church. Ambrose, who died in 397 A.D., said, "As Christ alone opened the immaculate womb of Mary, so Christ also opened the silent, immaculate, fruitful womb of the Church, of the holy Virgin for the re-birth of the people of God."[18]

This straightforward parallelism between the virginity of Mary and that of the Church must certainly be examined more closely at the actual point of comparison. The point of comparison is total devotion to Christ. It is identical with the virginity which characterizes the Church as well as Mary, and by means of which both become fruitful, bringing forth Christ and his members.

If one asks more concretely what this total devotion means formally, one points to the faith of Mary, always regarded by the Fathers as central, as well as that of the Church. The virginity of the Church as total devotion to Christ is faith. In this faith, which is seen as spiritual virginity, Mary and the Church are one. In faith they commit themselves unreservedly to Christ and to no other. In this exclusivity of devotion to Christ they are, in the christological sense, fruitful.

One would misunderstand this typology if, in the case of Mary, one did not take it in the real, physical sense, including therefore bodily virginity. Even when the Fathers do not expressly mention and emphasize this factor, it is naturally included and is part of their meaning. Yes, in terms of the origin of this typology from the point of virginity, one may even more definitely assert: this typology, regarding the subject of virginity, could never have been constructed, if Mary had not been a virgin in the physical sense and had not conceived Jesus *de Spiritu sancto*. Spiritual virginity was never separated from this bodily virginity, because the Fathers recognized that Mary had first to conceive in faith before she could, as a virgin, receive Christ physically. Spiritual and physical virginity are fully inseparable from one another in this concrete-symbolic way of looking at things.

[18] Espos, in Luc. [Exposition in Luke] II, 57.

Nonetheless, the question could arise here, whether, for the Church, virginity could be meant only in a spiritual or religious-existential sense because the Church, one could on first reflection believe, could not in the bodily sense be a virgin. As a result, the typology would in fact be completely lost. It would not be rigorously developed on the two sides: that of the Church and Mary, according to their two elements, of spiritual and bodily virginity. The position of St. Augustine proves that virginity for the Church was understood in the realistic sense. He also took up the typology from the spiritual side above all, that is, from the point of view of faith. In this regard he declared: "Christ has formed his Church as a virgin. She is a virgin in faith."[19] In this familiar explanation a new factor is introduced, that of the material-physical virginity of the Church, which naturally can be limited to only a small number of members. He adds immediately that: "The Church has only a small number of consecrated virgins according to the flesh. According to faith, all must be virgins, men and women." According to Augustine, the marian virginity of the Church concretizes itself also in the bodily-physical, and, to be sure, since there is no alternative, in people who live unwed and virginally, above all in the state of those of both sexes who live virginally. Augustine is of the opinion, which is the general opinion of the Church, that the state of virginity, the state of the evangelical counsels, in which true personal virginity has its place, belongs to the Church. The importance of this factor for Augustine shows itself in that he repeatedly emphasizes this thought in his addresses to virgins. He does not do this, to be sure, from purely ascetic reasons, but from a fundamental mariological basis that can be approximately formulated as follows: because of her spiritual marian character, the Church stands in need of people of a special state, who in the sense of a concrete way of living actualize virginity. Otherwise the Church would not be truly marian in structure. The parallels would not be completely drawn, so to speak.

Therefore he turns again in an especially expressive way to the virgins:

> Rejoice, you virgins of Christ, your companion is the Mother of Christ. You cannot truly bear Christ, but for the sake of Christ you desire not to bear. He who was not born by you is born to you. And

[19] Sermon, 213.

when you think of his word, as you should think of it, then you are also mothers of Christ, because you fulfill the will of his Father.[20]

In this word the virgins are designated as particularly intimate companions of Mary. The reason is, as with Mary, their special obedience to Christ, in which they eschew marriage. What is remarkable, however, consists in the fact that this renunciation of bodily fruitfulness leads in the Church to a spiritual maternity, for these virgins are literally also called "mother of Christ". They fructify the life of faith of the Church, they give birth to new faith and new believers.

Augustine emphasizes the fact and the necessity of virginity still more strongly when he relates it to all classes in the Church and declares that widows and married people make virginity real in the chastity which is appropriate to them, without which the Church cannot exist. He says concerning them,

> Rejoice, you widows of Christ, you have promised holy abstinence to him who let virginity be fruitful. You, noble marital chastity, rejoice as well, and all who live with their spouses faithful to you. Possess in the heart what you relinquished in the body. Your conscience is virginal in faith, as the whole Church is a virgin. In Mary pious virginity has given birth to Christ. In Anna aged widowhood recognized the little Christ. In Elizabeth, Christ has consecrated marital chastity and delayed fruitfulness. All states of believing members have contributed to the head, what they, through grace, could contribute.[21]

What Augustine achieves here is a universalization of virginity with its analagous possibility of being realized by all classes and groups of the Church, and, to be sure, always with incorporation of the bodily element. So, in the sense of marital chastity, married people can also safeguard virginity. That does not mean abstinence, but rather the spirit-filled marital devotion related to Christ. According to Augustine, the Church is so intensively marian that it always realizes virginity and chastity, even, to be sure, in a true, bodily way.

He who attentively considers and appraises the testimonies presented

[20] Sermon, 132.
[21] Ibid.

will hardly be able to say that they are no longer capable of addressing modern man and that taken together they would be unmodern. This holds first for the first element of virginity, the spiritual-existential, which is identical to devotion in faith to Christ.

In this respect there is no difficulty in extending the meaning of virginity to the Church and, conversely, in recognizing the virginity of Mary as the model and prototype of the Church, of the community of faith, and of believers. The importance of faith for Christianity and the Church is generally recognized. And the link between faith and the notion of spiritual virginity is thoroughly appreciated as a special nuance of the understanding of the faith.

Today in considering the appropriation of the bodily factor of the virginity of Mary by certain states in the Church, the objection could arise: high esteem for virginity must or could lessen the value of marriage. That is not, however, justified, even if one points out former tendencies in the Church which were hostile to the body or to marriage. They were, in any case, never as hostile to the body as currents in Gnosticism. That the Church in this respect is still subjected to such insinuations is explained in part because a differentiation among merits is viewed as opposition, and objective gradations of merit are judged to be pejorative. When, therefore, the objective distinctiveness of virginity is appreciated as an unconditional surrender to Christ as an eschatological sign and its high value is stressed, then there is in no way a lessening of the value of marriage. In reality, both these values are dependent on each other. A loss in appreciation of one results in a loss in appreciation of the other, as one can easily demonstrate in view of certain phenomena of the times in the contemporary Church.

Again the virginity of Mary, which is always to be viewed together with her maternity, shows itself to be not just a significant isolated truth for the Church. It develops in the Church a structure, which can be seen as an important enlargement of the hierarchical structure. Contemporary criticism is raised against the Church's hierarchical character and opposes to it the demand for the gentle servant character of the true Church of Jesus Christ. However in its foundation this critique of the hierarchy and the alleged power structure of the Church does not go much beyond borrowings from sociological-democratic models, which in this fashion cannot be applied to the Church. Sometimes the suspicion even arises that the so-called democratic restructuring does not seek to limit power and introduce the right balance, but only intends a distribution of power to other groups.

In contrast, the "marian principle", the principle of serving devotion and humble receptivity, provides a genuine balance and enlargement of a hierarchical principle that tends to become onesided. The inclusion of Mary as Virgin and Mother in the order of salvation imparts to the Church, which is the outstanding place of continuing salvation, in a totally special way, profoundly sensitive, deeper human maternal and even mystical characteristics.

Arrayed with such characteristics, the Church can provide to men of all states and dispositions the protection, the security, and the familiarity which flow from a maternal-virginal being. The post-Counciliar Church is in danger of losing these characteristics and to becoming an apparatus of masculine intellectuality, which despite the greatest efforts is basically unproductive. About this happening in more recent times, one could say in criticism:

> Without mariology Christianity is in danger of becoming inhuman. The Church becomes functionalistic, without soul, a hectic enterprise without resting place, alienated by over-planning. Because in this male-masculine world one new ideology replaces another, everything becomes polemical, critical, bitter, humorless, and ultimately boring. People desert such a Church in droves.[22]

These consequences for the Church with an atrophied faith in the Virgin Mother are also confirmed occasionally by Protestants' awareness of their faith and are applied self-critically to their own situation when it is said: "When in the Church the attention which one pays to Mary declines, then . . . the Church as successor to Mary becomes more or less unfeeling."[23] Then to all that is human, which is part of all that is Christian, something crucial is lost. "The loss of this [marian] devotion appears . . . to be a far-reaching step resulting from the Reformation . . . in

[22] Hans Urs von Balthasar, *Klarstellungen. Zur Prüfung der Geister* [Straight thinking: for a testing of spirits] (Freiburg, 1971), 72.

[23] H. Asmussen, loc. cit., 26f.

respect to the entry of spiritual forces into the developmental process of the soul."[24]

With this statement it is also hinted that proper devotion must correspond to the meaning of Mary in the theology of salvation. There have been many complaints about the hypertrophy and excessive growth in the Catholic Church of the devotion to Mary.[25] They ought not to be ignored and withdrawn from critical scrutiny.[26] However, they do not negate the legitimacy, the fruitfulness, and the inner necessity of this devotion or eliminate a reverence which really begins in Scripture.

It is an astonishing proposition, on the consequences of which one cannot reflect deeply enough, which the otherwise usually critically inclined Protestant dogmatic historian W. Delius advances, when he states, in reference to chapter 1 and 2 of Luke's Gospel and in reference to the so-called "infancy narratives": "With the hand of a master, Luke has drawn a picture of Mary that contains in it almost all important characteristic features of the veneration of Mary in its centuries-long development."[27]

That means nothing less than that the veneration of Mary, which already begins in the mouth of Elizabeth, rests on a biblical foundation. From the point of view of Catholic faith, it can be added that veneration of Mary in its subsequent history has never departed from that foundation.

This biblical foundation can contribute more in answering the question of what is specific in the veneration of Mary in contrast to the general cult of the saints. It can be said somewhat formally in response to that: the biblical is—generally speaking—the history of salvation. Therefore one may conclude just from the inclusion of Mary in holy Scripture and from the anchoring of her veneration in the genuine witness of the history of salvation, that marian veneration has its special foundation and its individuality in its special place in the history of salvation. It follows then that the specific foundation of marian veneration does not lie in her exceptional, personal holiness or in her being full of grace. On the

---

[24] V. von Weizsäcker, *Menschenführung* [Leadership of men] (Göttingen, 1955), 48.

[25] Compare W. von Löwenich, *Der moderne Katholizismus* [Modern Catholicism] (Witten, 1956), 268ff.

[26] Compare to it the encyclical of Paul VI, *Marialis cultus* (Feb. 2, 1974), 38.

[27] W. Delius, *Geschichte der Marienverehrung* [History of marian devotion] (München, 1963), 26.

contrary, it is found, somewhat abstractly stated, in that which caused this fullness of grace and which was its higher meaning and goal: that is and was Mary's mission, her vocation, her work in the history of salvation—as a conceiving and transmitting coworker beneath Christ, but at the pinnacle of humanity. The specific foundation of marian devotion rests in her place in the history of salvation, within the realization and extension of the salvation effected by Christ within humanity and the Church.

6

JUTTA BURGGRAF

WOMAN'S DIGNITY AND FUNCTION IN CHURCH AND SOCIETY

Translated by Lothar Krauth

Already Pope John XXIII considered as one of the signs of our time "the entry of women into public life, a process occurring perhaps more rapidly in Christian nations, more slowly yet steadily growing also in nations of other traditions and cultures."[1] In our day, the woman generally is no longer excluded from the world of culture, nor is she prevented from making her own decisions. She is no longer diagnosed as inherently deficient because of less intelligence and greater dependence. Women are increasingly able to enjoy security in their life and work; more and more they have access to public office in society and politics. The long centuries of women's degradation seem to be over.

In spite of these outward successes it remains a question whether our society is indeed on its way to promote the dignity of women. Cinema, theater, poetry, and the fine arts tell a different story. Mass magazines and the media today threaten women with deeper humiliation than was effected by political and social injustice. On the one hand, a woman's fundamental rights are loudly proclaimed; on the other, there is the tendency to confine her to an inhuman existence, often treating her more as a commodity than an independent person. Increased respect for women on a superficial level goes hand in hand with pagan contempt. This ambiguous attitude can find an explanation when it is seen in relation to the contemporary decline of faith. Peter Ketter aptly remarks: "The more a culture discards its ties to the eternal and the divine, the more it turns

[1] Pope John XXIII, Encyclical *Pacem in terris*, 1963, no. 41.

against women."[2] Social changes will not truly liberate women unless they spring from a changed mental attitude. Only if we are willing to respect the woman as a person can we really acknowledge and substantiate her dignity. This in turn is possible only if we consider the aspect of her fundamental relation to God, and her immediacy to the Creator.

God created man as well as woman "in his image and likeness."[3] Both share the same essence of being, inalienable freedom, and a high destiny. Their common task bids them to grow into "God's likeness" and mirror him in their lives. Christian anthropology has always defended the equality in rank and dignity of the sexes, which does not mean that it ever taught equalization as an ideal. Man and woman are of equal dignity in their essence; yet this essence is realized differently in each.

The woman's humanity is realized in the specific ways of a woman. She is a complete human being no less than the man, but according to *her own* nature. Her sex is not a mere accidental condition which could be abstracted. Her sex, on the contrary, is a reality which fundamentally defines her being and acting and corresponds to the specific design of the Creator. Her physical and psychological qualities proclaim clearly what it truly means to be a woman.

Though woman has been created equal to man, it is still inherent in her nature to have a vocation and function different from that of the man. God has given her the call to be at man's side as companion and "helpmate".[4] Basically, the word "helpmate" means that the woman helps the man to be fully human. For nature itself is arranged in such a way that both sexes complement each other, and each is superior to the other in its own domain. The man and the woman are each endowed with their own specific mental values and qualities.

And yet, in honest reflection, man and woman will be aware of various gaps and deficiencies in their specific natures. The man may well pride himself on his generally more rational thought and practical judgment; yet how many times will untempered reason lead to coldness of heart and obstinate formalism! The woman may well be content to

---

[2] Peter Ketter, *Christus und die Frauen* [Christ and women], vol. I: *Die Frauen in den Evangelien* [Women in the Gospels] (Stuttgart, 1948), p. 5.

[3] Cf. Gen 1:27.

[4] Cf. Gen 2:4–25.

rely on emotion and intuition; yet how many times will these lead to confusion and injustice! The male and the female natures stand each in need of a substantial infusion of the other's qualities to achieve harmony and balance in the human person.[5]

The differences between man and woman may find various expressions in different cultures. These differences nonetheless show invariably that the woman completes the man. She is indeed "helpmate"—in another, deeper sense. The woman is entrusted with the birth, nurture, and care of life, that is, the concrete life of this unique individual person with his countless needs. Every human being starts out as a helpless child and would feel quite lost in this world without the woman—as mother, spouse, and companion—acting as helpmate to find his way in the vast reality around him. The woman possesses the special talent to nurture an individual life into its full development. For our life consists, not just in planning and realizing grand designs for society, but also in those hundreds of little daily things which need to be mastered before we can set out for greater things. The specific vocation of the woman becomes evident in this: she is entrusted with the task of imitating God's special care and with showing how God is at every moment concerned with the individual.

The woman tends to be more interested in the individual person, the man more in general concepts. He is more concerned with the common good, the always valid general order, without which human life could hardly endure in the long run. Thus the man, too, stands in the service of life, bearing equal responsibility, but from a greater distance.[6] This finds its expression especially in marriage and family life.

Everywhere in the universe we discover a graduated order as the fundamental principle; so, too, we see this order in the relationship of the sexes to each other. In the temporal order of the family, the difference between the call of the man and the woman who makes her activities, as it were, oriented toward his activities. This orientation, however, should by no means be conceived as absolute. For the woman was not created

[5] Cf. Peter Ketter, op. cit., p. 76.

[6] Cf. Johannes Betz, "Vom Charisma der Frau in der Kirche" [The charisma of women in the Church] in *Deutsche Tagespost*, 25 (Feb. 28, 1984), p. 5.

for the man but for God. Even so, within the family the man can claim a certain privileged position. This position is provisional and temporary. At the end of time a different order of rank will prevail, one not determined by sex or any other created category, but exclusively by the sanctity of each individual.

Originally, the relations between man and woman were in full harmony. They mirrored the relation of the Father to the Son who willingly "emptied himself"[7] and, though of the same essence, subordinated himself to the Father. Love inherently is ready for self-sacrifice and service. Love desires to give the other everything, the total self. In love, there is no room for calculating demands or selfish insistence on one's own rights. After the Fall, however, mankind was separated from God, in a state of rebellion against his creation. The relation between the sexes is inevitably disturbed as well. The consequences are evident in many cultures and civilizations: men degrade and suppress women who in turn fight such humiliation.[8]

Jewish culture toward the end of Old Testament times definitely treated women as inferior beings. Werner Neuer states, "The woman was considered inferior to the man in religion, law, and ethics", and that "this underestimation led to her suppression in religion and society."[9]

In contrast, the position of women was radically changed by Jesus and his teachings. Jesus again reconciled mankind with God and with each other. In dealing with women, he showed himself free from the prejudices and restraints of a society dominated by men. Unlike those around him, he treated women as equals. From the beginning until the end on the Cross, women were his faithful companions. And women showed more courage than his disciples, and were privileged to be the first witnesses of his resurrection.[10] Yet, when Jesus chose the Twelve to be the foundation of his Church,[11] he did not choose any women, only

---

[7] Phil 2:7.

[8] Cf. Edith Stein, "Frauenbildung und Frauenberufe" [Education and professions of women], 2nd ed. (Munich, 1951), pp. 152f.

[9] Werner Neuer, "Man und Frau in christlicher Sicht" [Man and woman in Christian conception] (Giessen, 1981), p. 85.

[10] Cf. Mt 28:9–10.

[11] Cf. Eph 2:20.

men. Later on, the apostles again entrusted other men with the leadership in the Christian communities.[12] Thus the order of creation was restored: as the man presides over the family, so some men, called by God, preside over the great family of the Church. Their decisions, however, are not to be imposed under coercion but should be accepted in freedom and on the basis of equality. In this respect St. Paul states: "There is neither Jew nor Greek, there is neither slave nor free, there is neither male nor female; for you are all one in Christ."[13] Monsignor Escrivá de Balaguer points out that "the man and the woman—because they complement each other—are equally to be considered main actors in salvation history."[14]

Acceptance of God's will in freedom is the secret which will restore the corrupted order. The one who understood this perfectly is Mary; she was God's unique instrument in his plan of salvation. While human history shows how low into the abyss of vice and corruption a woman can sink, Mary shows how high she can ascend in Christ and through Christ.[15] The question as to the guiding ideal of the woman is not to be answered with theological and philosophical definitions, but rather with the living reality of Mary. In her, all degradation of women loses any pretense of being justified.

Reflecting on the person of Mary sheds light on the specific qualities of a woman, such as her special sense of gratitude and helpfulness; her sense for contemplation; her grasp of the importance of beauty in human life; her capacity for love, support, compassion, warmth, and togetherness. Thus "it is urgent, as in few other epochs of Church history"[16] to return to Mary. Her being virgin and mother gives the vocation of women its Christian expression.

Mary is "ever virgin", the spouse who receives the Holy Spirit. God

[12] Cf. Acts 6:3, 14:23; Tit 1:5f.; I Tim 4:14.

[13] Gal 3:28.

[14] Msgr. Josemaría Escrivá de Balaguer, "Gespräche" [Conversations]. 3rd. ed. (Cologne, 1981), no. 14.

[15] Cf. Pope Pius XII, "An die katholischen Frauen der Welt" [Address to the Catholic women of the world] (Sept. 29, 1957). German edition (Cologne), p. 13.

[16] Joseph Cardinal Ratzinger with Vittorio Messori, The Ratzinger Report: An Exclusive Interview on the State of the Church (San Francisco: Ignatius, 1985), p. 105.

works in Mary with exceptional gifts of grace; witness her sanctity which, according to Suarez, is greater than that of the angels and saints combined;[17] and not least her physical incorruption. In his salvific work, God lays on Mary a total claim, and she accepts this claim without any reservation. Her physical virginity is sign and expression of her spiritual attitude. The Church Fathers are justified when they state that Mary had conceived first in her mind and heart, and only then also in her body. All her capacities of soul and mind are surrendered to God. Her heart is not divided in its purpose: the dedication is total.

Mary's obedience has overcome Eve's pride. For this reason she is called the "new" woman. Scheffczyk explains that "new" in biblical and Christian thinking means something that has not existed so far, something that is unique and definitive. Mary as the "new" woman does not mean she should be defined in terms of our modern conceptions. The reality of Mary cannot be expressed in socio-political terms. "New" within the context of salvation history denotes rather "a reality which is *ever* new compared with what is old and discarded; a reality which is so overflowingly rich that it can never become old or depleted. 'New' here means something definitive and timeless which lies beyond the claim and disposal of any particular age."[18] "New" thus denotes a permanent reality which offers its wealth to any and all generations.

Mary is the "new" woman, the complete human being. She demonstrates what truly makes a Christian: not simply a specific outlook and frame of mind as other religions expect, but rather community with Christ, which takes possession of the mind and molds a person's entire physical and spiritual life. To be a Christian means to continue the incarnation of God in the Church and her members, just as this occurred the first time in Mary.

The reality embodied in Mary is much too radical and profound to allow its definition in any political or sociological terms. For the total change of the human condition, accomplished in and through Mary,

[17] Cf. F. Suarez, "De mysteriis vitae Christi" [Mysteries of Christ's life], Disp. 18, section 4, no. 14, in *Opera omnia,* ed. L. Vivès (Paris 1956–61), vol. 19.

[18] Leo Scheffczyk, "Maria—die neue Frau und vollkommene Christin" [Mary, the new woman and perfect Christian]. In: *Christliche Innerlichkeit,* vol. 18, no. 5 (Mariazell, Sept./Oct. 1983), p. 213.

originates at the roots, effecting deliverance from sin, conversion of heart, and transformation of a person's innermost being. No external revolution could even begin to achieve this.[19]

Mary perfectly accepts God's plans and makes them her own. Sometimes her attitude is disparagingly called "passive". Yet it should not be overlooked that virtues like self-surrender, humility, obedience, willingness to sacrifice and serve, require elevated spiritual processes that rise above the person's own needs and desires. Mary's is not an attitude of servility but one of freedom and responsibility.

On the other hand, seen in the light of faith, a passive attitude by itself does not appear totally negative as in the philosophies of antiquity. It is a prerequisite, as it were, for a true Christian: only by surrendering ourselves to God can we be seized by God and receive his graces. Such surrender alone opens the way to realize the full human potential. The *ancilla Domini* [maidservant of the Lord] is also the *regina coeli* [Queen of Heaven].

Mary is the perfect model for a Christian; she is Virgin of virgins and Queen of Heaven. Above all, she is Mother. God has revealed the dignity of women in Mary's motherhood. Her maternity, further, underlines the recognition and honor which womanhood can rightly claim.

Mary cooperated in the work of salvation precisely as a woman. As a woman she received, preserved, and transmitted God's grace. As a woman she absorbed and internalized, in exemplary fashion, the spirit of dedication toward God and toward others. She walked the path of quiet, unpretentious, unselfish service. She is helper in need, refuge for the afflicted, and heavenly intercessor, thus reflecting God's own mercy. Her female qualities gloriously complete the man's role in the work of salvation.

Mary is mother, not priest. Her specific vocation extends into the areas of motherly care and love, not into the domain of the hierarchy. Mary never stood in front of Jesus nor at his side, always behind him. So, too, after his death: she did not position herself in front of the apostles or at their side, always behind them.[20] For a mother is fully mother not in herself but in her child.

[19] Cf. ibid. pp. 221ff.
[20] Cf. Msgr. Josemaría Escrivá de Balaguer, *Der Weg* [The Way]. 9th ed., Cologne 1983, no. 509.

In this, Mary's mission in the Church is intimately connected with the very nature of the Church. For the Church herself, taken as a mother, fulfills her mission by working with others; the main operator in her is Christ.

In her essence, Mary represents mankind and the Church as they receive God's salvation. Her trusting acceptance of God's message thus becomes model and example for every Christian, female or male. And yet, Mary's fundamental attitude offers a particular lesson for women.

Fulfillment as a woman is not to be sought in imitating the man. Any attempt to measure the woman with male categories distorts her nature rather than defines it. Such attempts misunderstand the woman's specific role and qualities. A woman will not find fulfillment in the dogged pursuit of liberation from all restraints, but only in the unreserved acceptance of creation's order and her own nature. Here, Mary has shown the way.

Mary's motherly attitude offers a ray of comfort in an era marked by selfishness and arrogance. Gertrud von Le Fort stated years ago: "Nothing defines the condition of our time more profoundly and tragically than the total absence of all motherly dispositions."[21]

Imitating Mary means to renounce all ambitions, all pretentious self-promotion. It means further not to seek one's own interests and "fulfillment" but to devote oneself to others and be for them perhaps their only refuge of patience, kindness, and understanding. The true woman and mother will be able to wait in silence. Her approach adds a logical completion to that of the man. She enjoys the privilege of ignoring occasionally some wrongdoing or a weakness, the privilege of sparing and excusing others. According to von Le Fort, it is one of the world's most fateful errors—and part of the basic reason for its lack of peace—that it feels obligated in every instance to expose and condemn any and all wrongs.[22] The true woman and mother, by her caring and understanding, knows how to lighten for others the burden of life. Thus she becomes the great conqueror of everyday life. Every day she conquers anew by making the trivialities of life bearable. And should no one even notice, her conquest has been thorough indeed.

---

[21] Gertrud von Le Fort, *Die ewige Frau* [Eternal woman] (Munich 1950), p. 128.
[22] Cf. ibid. p. 118.

True promotion of the woman's position requires that the values of motherhood and family be clearly acknowledged. Her most genuine and specific domain will always be the family. The woman is the supporting center of the home, the heart of the family. If she neglects her responsibilities as spouse, mother, and guardian of the home, the welfare of society at large will suffer.

It cannot be a legitimate aim to "emancipate" husband and wife, parents and children from each other. On the contrary, the spouses should ever more realize how noble their relationship is; it is so great, in fact, that in its intimacy it mirrors the union of Christ with his Church.[23]

This may well be the most profound and sublime statement ever to describe the relation between the sexes. It points to the truth that man and woman are created to serve each other in voluntary mutual submission based on love. Such service is entirely oblivious of its own "rights", and such love does not ask for anything it would not happily give itself. When spouses are ready to give themselves to each other in unconditional love, only then do they fulfill the meaning of their union and only then do they find the completion of their own specific qualities.

A Christian mother will strive for her family to be a place where God can be found, even today. Her unselfish, hidden activity has always testified to the belief in the common priesthood of all the faithful, and has transformed her family into that "domestic Church", a favorite notion also in modern Church teaching.[24]

All this does not mean that the woman must be confined to a "small world". The forms of service are as varied as life itself. Acknowledging the value of domestic tasks should not lead us to overlook this other fact: those mental abilities and qualities—intuitive and person-oriented on one side, objective and more general in thinking and planning on the other—have not been exclusively bestowed on one or the other of the sexes respectively. They cannot be ascribed in any strict either/or fashion, only as more or less prevalent tendencies within a common mental capacity. Both sexes are in principle capable of any mental

[23] Cf. Eph 5:22ff.
[24] Cf. Pope John Paul II, "Apostolisches Schreiben Familiaris consortio" [Apostolic Letter *Familiaris Consortio*] (Nov. 22, 1981), no. 49.

activity. Equal obligation and responsibility of man and woman fully justify the woman's access to the public domain. The man in turn is asked to recognize in all honesty the abilities of the woman. Her abilities do not limit his worth but underscore and augment all human values. Specific female qualities, such as her desire to mediate and reconcile opposites, her understanding and sensitivity, are also effective contributions to a more humane atmosphere at the workplace.

The unmarried woman, too, can find fulfillment by following Mary's lead. For Mary is virgin as well as mother. Virginity as such is not an essential prerequisite for the unmarried, but has always been accepted as the natural expression of unmarried life. In our day, virginity is not discussed, and we are oblivious to the fact that it represents not only a state of life, but rather a value in itself. Virginity is a religious value if chosen freely and deliberately out of love for God, *propter regnum coelorum*[25] [for the sake of the Kingdom of heaven].

While marriage is but a sign of God's love for mankind, the virgin testifies directly to this love. The *mysterium caritatis* [mystery of love], only symbolized in marriage, is intimately incorporated in the virgin's life, where it is lived out on a level higher than the natural level. The virgin lives in a direct I–Thou relationship with Christ, in exclusive surrender to him.

The Magisterium, time and again, has stated that virginity, freely chosen "for the sake of the Kingdom",[26] surpasses the dignity of motherhood. For the value of a particular love or devotion depends on *who* it is we love or are devoted to. Christian virginity has chosen God himself as its immediate aim and purpose.

We are never able to merit by our own doing such a vocation to total dedication. God alone offers it as a gift. But every Christian woman and every Christian man should be willing to accept this gift. And if someone in fact hears God's special call, he should be courageous enough to leave a secure, familiar position and—like Mary—surrender to the plans of God's providence.

The virgin is a living sign of that religious truth which holds that the

[25] Mt 19:12.

[26] Cf. Council of Trent, *De sacramento matrimonii.* Session XXIV (Nov. 11, 1563), can. 10, DS 980. Pope Pius XII, Encyclical *Sacra virginitas* (1954). Pope John Paul II, *Familiaris consortio,* loc. cit., no. 16.

ultimate value of the human person is based on her immediacy to God. It is therefore logical that the liturgy places her side by side with the martyrs; for she, too, proclaims the absolute value of the soul by surrendering her earthly life.

The more we give ourselves up in the worship of God, the more our personality is deepened and enriched. The more we concentrate on ourselves and our own status, however, the more we grow poor, shallow, and dull. It is not by accident that today the instances of depression and nervous breakdowns are on the rise among women whose sense of identity is confused. We should not forget that only by our living contact with the personal God can we grow beyond our own inner limitations.

It certainly is not easy to pursue the Christian vocation all the way to its ultimate consequences. It certainly demands total dedication to live a true life of love. Mary's Yes at the moment of her call was also a Yes to the sacrifice on Calvary. The Yes of a Christian woman to marriage or virginity has to be modeled after Mary's attitude.

We know many women mystics and theologians who speak of God's love with poetic height and speculative depth, including Hildegarde of Bingen, Mechtild of Magdeburg, Bridget of Sweden, Catherine of Siena, Teresa of Avila, up to Gertrud von Le Fort, and Edith Stein. These women have much to teach men about love of God and love of his Church. And women like these acknowledge and support men in their service to the Church.

The fact that women are not admitted to the priesthood has to be seen as a defense of the woman's specific call. Whoever interprets this exclusion as a degradation of women seems to misunderstand the role of office in the Church. It is not, of course, a right which anybody may claim; nor is it a position of power that may be coveted to improve social standing. If the priesthood were such, then it might indeed be an injustice to exclude women. But priestly ordination is not conferred for honor and privilege, but for service and sacrifice. The priest, too, has to learn from Mary, "a creature of courage and obedience",[27] who was neither priest nor bishop but always Church.

Not by accident is the word "Church" of female gender. It is not the

---

[27] Joseph Cardinal Ratzinger, op. cit., p. 109.

man, with his pursuit of results, who expresses the true nature of Church, but the woman and her specific approach. This symbolic reality is emptied of its meaning whenever the woman is "masculinized". No wonder, then, that our present male-dominated society finds it so difficult to discover the mystery of the Church, and to entrust itself in love and gratitude to the Mother of all.

To belong to God and serve him is the call of every Christian, priest and layman alike, man as well as woman. We all have the duty to integrate and cultivate in different ways our natural talents; we can and must go even further and transcend them. For in a specific and unique way, God has called each of us by name.[28]

The more a Christian lives the faith, the more he resembles Christ who is the ideal model of human perfection. In Christ, all one-sidedness, all shortcomings are overcome; the best qualities of man's as well as woman's nature are united. Thus we witness in holy men true kindness and motherly care for souls, in holy women manly courage, firmness, and decisiveness. This ability to transcend our own limitations is the effect of grace which God gives to all who humbly submit to the divine order.[29]

Here, then, the struggle of the sexes against each other is transformed into the blessing of working with each other. United in Christ's love men and women can live together as equals, together shouldering the responsibility for a more humane world to come.

---

[28] Cf. Die Deutschen Bischöfe: "Zu Fragen der Stellung der Frau in Kirche und Gesellschaft" [The German Bishops, Questions regarding the role of women in Church and society] (Bonn, Sept. 21, 1981), p. 14.

[29] Cf. Edith Stein, *Frauenbildung und Frauenberufe,* op. cit., p. 171.

III

REFLECTIONS ON THE RELATIONSHIP OF THE DEACONESS TO WOMEN

7

MANFRED HAUKE

OBSERVATIONS ON THE ORDINATION OF WOMEN TO THE DIACONATE

Translated by Graham Harrison

Turning its attention to the role of the laity, the 1987 Synod of Bishops was also concerned about the significance and responsibilities of women in the Church.[1] In this context a question arises which, while it does not belong directly to the topic of "laity", is certainly related to it, namely, the question of restoring the office of deaconess, that is, ordaining women to the diaconate. As is well known, this issue provoked lively and controversial debate at the Würzburg Synod. In 1975 the Synod requested the Pope "to examine the question of women deacons in accord with modern theological knowledge", recommending that, "taking account of the concrete pastoral situation, women should be admitted, where possible, to ordination to the diaconate."[2] The German bishops' statement "On Questions Relating to the Position of Women in Church and Society" was taken up and discussed at the 1981 Synod, where it was added that "this question needs further and deeper discussion, but above all it needs a greater degree of unanimity in the whole Church."[3]

The debate concerning women deacons is often conducted at a strongly emotional level; frequently it is not backed up by basic and essential knowledge in theology and history. Unfortunately there is still no exhaus-

---

[1] Cf. "Der Laie in Kirche und Welt. Stellungnahme der deutschen Bischöfe zur Bischöfssynode 1987", section 2.6: *Herder Korrespondenz* 40 (1986): 328.

[2] Resolution: "Die pastoralen Dienste in der Gemeinde", 7.1 votum 3: *Gemeinsame Synode der Bistümer in der Bundesrepublik Deutschland, Beschlüsse der Vollversammlung* (Freiburg, 1976), 634.

[3] Sekretariat der Deutschen Bischofskonferenz (ed.), *Zu Fragen der Stellung der Frau in Kirche und Gemeinschaft* (Bonn, 1981), 24.

tive monograph on the topic apart from a few detailed historical studies.[4]
Nor can the following essay present a comprehensive treatment of the
subject; what it does attempt to do is to bring out crucial theological
factors without which all debate is doomed to fruitlessness.

I. THE SIGNIFICANCE OF THE THEOLOGY
OF THE DIACONATE

In general, the debate on women deacons starts from the following
question: Is it theologically possible and pastorally meaningful to admit
women to the diaconate which already exists and has an established
sacramental form?

To answer this question we need an adequately clear notion of what
the diaconate is. For centuries, in the Western Church, the diaconate was
regarded, in practice, as nothing more than a transitional stage to the
priesthood; it had no contours of its own. Even in 1962 a contributor to
the book *Diaconia in Christo* could remark, laconically: "There is no
theology of the diaconate."[5]

Up to the present his remark still seems to apply. In what follows we
shall discuss two questions in this area, which call for distinctive treatment:

[4] Important older studies: A. Kalsbach, "Die altkirchliche Einrichtung der Dia-
konissen bis zu ihrem Erlöschen": *Römische Quartalsschrift Supplement* 22 (Freiburg,
1926); idem, article "Diakonisse" in RAC III (Stuttgart 1957), 917–28. Even more material is brought to light in R. Gryson, "Le ministère des femmes dans l'Église ancienne":
Recherches et synthèses, section d'historie IV (Gembloux, 1972); esp. A.-G. Martimort,
"Les Diaconesses. Essai historique" in *Bibilotheca "Ephemerides Liturgicae"*, Subsidia 24
(Rome, 1982).

The question of "women deacons" has been very widely discussed in recent years. In
addition to the publications noted further below, the following are characteristic:
J. M. Barnett, *The Diaconate, a full and equal order* (Minneapolis, 1981), which is in
favor of the female diaconate; C. Zedda, "Ministerium feminarum?" and R. Goldie,
"Diaconato femminile?" in *Il diaconato permanente* (Naples, 1983), 237–45 and 305–13
(both opposed to women deacons); A. Frotz, "Zu der Frage: Diakonat der Frau" in
Pastoralblatt 32 (1980): 25f. (also negative).

[5] A. Kerkvoorde, "Die Theologie des Diakonates" in K. Rahner and H. Vorgrimler
(ed.) *Diaconia in Christo. Über die Erneuerung des Diakonates*. QD 15–16 (Freiburg,
1962), 221.

1. How is the diaconate related to the other two degrees of ordination, i.e., episcopacy and priesthood?

2. What is the theological difference between the lay ministries and the diaconate?

With regard to the first question the following models can be envisaged:

a. Ordination to the diaconate is completely independent of episcopal or priestly ordination. In this case the problem of admitting women to the diaconate can be kept separate from the question of women priests or bishops. The Würzburg Synod resolution seems to tend toward this model when it says: "The diaconate is a separate form of the sacrament of ordination, theologically and functionally distinct from priestly ministry." And: "The question of admitting women to the sacramental diaconate is distinct from the question of women priests."[6]

b. Ordination to the diaconate is a constituent part of the sacrament of ordination and is closely connected with the other stages. In this case the diaconate can only be properly interpreted in close relation to priesthood and episcopacy.

These divergent views are illustrated, even more clearly than in Western theology, in the controversy between two Greek Orthodox theologians. Professor Karmiris emphatically sees the diaconate as the third level of the sacrament of ordination, to which, for fundamental reasons, the Orthodox Church cannot admit women.[7] Professor Theodorou, on the other hand, attributes an independent significance to the diaconate, regarding it as clearly distinct from priesthood. Women too could be admitted to such an independent office that is not oriented to the priesthood.[8]

In the face of this controversy it is appropriate to note the foundations on which Vatican II restored the permanent diaconate. After discussing the episcopal and priestly office the Dogmatic Constitution on the Church turns to the diaconate:

[6] *Gemeinsame Synode* (cf. note 2 above), 617.

[7] J. Karmiris, Ἡ θέσις καὶ ἡ Διακονία τῶν Γυναικῶν ἐν τῇ Ὀρθοδόξῳ Ἐκκλησίᾳ (Athens, 1978).

[8] E. Theodorou, Ἡ "Χειροτονία" ἢ "Χειροθεσία" τῶν Διακονισσῶν (Athens, 1954); idem, "Das Amt der Diakoninnen in der kirchlichen Tradition" in *Una Sancta* 33 (1978): 162–72.

At a lower level of the hierarchy are to be found deacons, who receive the imposition of hands "not unto the priesthood, but unto the ministry". For, strengthened by sacramental grace they are dedicated to the People of God, in conjunction with the bishop and his body of priests, in the service of the liturgy, of the Gospel, and of works of charity.

After describing the responsibilities of the deacon, the Constitution resolves, "It will be possible in the future to restore the diaconate as a proper and permanent rank of the hierarchy."[9]

Here the diaconate is seen as a distinct step of the sacrament of ordination, not identical with priesthood and episcopacy.[10] On the other hand, like the priest, the deacon is a constituent part of the ordained hierarchy which finds its source and its highest expression in the episcopal office:

Christ ... has, through his apostles, made their successors, the bishops namely, sharers in his consecration and mission; and these, in their turn, duly entrusted in varying degrees various members of the Church with the office of their ministry. Thus the divinely instituted ecclesiastical ministry is exercised in different degrees by who even from ancient times have been called bishops, priests, and deacons.[11]

Thus the deacon shares in the particular ministry of the apostolic succession. In distinguishing the office of deacon from the office of priest, we must therefore keep in mind that both offices originate in the full authority of the bishop. Both share in the one sacrament of ordination.

In some authors we find the view that, as compared with the priest (and the bishop), the deacon does not act *in persona Christi.*[12] Such a view

---

[9] *Lumen gentium* 29 in A. Flannery (ed.), *Vatican Council II* (Dublin, 1975).

[10] In the Council document, "priesthood" means the presbyterate *and* the episcopate. Cf. A. Kerkvoorde, "Elemente zu einer Theologie des Diakonates" in G. Baraúna (ed.), *De Ecclesia II* (Frankfurt, 1966), 231.

[11] *Lumen gentium* 28 in A. Flannery (ed.), *Vatican Council II* (Dublin, 1975).

[12] For example, Y. Congar, "Gutachten zum Diakonat der Frau"; *Synode. Amtliche Mitteilungen der Gemeinsamen Synode der Bistümer in der BRD* 7 (1973): 26: the deacon "is not in the same position as the priest, who acts 'in persona Christi' in administering the sacraments". Or: H. J. Pottmeyer, "Thesen zur theologischen Konzeption der pastoralen Dienste und ihrer Zuordnung" in *Stimmen der Zeit* 195 (1977): 326: "The 'repraesentatio Christi' performed by the deacon has a different basis and character from that of the

might find support in the fact that, in the liturgical celebration, the deacon's role is normally only supportive and preparatory. On the other hand it can hardly be denied that, in certain of his tasks, the deacon does represent Christ the "Head" (and is sacramentally assisted in doing so), e.g., in baptizing, administering communion, and preaching. The Council of Trent affirms it to be a binding dogmatic teaching that sacramental character is imprinted in the sacrament of ordination;[13] it does not exclude the deacon from this.[14] But this same *character indelibilis* is the basis for acting *in persona Christi*,[15] so we can say that the deacon "symbolically represents" the "diaconal dimension of the three offices of Christ".[16]

If women receive sacramental ordination as deacons, it would be hard theologically to justify their exclusion from the other stages of the one sacrament of ordination. Thus the decision whether or not to admit women to the sacramental diaconate is inseparably linked to the question of their admission to priesthood and episcopacy.[17]

Moreover, the question arises whether the restored office of deacon is not closer to the priestly and episcopal office than it was before the Council or even in the Eastern Church. At all events, the deacon's area of independent responsibility has been substantially expanded. The deacon can now impart blessings and assume much more leadership in liturgical celebrations, whereas historically his role was much more that of service

---

priest; it follows, therefore, that in ordination to the diaconate neither the sacramental power to act 'in persona Christi' (eucharist, penance, ordination) nor jurisdiction over the community are conferred."

[13] DS 1767, 1774.

[14] On the character imprinted on the deacon in ordination cf. Kerkvoorde, 225f.

[15] *Presbyterorum ordinis* 2: A. Flannery (ed.) *Vatican Council II* (Dublin, 1975), 865.

[16] H. J. Weber, "Zur theologischen Ortsbestimmung des Diakonates im einen Weihesakrament" in J. G. Plöger and H. J. Weber (eds.) *Der Diakon. Wiederentdeckung und Erneuerung seines Dienstes* (Freiburg, 1980), 110. Also J. Auer, *Die Kirche—Das allgemeine Heilssakrament* = KKD VIII (Regensburg, 1983), 281.

[17] Cf. the author's dissertation on this subject: M. Hauke, *Die Problematik um das Frauenpriestertum vor dem Hintergrund der Schöpfungs- und Erlösungsordnung,* Konfessionskundliche und kontroverstheologische Studien XLVI, 2nd ed. (Paderborn, 1986), English edition: *Woman in the Priesthood?* (San Franciso: Ignatius, 1988).

and administration in the community.[18] Since Vatican II the deacon has been moved much closer than ever before to priestly ministry. No doubt the decisive reason for this is the wish to respond to the lack of priests.[19] This (merely negative) main argument for the permanent diaconate is bound to lead to difficulties in the way the deacon understands his role.[20]

However, the deacon's expanded area of responsibility does not have to be seen in purely negative terms.[21] At least it shows the relative flexibility with which the office of deacon can be an extension of the episcopal office. And theologically speaking it is an open question whether priesthood and diaconate are purely historically determined extensions of the apostolic office.[22] From this point of view, too, it seems questionable to dissociate the issue of "women deacons" from the whole issue of the ordination of women.

As well as clarifying how the diaconate is related to the other degrees of ordination, there is also the question of its relationship to the lay ministries. Immediately a difficulty arises at this very point. Even in preconciliar canon law "among the powers imparted to the deacon in ordination there is not a single one that the Church could not grant even without ordination."[23] The deacon's area of responsibility cuts across functions that any layperson can perform, either by being given a canonical mission or simply in virtue of baptism and confirmation. In that case, what is specific to the diaconate?

[18] Cf. H. Brakmann, "Zum Dienst des Diakons in der liturgischen Versammlung": Plöger and Weber (see note 16 above), 155.

[19] N. Trippen, "Die Erneuerung des Ständigen Diakonates im Gefolge des II. Vatikanischen Konzils": Plöger and Weber, 91: "The central argument for its renewal was pastoral necessity in the face of a lack of priests."

[20] Thus, for instance, the criticism of J. Caminada, Der Diakon. Reflexionen uber die Dogmatik des eigenständigen Dienstamtes in der Kirche (Munster: Diss, 1970), 4. The practical problems involved are described by K. Nientiedt, "Auf der Suche nach dem eigenen Profil. Zur Erneuerung des Ständigen Diakonats" in Herder Korrespondenz 39 (1985): 428–32.

[21] In reference to the Eastern Church: P. Plank, "Der Diakon: Gedanken und Anmerkungen für Weihbischof Augustinus Frotz" in Liturgisches Jahrbuch 32 (1982): 240.

[22] K. Rahner, "Die Theologie der Erneuerung des Diakonates" in Rahner and Vorgrimler, Diaconia in Christo, 290, 315.

[23] H. Flatten, "Der Diakon nach dem heutigen Recht der lateinischen Kirche" in Rahner and Vorgrimler, Diaconia in Christo, 131.

With regard to liturgical actions such as preaching and the solemnization of baptism, Paul Winninger says: "It is true that laypeople could do these too, but only in an 'acting' capacity and occasionally, in exceptional circumstances. Normally these actions have a hierarchical quality; their regular and continuous performance belongs to those in the ordained state."[24] Johannes Auer speaks in the same terms: in what the deacon does he "represents what Christ does, even when he does the same things that he did as a layman, prior to his ordination".[25]

In its Decree on the Church's Missionary Activity, Vatican II concluded, therefore, that particular tasks of the lay apostolate should be anchored in diaconal ordination:

> It would help those men who carry out the ministry of a deacon— preaching the word of God as catechists, governing scattered Christian communities in the name of the bishop or parish priest, or exercising charity in the performance of social or charitable works—if they were to be strengthened by the imposition of hands which has come down from the apostles. They would be more closely bound to the altar and their ministry would be made more fruitful through the sacramental grace of the diaconate.[26]

In this perspective there arises the critical question, whether the same argumentation could not also apply to women, i.e., those who do parish work as pastoral assistants, etc. The Würzburg Synod regards "the exclusion of these women from ordination" as introducing "a theologically and pastorally indefensible dichotomy between function on the one hand and the sacramentally mediated power for salvation on the other".[27]

---

[24] P. Winninger, "Diakon und Laie" in Rahner and Vorgrimler, *Diaconia in Christo*, 385.

[25] J. Auer (see note 16 above), 281.

[26] *Ad gentes* 16: M. A. Flannery (ed.) *Vatican Council II* (Dublin, 1975), 833.

[27] Resolution: "Die pastoralen Dienste in der Gemeinde" 4.2.2 (see note 2 above), 617.

2. DEACONESSES IN THE ANCIENT CHURCH:
A HISTORICAL SKETCH

In considering whether such an ordination is possible, we need to examine tradition closely. The ancient Church was acquainted with the institution of deaconesses. The crucial question here is whether these deaconesses of the ancient Church, seen from the modern standpoint, belonged to the sacramental diaconate or not. At first glance the problem seems to be anachronistic, since our concept of what a sacrament is did not exist prior to the twelfth century. Yet we can ask whether these deaconesses were ranked with the male deacons in terms of responsibilities and honor.

The more recent historical studies of Gryson (1972) and Martimort (1982)[28] come to an initially surprising conclusion: the existence of a firmly-established office of women called "deacons" or "deaconesses" can only be demonstrated since the third century.

In itself, the New Testament is inconclusive. "Phoebe, a servant of the church at Cenchreae" (Rom 16:1 AV) indicates a permanent responsibility, recognized by the community.[29] But it remains doubtful whether we can speak of a "deaconess" (cf. RSV) in the technical sense here, since this is only the beginning of a development of offices in the Church.[30] Furthermore we must remember that the words "serve" and "service" belong to a large constellation of meaning in the New Testament.[31]

Similarly, it is hard to know how to interpret that section of the First Letter to Timothy which holds a mirror up to church officials and refers,

---

[28] See note 4 above. On Martimort cf. E. J. Lengeling's (favorable) review in *Theologische Revue* 80 (1984): 227–30; similarly B. Kleinheyer, "Zur Geschichte der Diakonissesn" in *Liturgisches Jahrbuch* 34 (1984): 58–64; H. Moll in *Römische Quartalschrift* 79 (1984): 272–75; E. D. Theodorou in *Theologia* 53 (1982): 819–21.

[29] Cf. the more recent commentaries on Romans, e.g., H. Schlier, *Der Römerbrief* (HThK VI, Freiburg, 1977): 441.

[30] Martimort, 14f.; Gryson, 22–24; Congar, 23; P. Hünermann, "Gutachten zum Diakonat der Frau" in *Synode. Amtliche Mitteilungen* (see note 12), 28; H. Vorgrimler, "Gutachten über die Diakonatsweihe für Frauen" in *Synode. Amtliche Mitteilungen* (see note 12), 34; B. Weiss, "Zum Diakonat der Frau" in *Trierer Theologische Zeitschrift* 84 (1975): 15.

[31] Cf. Gryson, 22f.

in the passage on deacons, to women (1 Tim 3:11). Is it speaking of women in general, of deacons' wives, of the deacons' female coworkers, or of women deacons? The best arguments seem to indicate a service rendered by women in some connection with the deacons.[32] The term *diakonoi* may even include such women.[33]

A source from directly postapostolic times is a letter of Pliny the Younger, Administrator of Bithynia, written to the Emperor Trajan around the year 112. Pliny writes that he found it necessary to examine under torture two maidservants whom the Christians called *"ministrae"*, in order to find out the truth about the Christian faith.[34] *"Ministra"* may possibly be a translation of the official title *"diakonos";* but as to the functions of these women we learn as little as in the case of the "women" of 1 Timothy 3:11.

The basic reason for the reserved interpretation of these three sources is the fact that the postapostolic age makes no reference to the existence of women deacons. There are no traces of them, either in the Eastern Church (Ignatius of Antioch, Polycarp of Smyrna) or in the Western (Tertullian, Hippolytus). Nor are the Egyptians, Clement of Alexandria and Origen, acquainted with women deacons; when they mention 1 Timothy 3:11 or Romans 16:1, they essentially only expound the text as such, making no reference to any parallel institution of their own times.[35]

Martimort concludes that, had the apostolic age instituted women deacons, a tradition of that kind would have been continued and probably developed further in the succeeding age.

However, we should not forget that women's collaboration was considerable in the early Christian communities and in the postapostolic age. Women helped to spread the faith and devoted themselves to charitable and social work on a broad front. Diaconal and caring service was given

[32] Gryson, 30f.; Martimort, 16–19.

[33] This was regarded as certain in the older literature: Kalsbach, "Diakonisse" 13; also G. Lohfink, "Weibliche Diakone im Neuen Testament" in G. Dautzenberg et al. (ed.), *Die Frau im Urchristentum* (QD 95, Freiburg, 1983), 333. Also H. Frohnhofen, "Weibliche Diakone in der frühen Kirche" in *Stimmen der Zeit* 111 (1986): 270, who surely goes beyond the text when he speaks of the "female deacons" enjoying "full and equal rights".

[34] *Epp.,* X, 96, n. 8; cf. Martimort, 21f.

[35] Martimort, 74–80; contrary to Frohnhofen, 271.

by the oft-mentioned "widows and virgins"; but these women were not given the title "deacons".

The office of deaconesses is mentioned for the first time in the Didaskalia, a community rule of the third century which reflects the conditions in a small community in the East, possibly in Syria.[36] The women deacon (ἡ διάκονος) appears to be an innovation requiring special justification. The author of the *Didaskalia* does not trace the women deacon back to Phoebe and the women in 1 Timothy 3:11, but to the women who ministered in Jesus' entourage.[37] The introduction of the deaconess is recommended, not laid down as binding. Essentially she has two responsibilities:

1. She helps with baptisms: once the bishop has anointed the head of newly-baptized women, she anoints the rest of their naked bodies; in an emergency, however, some other woman can perform this service.

2. She looks after sick women and visits women in the houses of non-Christians, where the appearance of a male deacon would be regarded as improper.

Deacons and deaconesses are often mentioned in the same breath. On the other hand male and female deacons are seen according to different typologies: the deacons are held in honor as representing Christ, the deaconesses as representing the Holy Spirit. Then, too, deacons and deaconesses have quite distinct areas of work. Even in the case of women candidates, the anointing of the head and the act of baptism itself is reserved to the deacon or priest. Deaconesses are also forbidden to preach.[38] Thus the offices of male and female deacons cannot be simply equated.

The new ministry of deaconesses presupposes a relatively strict separation of the world of men from the world of women. Consequently the office of deaconess remained restricted to the eastern part of the Roman Empire, whereas, in the more liberal west and in Egypt, deaconesses were superfluous. In all probability, deaconesses were only introduced in the East in the third century as a result of the growth of the communities,

---

[36] Martimort, 40f.

[37] Cf. Lk 8:2f.

[38] *Didaskalia* III, 12, 7–13, 1; cf. Martimort, 31–41.

which called for new ministries. What had formerly been done at a more "family" level, now acquired an institutional framework.[39] It also presupposed the baptism of adults, a feature which went into the background in a Christianized society.

The historical influence of the *Didaskalia* was primarily due to its being taken up in the Apostolic Constitutions (end of the fourth century). According to canon 19 of the Council of Nicaea (325),[40] this is the first time that the title "deaconess" (διακόνισσα) appears. In the Apostolic Constitutions, for the first time, we have a testimony to the ordination of deaconesses with the imposition of hands and the invocation of the Holy Spirit; however, subdeacons and lectors were also ordained with the imposition of hands and with prayer. Also, for the first time, we are given a prayer of ordination, following immediately after the prayer for the deacon. The two prayers, however, are different in content. As the deaconesses' prototypes the Apostolic Constitutions take the Old Testament prophetesses, Mary the Mother of God, and the female doorkeepers of the Tent of Meeting.[41] The difference in content between the ordination formulas for men and women deacons is also maintained in all later-documented liturgical texts. Historically speaking, one cannot talk in terms of an "absolute equality and parallelism of ordination formulas for men and women".[42]

Furthermore, the male and female diaconates are expressly distinguished: "The deaconess cannot impart a blessing, nor does she carry out any of the functions which the priest or the deacons exercise; she is only a doorkeeper and helps the priests in administering baptism simply for the sake of decency."[43]

[39] Martimort, 39.

[40] See below.

[41] Ex 38:8; 1 Sam 2:22. *Apostolic Constitutions* VIII, 20: F. X. Funk (ed.), *Didascalia et Constitutiones Apostolorum II* (Paderborn, 1906), 524.

[42] Thus P. Hünermann, "Diakonie als Wesensdimension der Kirche und das Spezifikum des Diakonates. Ein systematisch-theologischer Beitrag zur gegenwärtigen Situation": *Wann bestellt die Kirche ihre Diakoninnen? Diskussionsbeiträge,* ed. International Diaconate Center (Freiburg, 1985) 53; appeared first in *Diaconia XP* 13 (1978): 3–22.

[43] *Apostolic Constitutions* VIII, 28, 6: Funk II, 524. It is baffling how Frohnhofen (277) manages to find "a total equivalence of male and female deacons" in the Apostolic Constitutions, of all places.

The Council of Nicaea (325) refers to deaconesses as laywomen and rejects the idea of their being ordained by the imposition of hands.[44] But later the Council of Chalcedon (451) includes the deaconess among the ecclesiastical offices (τὸ ἐκκλησιαστικὸν τάγμα) and envisages an ordination involving the imposition of hands and prayer, similarly to the Apostolic Constitutions.[45] In the legislation of the Emperor Justinian (535), again, the deaconess is regarded as one of the Church officials, though distinguished from the "clerics" (κληρικοί).[46] Sometimes the deaconess is included among the ordained, after the deacon; sometimes, however, she is mentioned after the list of clerics, which points to her special position. As early as the end of the fourth century Epiphanius includes the deaconess among the ecclesiastical offices (τὸ ἐκκλησιαστικὸν τάγμα), to which all "church appointees"—right up to the doorkeeper and sexton—belong. On the other hand the Bishop of Salamis expressly excludes the deaconess from the priestly hierarchy (ἡ ἱερωσύνη), which extends from the bishop to the subdeacon.[47]

From the fourth century on, increasingly, the superiors of convents of women were appointed deaconesses, no doubt because there was as yet no form for the consecration of abbesses.[48] In the remote convents of the Syrian Monophysites (fifth century) the ordained deaconesses were permitted to distribute Communion to their sisters and to children up to four years old and to read the Epistle and Gospel at a service of worship exclusively for women. All these rights were suspended, however, if a priest or deacon were present.[49]

Deaconesses assume a particularly important role in the Byzantine Rite. Their ordination has a "morphological similarity to the *cheirotonia* of the higher clergy" and is similarly incorporated into the rite of Mass.[50] As with the deacons, the ordination of deaconesses takes place in the sanctuary after the anaphora, whereas the subdeacon is ordained at

---

[44] On the interpretation of can. 19 cf. Martimort, 99–101.
[45] Martimort, 106.
[46] Martimort, 109.
[47] Gryson, 134; Martimort, 111.
[48] Martimort, 134–37.
[49] Kalsbach, "Diakonisse" 922; Martimort, 137–42.
[50] Theodorou, "Diakoninnen", 169.

an earlier point in the liturgy and outside the sanctuary. As in the case of the ordination of bishops, priests, and deacons, the bishop uses the proclamatory formula Ἡ θεία χάρις (the grace of God), which is not used for the subdeacons and other ministries. Yet in other liturgical traditions the same formula is used for subdeacon and lector too.[51] In addition the deaconess, like the deacon, is handed a stole and a chalice.

For the liturgical scholar Vagaggini these signs of external equality indicate the inner identity of the ordination of deacons and of deaconesses. Thus he designates deacon and deaconess as two branches of the same office.[52] However, Vagaggini's colleague, Martimort, comes to the opposite view; he points out crucial differences between the two ordinations:[53] the stole given to the deaconess in the rite of ordination is not worn in the manner of the deacon but in that of the subdeacon, who was not authorized to distribute Holy Communion. Moreover the stole is put on under the veil. Whereas the deacon, having been handed the chalice, may distribute the sacred Blood, the deaconess immediately puts the chalice back on the altar. In contrast to the deacon, she does not assume a ministry at the altar. At the ordination the priest kneels and the deacon genuflects; in doing so both of them touch the altar with their heads, which, according to Pseudo-Dionysius, indicates a difference of power with reference to the Eucharist; the deaconess, however, remains standing at her ordination.

Just as the external form of the ordination of deaconesses differs from that of the deacons, so does the interpretation of the ministries as expressed in the ordination prayer. The deaconess' ordination prayer speaks of the example of the Mother of God, the descent of the Holy Spirit on women as well as men, and the case of Phoebe, who received grace for service.[54] The ordination prayer for deacons has a different content.

Their tasks are also distinct. The deaconess is "forbidden" to "preach in

---

[51] C. Vagaggini, "L'ordinazione delle deaconesse nella tradizione greca e bizantina" in *Orientalia Christiana Periodica* 40 (1974), 184; Martimort, 152.

[52] Vagaggini, 151.

[53] Martimort, 152–55; cf. also Theodorou, "Diakoninnen", 169.

[54] Martimort, 147f.

the ecclesial assembly, to baptize and carry out other priestly duties".[55]
The deaconess' area of responsibility is not the liturgical ministry but,
apart from helping in baptism, primarily caring for the sick and needy
and looking after Christian women.[56] Martimort draws this conclusion:

"However great the solemnity which accompanied the (Byzantine)
rite (of ordination of deaconesses), and however similar, externally, to
the ordination of deacons, the Byzantine deaconess is not a deacon: the
office is totally different."[57]

After the eighth century, traces of these deaconesses become more and
more scarce. By the tenth or eleventh century women deacons have
vanished in the East. A basic reason for this was the cessation of adult
baptism. Abbesses too no longer receive ordination as deaconesses, probably because a special rite for their institution had been developed.[58]

In the West, deaconesses are never mentioned until the fourth century.
Whereas Ambrosiaster regards deaconesses as a heretical invention of the
Cataphrygians (Montanists), Pelagius knows something of the Eastern
usages, which he regards as apostolic.[59] In Gaul several Councils energetically proscribe the ordination of deaconesses: what they object to is a
"ministerium leviticum" on the part of women, i.e., a female diaconate
equivalent to the male.[60]

Nonetheless the Eastern influence occasionally makes itself felt in the
West. Remigius, Bishop of Rheims, gives his daughter Hilaria the epithet
"Deaconess"; Radegunde, the wife of King Clothar I, is ordained deaconess by the imposition of hands.[61] In addition, the wives of deacons are
referred to as "deaconesses". From Carolingian times we have an ordination prayer for "deaconesses" that is concerned with widows.[62] Under
Byzantine influence, from the seventh century on, there are also deaconesses
in Rome and Ravenna;[63] in the tenth century, in Rome and Nepi, three

[55] Theodorou, "Diakoninnen", 169.
[56] Theodorou, "Diakoninnen", 170.
[57] Martimort, 155.
[58] Martimort, 183f.
[59] Martimort, 191f.
[60] Martimort, 193–96.
[61] Martimort, 199f.
[62] Martimort, 211.
[63] Martimort, 204f.

abbesses are referred to as deaconesses.[64] In the twelfth–thirteenth centuries this circumscribed institution of deaconesses falls into disuse. An echo is heard in a few convents of the fourteenth–seventeenth centuries: the "deaconess" is allowed to read the Gospel and the homily at the conventual Matins, and receives a special blessing for the purpose.[65]

3. ASSESSING THE HISTORICAL EVIDENCE

First it must be said that there is no homogeneous picture of the nature and responsibilities of the office of deaconess. The first historically ascertainable women deacons in the third century are basically assistants in baptism and in looking after women (Mesopotamia, Chaldaea, Persia). In other areas of the East, the ordination of deaconesses is primarily a solemn mark of honor for the wives of priests and deacons, for widows involved in parish work, and for abbesses. In many times and regions the deaconesses are more oriented to ascetical or religious life than to parish work.[66]

The greatest similarities between deacon and deaconess appear in the Byzantine rite of ordination of deaconesses. But at this very point, as we have seen, substantial differences come to light between the deacon and the deaconess. In spite of the variety of liturgical traditions, the deaconess was no more permitted to perform any service at the altar than to exercise the public ministry of preaching. The reasons for this lie in the exclusion of women from the office of priesthood.[67] The decision for or against the sacramental ordination of women to the diaconate is therefore dependent on a clarification of the issue of "women priests".

At all events it would be right to say, with Galot, that female ministries in the ancient Church are profoundly different from those of the male

[64] Martimort, 206.
[65] Martimort, 231–43.
[66] Martimort, 245–47.
[67] Cf. the historical references from the Fathers in Hauke, 399–440.

ordination hierarchy. They are not along the lines of the priestly office.[68]

> It is true that, in its explicit form, the distinction between the sacramental and the sacrament only emerges in scholasticism; but if we consider the "embryonic stage" of the development objectively, the ordination of deaconesses does not seem to point in the direction of sacrament.[69]

The history of the institution of deaconesses offers no solid basis, therefore, for the introduction of a sacramental female diaconate.[70] The ancient Church was unacquainted with a female diaconate equivalent to the male diaconate.

4. THE RENEWAL OF THE OFFICE OF DEACONESS IN ORTHODOXY, ANGLICANISM, AND PROTESTANTISM

Even if tradition cannot be adduced in favor of a sacramental female diaconate, the question arises whether a specific office of woman deacon could be introduced as something entirely new. The institute of deaconess in the ancient Church was, in its time, a new creation by the Church, which became a firmly established office, anchored in an ordination. In modern terminology we would not speak of a sacrament here, but of a sacramental, but this in no way disparages the great significance of the deaconess' ordination. Would it be meaningful today, therefore, to introduce an ordination of deaconesses as something new, suited to modern conditions?

[68] J. Galot, *Mission et ministère de la femme* (Paris, 1973), 61.

[69] Hauke, 440.

[70] Cf. A. Heinz, "Die liturgischen Dienste der Frau. Studientagung 1978 der Arbeitsgemeinschaft Katholischer Liturgiker im deutschen Sprachgebiet" in *Liturgisches Jahrbuch* 28 (1978). He sums up the results of this liturgical congress thus: "There was unanimity that history could provide no solid basis ... for a female diaconate" (130). At the same congress Maria B. von Stritzky urged that the historical argumentation of the Würzburg Synod (which had based itself on the deaconesses of the ancient Church) should be corrected: "Der Dienst der Frau in der alten Kirche" in *Liturgisches Jahrbuch* 28 (1978), 154. Similarly Kleinheyer, "Zur Geschichte ... " 64; idem, "Ordinationen und Beauftragungen" in *Sakramentliche Feiern II: Gottesdienst der Kirche. Handbuch der Liturgiewissenschaft*, part 8 (Regensburg, 1984) 17f.

Here it is helpful to look at other Christian denominations. First of all we must mention the Orthodox Church, in which the permanent diaconate has persisted down through history; the deaconesses of the ancient Church flourished primarily in its area of influence. Here too, however, there is no homogeneous picture. In the 1960s, Irenäus Doens reported that the permanent diaconate was dying out in Greece.[71] Simultaneously Robert Clément observed that there were no permanent deacons in the Greek-Orthodox Patriarchates of Alexandria and Antioch, or in the Egyptian Coptic Church.[72] In countries oppressed by Islam the office of the permanent deacon is regarded as a luxury; the liturgical functions of the deacon are mostly performed by subdeacons and lectors.[73]

The amplest tradition with regard to the permanent diaconate is to be found in Russia, especially in pre-Revolution times. It was in Russia that ideas first arose to restore the ancient Church's office of deaconess. The first historically influential suggestions date from 1860, and were supported by the sister of Tsar Nicholas I, the Grand Duchess Elena Pavlovna. In 1906 there was a discussion of the issue at the Holy Synod, but it rejected the idea of restoring the office. These attempts were then totally nullified by the confusions of the Russian Revolution.[74]

Nonetheless it is instructive to examine more closely that movement in favor of the office of deaconess. The future deaconess' role was seen primarily as the pastoral care of the poor and needy.[75] One of the movement's spokesmen, Alexios von Maltzev, observed with regard to the deaconesses of the ancient Church: they "did not receive the sacrament of ordination, though they received cheirotony".[76]

---

[71] Irenaeus Doens, "Der Diakonat in den griechischen und slawischen Kirchen", in Rahner-Vorgrimler, *Diaconia in Christo,* 145.

[72] Robert Clément, "Der Diakon in den orthodoxen und unierten Kirchen des Ostens in der Gegenwart", in Rahner-Vorgrimler, *Diaconia in Christo,* 183.

[73] Clément, 186.

[74] Doens, 165; Kyriaki Karidoyanes Fitzgerald, "The Characteristics and Nature of the Order of the Deaconess", in Thomas Hopko, ed., *Women in the Priesthood* (Crestwood, New York: St. Vladimir's Seminary Press, 1983), 89f.

[75] Sergei Hackel, "Mother Maria Skobtsova: Deaconess Manquée?", in *Eastern Churches Review* 1 (1966–67): 265f.

[76] That is, to receive ordination by the laying on of hands.

They were not commissioned "to serve at the holy mysteries".[77]

Whether the deaconesses of the ancient Church received a higher consecration, i.e., sacramental ordination, is a disputed question among Orthodox theologians.[78] Theodorou and Zernov,[79] for instance, regard the ordination of deaconesses as sacramental, whereas many others hold it to be non-sacramental.[80] But even those who advocate a sacramental ordination clearly distinguish it from priestly ordination. The presupposition here is that the deacon does not impart blessings and act in general as a liturgical image of Christ.[81] The model of the deaconess is held to be Mary, who assisted in Christ's redemptive work.[82]

The first Orthodox deaconesses of modern times are found in Greece. In the years prior to the First World War the Archbishop of Athens appointed a number of women religious as subdeacons, but gave them the title "deaconess". The functions of these women religious were to decorate the church and to administer incense; in the absence of a priest they were authorized to read the Gospel and distribute communion to their sick sisters. Even in the 1950s there were some Greek convents of women with monastic deaconesses;[83] the present author has no information about their activities.

Since 1952 there have also been "deaconesses" in parishes in Greece. However, this is explicitly regarded as a lay ministry: the women are not ordained. The duties of "deaconesses" roughly correspond to those of our women parish assistants and community workers.

In 1976, in Agapia (Rumania), there was a multi-national congress on

[77] Alexios von Maltzew, *Die Sakramente der Orthodox-Katholischen Kirche dès Morgenlandes* (Berlin, 1898), appendix, 10–12.

[78] See Kallistos Ware, "Man, Woman, and the Priesthood of Christ", in Hopko, 32f; Fitzgerald, 84–89.

[79] Militza Zernow, "Women's Ministry in the Church", in *Eastern Churches Review* 8 (1975): 34–39; on Theodorou, see above, footnote 8.

[80] For instance, Karmiris: see footnote 7; Nicolae Chitescu, "Das Problem der Ordination der Frau", in *Zur Frage der Ordination der Frau*, of the series "Studien des Ökumenischen Rates der Kirchen", 1 (Geneva, 1964): 67–71; Georges Khodre, "Die Ordination der Frau", likewise in: *Zur Frage . . .*, 72–75.

[81] Ware, 33.

[82] See the Byzantine prayer of ordination discussed above, and Zernow, 38.

[83] Fitzgerald, 90.

"The Work and Involvement of Women in the Orthodox Church". A call was issued to study the office of deaconess and possibly to instil new life into it. An ordination of deaconesses, however, was not in any way to be understood as the first step toward priestly ordination. There was a similar conference in 1980 in New York.[84] The only other concrete example of "deaconesses", apart from Orthodox Greece, is in the Old Coptic Church of Egypt, where they have been introduced as an experiment.[85]

In the Anglican Communion[86] it was the Bishop of London who, in 1862, ordained a number of women as deaconess, by imposition of hands. Others followed this example. The work and external appearance of the deaconesses were quite different from diocese to diocese. The Lambeth Conference of 1920 suggests that the deaconesses share in the ordained priesthood ("Holy Orders"); but neither this, nor the identity of their office with that of the male deacons, is explicitly stated. The work of the deaconess is to care for the sick and needy, but also to engage in catechesis in the parish. It is a matter for the local bishop whether she may preach or not. In 1930, however, the Lambeth Conference explicitly excluded deaconesses from the threefold ordained office. The office of deaconess is affirmed to be essentially different from the hierarchical offices, but complementary to them. Here the deaconess' responsibilities correspond to those of a parish assistant and almoner. Yet, in spite of this interpretation, an ordination of deaconesses is envisaged which involves the imposition of hands by the bishop and the use of the same formula as for the male deacon; Anglican writers are no doubt correct to speak of "confusion" here.[87]

A specific difficulty arose with regard to the Anglican deaconesses in

[84] Fitzgerald, 91.

[85] Elisabeth Behr-Sigel, "The Participation of Women in the Life of the Church", in Ion Bria, ed., *Martyria/Mission: The Witness of the Orthodox Churches Today* (Geneva, 1980), 58; Behr-Sigel gives no information on the theological status of deaconesses.

[86] On what follows, see Hugh McCullum, "The Experience in Anglicanism", in M. P. Hamilton and N. S. Montgomery, eds., *The Ordination of Women: Pro and Con* (New York, 1975), 136–51; Paula Schäfer, "Das Diakonissenamt in der anglikanischen Kirche", in *Eine heilige Kirche* 21 (1939) 76–79.

[87] "Confusion", McCullum, 138; Report of the Archbishops' Commission on Women and Holy Orders (London, 1966), 34.

that they were in "competition" with the newly established female religious orders which arose likewise in the nineteenth century and attracted substantially more members. In 1939 Paula Schäfer reports "regret over the lack of deaconesses".[88]

A new situation came about in 1968, when the Lambeth Conference—as in 1920 and contrary to 1930—expressly included the office of deaconess among the "Holy Orders". Since the 1970s practically all Anglican member-Churches have had a sacramentally-understood ordination of women to the office of "deacon", distinct from the non-sacramental office of "deaconess". In the Anglican Church the question of the ordination of deaconesses is closely linked with the problem of women's ordination as a whole. In 1970, after the Lambeth Conference, the first female deacons were ordained in Canada, and in 1975, the first female priests. In Limuru in 1971 the Anglican Consultative Council left the question of the ordination of women to the discretion of the individual member churches; that same year saw the first "ordinations to the priesthood" in Hong Kong.

In the Anglican Communion the sacramental ordination of women deacons is seen as a stepping-stone to the other ordinations. All the same, the issue of the ordination of women is still just as contentious in Anglicanism: the Church in the United States split as a result, and the General Synod of the Church of England is experiencing strong opposition to its plans to introduce the ordination of women in England.[89]

In Protestantism there have been "deaconesses" for about 150 years, comparable with Catholic communities of sisters,[90] but there is no analogy here for the introduction of the sacramental female diaconate. In addition, since the beginning of the Seventies, some member-churches of the German Evangelical Church (EKD) have begun to use the official term *Diakonin*. This refers either to female graduates of the Diaconate Colleges (to which women have been admitted since the Seventies) —working as youth workers, social workers, and teachers of religion—or to those who were formerly called "women parish assistants": e.g., in the

---

[88] Schäfer, 79.

[89] *Herder Korrespondenz*, 40 (1986): 361f.

[90] *Die Frau in Familie, Kirche und Gesellschaft,* 2nd ed. (Gütersloh, 1980), 156f.

Evangelical Church of Baden these are now called "parish deaconesses" (*Diakoninnen*). In the Diaconate Colleges both deaconesses and deacons, having completed their training, are jointly blessed as they are sent forth.[91] The "call to service" of the Protestant deaconess or *Diakonin*, however, must be clearly distinguished from ordination to the office of pastor.

5. A NEW OFFICE OF DEACONESS?

Our glance at the other denominations has shown that the term "deaconess" or *Diakonin* can refer to very diverse concepts of service. The spectrum extends from the female deacon, regarded as a constituent part of the ordained hierarchy in the Anglican Communion, to the non-ordained parish assistant in Orthodox Greece and in Protestantism. The Orthodox Church evinces a certain uncertainty as to the theological position of deaconesses in the ancient Church. Consequently there is a reluctance simply to take up the practice of the ancient Church. There is unanimity that the ordination of deaconesses must not imply any step toward the priestly office. In the Anglican communion the ordination of female deacons, although it is diversely interpreted, signifies a decisive step in the direction of ordination to the priesthood. The situation in Protestantism is less comparable to that in Orthodoxy and Anglicanism in that, in the former, "deaconesses" and *Diakoninnen* carry no great implications for the theology of ministry.

The Protestant deaconess, however, is a significant pointer to something which has continued the ancient Church's institution of deaconesses, namely, religious life. It was particularly the deaconesses' caritative work that was subsequently carried on and developed by the religious orders. Other responsibilities of the deaconess in the ancient Church have become obsolete today, e.g., the assistance at baptism and the visitation of women isolated in the world of the harem. On the other hand, the woman engaged in pastoral work is faced with new and important tasks: parish

----

[91] U. Roland, "Die Diakonin in der Evangelischen Kirche in Deutschland": in *Wann bestellt . . .* (see note 42 above), 12–15.

catechesis, personal counselling, the inexhaustible realm of caring . . .

It should be beyond question that woman's service in the Church is just as important as man's. But the admission of women to sacramental ordination to the diaconate raises theological problems involving the God-given distinction of the sexes and the structure of the Church as established by Christ. A sacramental female diaconate would pre-empt the decision concerning a female priestly office—which, on principle, the Church rejects. And, as for regarding the ordination of female deacons as the "second step" on the way to the "tenth step"—priestly ordination—is this really the most honest way to pursue the ordination of women?[92]

It would be a different situation if the diaconate could be seen as a sacramental office with no inner connection with the other ordained offices, as a totally distinct office. But as we have shown in section I above, such a thesis is at least highly controversial. Taken to its logical conclusion, would it not imply an office conferred by sacramental ordination yet outside of the sacrament of ordination?

The Synod of Bishops on the role of the laity contributed to a new realization that the meaning of our Christian life does not depend on whether we are ordained or not. Through baptism and confirmation every Christian is richly equipped with gifts, to perform a service which is personal to him or her. Those who suggest, as a rationale for the sacramental ordination of women to the diaconate, that otherwise women are deprived of the grace they need for their work, are surely underestimating the charisms of the priesthood of all the faithful. Cannot we discern a hidden clericalism in this sort of argumentation, a clericalism that, since Vatican II, should be regarded as dead and buried?

At a period in the Church's history which has devoted so much intensive thought to the dignity of the laity, it would surely be strange to look for the Church's "ratification" and "recognition" in terms of sacramental ordination.[93]

It would be quite a different matter to link particular ministries of the

---

[92] This kind of strategic use of women's ordination to the diaconate is put forward, for example, by H.-R. Laurien in N. Sommer (ed.) *Nennt uns nicht Brüder! Frauen in der Kirche durchbrechen das Schweigen* (Stuttgart, 1985), 238.

[93] Cf. *Wann bestellt . . .* 5:17.

lay apostolate with a special blessing or solemn commissioning—which already occurs to some extent. One could envisage certain ministries being anchored in a (non-sacramental) consecration, already found in a specific form in religious communities, e.g., the consecration of an abbess or of virgins. However, an ordination of this kind is widely rejected within the movement for women deacons. A non-sacramentally ordained female deacon, perhaps performing the same tasks as a man, is felt, no doubt rightly, to be a contradiction. A deaconess ordained in such a manner would be a kind of "spoiled deacon". The female ministry in the Church has its own dignity: it does not need to be based on a clerical office.

It would be an impossible anachronism simply to revive the ancient Church's office of deaconess. The deaconess of former times has little in common, apart from the name, with the picture of the female deacon as envisaged today. Again, the demand for a sacramental ordination of deaconesses suffers from being seen as a kind of Trojan Horse for other aims.

The present author regards the sacramental ordination of women deacons as theologically impossible, and the (non-sacramental) diaconate as pastorally lacking in meaning. What is urgently needed, however, theologically and pastorally, is the committed service of men *and* women in the Church, where the charisms of all Christians complement each other in a wonderful way. Particularly at a time such as this, which in so many ways utters the *"non serviam"* — "I will not serve" — we all need the mind of Christ, who said of himself: "The Son of Man came not to be served but to serve, and to give his life as a ransom for many" (Mk 10:45).

8

BRUNO KLEINHEYER

REGARDING THE HISTORY OF DEACONESSES

A BIBLIOGRAPHICAL REFERENCE

Translated by Lothar Krauth

1. Any era desiring change should feel obligated to argue the theological implications carefully and without emotions. The Roman Catholic Church is at present engaged in a search for ways and means to include women in ecclesiastical ministry. The clearest manifestation of such tendencies, in this country [Germany], was the vote by the Common Synod of the Dioceses in the Federal Republic of Germany, saying: "This Synod petitions the Pope to evaluate the question of female deacons according to contemporary theological insights; and, in view of the present pastoral situation, to consider the possible ordination of women to the diaconate."[1] This vote 7.1.3 of the Resolution on "The Pastoral Ministries in the Parish" (May 7–11, 1975) is given its historical rationale in text 4.2 of "The Diaconate of Women":

> Based on biblical testimony regarding the role of women in Jesus' circle of disciples and the numerous and important services of women in the Church of New Testament times, the Eastern Churches, and during the early Christian centuries occasionally also the Churches of Latin rite, ordained women as deaconesses. According to the cultural and social conditions of the time, they were charged with a ministry of service especially for women and families. Their role in liturgy and sacramental ministry was scarcely developed, reflecting the general position of women in society at the time. In spite of their limited pastoral and, above all, liturgical responsibilities, these women, during

[1] Common Synod of the Dioceses in the Federal Republic of Germany. Official Complete Edition I. (Freiburg, 1976), 634 pp.

their time, contributed considerably to imbue the life of women and families with a Christian spirit. These historical facts have largely been forgotten in the Church.[2]

That the inclusion of women in ecclesiastical ministry was and still is an acute question, is shown by the choice of the theme for the 1978 Conference of the Association of Catholic Liturgists in German-speaking Areas, which was "The Liturgical Ministries of Women".[3] It is also shown in the discussion published in the Pastoralblatt Aachen (and elsewhere) at the beginning of 1983,[4] to quote but two instances.

Under these circumstances it is advisable and instructive to listen to some prudent voices. It becomes indispensable for the theological investigation of the diaconate for women, as advocated by the Synod of Würzburg. The French expert in liturgy A. G. Martimort now joins the discussion, speaking with caution and thorough knowledge, as was to be expected from him:

Aimé Georges Martimort, *Diaconesses: An Historical Study* (San Francisco: Ignatius Press, 1986), 268 pp.

In German-speaking countries, Martimort became widely known through his edition of the most recent important manual on the liturgy.[5] Among experts he enjoys a high reputation, based—with other works—on his finely chiseled key to the sources of E. Martène.[6] To say it right

---

[2] Ibid., 616f.

[3] Cf. the report by A. Heinz in *Liturgisches Jahrbuch: Vierteljahreshefte* 28 (1978): 129–35; cf. also the important presentation by M. B. von Stritzky, "Der Dienst der Frau in der alten Kirche" [The Ministry of women in the early Church]; ibid., 136–54.

[4] H. Moll, "Aus Treue zum Vorbild ihres Herrn" [Faithful to the example of the Lord]. The meaning of male priesthood in the Catholic Church. In *Pastoralblatt* Aachen et al., 35 (1983): 6–14. St. Schmitz, "Zu Helmut Moll . . ." [Reply to Helmut Moll] ibid., 86–89. Cf. also the review by H. Moll, ibid., 93–95 of Manfred Hauke's *Women in the Priesthood? A Systematic Analysis in the Light of the Order of Creation and Redemption* (San Francisco: Ignatius, 1988).

[5] A. G. Martimort, "L'église en prière" [The Church at prayer]. (Paris, 1960); in German: *Handbuch der Liturgiewissenschaft*, 2 vols., (Freiburg, I, 1963; II, 1965).

[6] A. G. Martimort, "La documentation liturgique de Dom Edmond Martène" [The liturgical documentation of Dom Edmond Martène]. Città del Vaticano, 1978, StL 279; cf. the review by L. Brinkhoff in *Liturgisches Jahrbuch. Vierteljahreshefte* 28 (1978): 182–85.

away: the work we introduce here is everything we would expect from such an author.

The book's introduction contains remarks on the present state of the discussion. Relating this introduction and the final summary to the index of subjects and proper names, it becomes evident that Martimort's study was prompted by some corresponding works which appeared in the early years of the last decade. There is a more distant link with A. Kalsbach's monograph;[7] Martimort wishes to continue and deepen the work of R. Gryson[8] and in so doing offers comments on related articles by P. Delhaye[9] and C. Vaggagini,[10] frequently contradicting them.

Martimort is always careful to let the many and quite different sources speak for themselves, without prejudice. He divides his work into twelve chapters. The first chapter deals with the first two centuries (pp. 17–32) and is followed by the two main parts of the book. Part I, containing chapters 2–8, treats the Churches of Greek and oriental languages (pp. 35–183). Part II, including chapters 9–12, is entitled "Deaconesses in the Latin Church" (pp. 187–240). Pages 241–250 offer some conclusions. The extensive indices are extremely instructive.

2.1. Testimonies of the first two centuries: What weight do we attribute to certain New Testament texts which occasionally are used to discuss the diaconate of women? It is commonly agreed that the 'Diakonos' Phoebe in Cenchreae (Rom 16:1) does not present the same formal meaning as 'Diakonos', e.g., in Philemon 1:1 and 1 Timothy 3:8,12. 1 Timothy 3:8–13 deals with deacons; in an abrupt transition in this passage, verse 11 speaks of women. Is this a later insertion? If not, to whom does it refer to: Women in general? Wives of deacons? Specific female helpers? The early

---

[7] A. Kalsbach, "Die altkirchliche Einrichtung der Diakonissinnen bis zu ihrem Erlöschen" [The institution of deaconesses in the early Church until its disappearance] RQ (Freiburg im Breisgau, 1926), p. 22.

[8] R. Gryson, "Le ministère des femmes dans l'Eglise ancienne" [The ministry of women in the early church] (RSSR. H4), (Gembloux, 1972).

[9] P. Delhaye, "Rétrospective et prospective des ministères feminins dans l'Eglise" [Past and future of women ministers in the Church]. In RTL 3 (1972): 55–75.

[10] C. Vaggagini, "L'ordinazione delle diaconesse nella tradizione greca e bizantina" [The ordination of deaconesses in Greek and Byzantine tradition]. In OrChrP 40 (1974): 146–89.

exegetes were not unanimous on this—much like modern biblical scholars. Nor is it clear whether the "widows" in 1 Timothy 5:9f. were somehow members of the hierarchy or not. It would be quite helpful for the interpretation of these texts if we only had related documents from the second century. The material available from the third century apparently is not connected with the situation in previous times.

It is of some significance that Tertullian treats the state of "widowhood" as an order. In this order widows share with clerics the decision for monogamy; but this does not make them clerics. Deaconesses are unknown to Tertullian. According to the Church Order of Hippolytus, the "traditional orders", as it were, are conferred through the laying on of hands, and prayer. All other groups, widows and virgins among them, do not receive the laying on of hands. "The ecclesiology of St. Hippolytus of Rome simply excluded the possibility of deaconesses" (p. 32).

2.2. Part One on the practice in the Churches speaking Greek and oriental languages is divided according to geographical, historical, and factual aspects. Following the sources, the survey begins at the Syrian, eastern border of the Empire (and in regions beyond). Chapters 2 and 3 introduce the most ancient Church Orders which originated in these districts or were compiled there. Then, chapter 4 looks at the regions along the Nile. Chapters 5 and 6 consider the other Eastern territories. Chapter 7 deals exclusively with the liturgy of ordination. Chapter 8, the last chapter of Part One, sketches the end of Deaconesses as an institution.

The most ancient reference to deaconesses, the *Didascalia* of the Apostles, comes from the early third century. The author writes in Greek, from a Semitic background. This ecclesiastical Order probably originated east of the Antioch region. In the *Didascalia,* deaconesses are mentioned in sections nine and sixteen, which also describes their activity. They are needed because society insists on strict separation of the sexes. Deaconesses minister to women who cannot be visited by deacons because of the pagans. Under the direction of the priests and deacons they are involved as helpers at baptismal celebrations, mainly to safeguard modesty at the baptism of women. After an ordained minister has initiated the anointing, they proceed to complete the anointing of the entire body of the candidate before baptism. In addition they instruct the newly baptized women.

It should be emphasized, against possible objections, that the passages on deaconesses in the *Didascalia* are not later insertions. The role of deacons is described extensively, that of deaconesses only in hints. The reason may be that the institution of deaconesses was new and still unsettled. It is significant that neither Romans 16, nor 1 Timothy 3, nor 1 Timothy 5 are invoked as biblical patterns; it is Matthew 27:55 that is considered the model for the ministry of deaconesses. Other texts of later date from these districts may at times tell more about the ministry of deaconesses but not always more clearly; thus, for example, the *Testamentum Domini Nostri Jesu Christi,* a successor text also of Hippolytus' Church Order. However, the ministry of deaconesses at the baptism of women is mentioned consistently. They further act as doorkeepers with regard to women. They ought to be sixty years of age when they begin their ministry (based on 1 Tim 5:9). Occasionally it is said that a deaconess should be chosen as the most worthy from among the circle of women who are called "Daughters of the Covenant" (Martimort: "Filles d'Alliance"). Here we find a hint of developments to come. A Persian manuscript from the fifth century shows that deaconesses were installed through laying on of hands but with a prayer different from the one given for the ordination of deacons.

A further important, though not totally unambiguous source are the *Apostolic Constitutions* which originated around 380 in Antioch (or Constantinople?). It is known that in these several more ancient Church Orders are compiled, sometimes in mosaic fashion. Elements of the *Didascalia* are enlarged or compressed, and the same with regard to deaconesses. Baptismal ministry and doorkeeping service are mentioned; not, however, home visitations. Book VIII incorporates Hippolytus' Church Order; its regulations concerning Holy Communion show clearly that deaconesses are considered laypersons, not clerics. The passages on the ordination of deacons are immediately followed by texts on the ordination of deaconesses. She receives the laying on of hands (as does, however, also the subdeacon and the lector). In this compilation there repeatedly appear two tendencies which cannot be reconciled one with the other. On the one hand, the deaconess is assimilated to the deacon; on the other, she ranks lowest in the order of Church ministries. This finding contributes to the opinion that the *Apostolic Constitutions* may not reflect much factual reality, if any.

The discoveries regarding Egypt and Ethiopia present a situation different from the area east of Antioch. No deaconesses are found there. This follows from an analysis of relevant texts by Clement of Alexandria and Origen. There, too, collections of Church rules which originated elsewhere are usually rewritten in such a way as to give the impression that deaconesses were unknown in Egypt. The *Canons of Hippolytus* (Alexandria, c. 340), a successor text to that Roman Church Order, treats baptismal nakedness and hence questions of modesty at the baptism of women as important topics; yet the helping service of women is not mentioned. The most ancient Egyptian rules for ordinations are silent on deaconesses. In baptismal rituals as well (and related commentaries) deaconesses are absent in the context of adult baptism.

Martimort then divides the material covering the rest of the vast area of the Eastern Church. He first discusses Church law and teaching. It becomes evident that toward the close of the fourth century deaconesses are commonly known. Canon 19 of Nicaea (325) limits itself to the question of how to deal with those deaconesses who, after having joined splinter groups, return to the Mother Church. In Canon 15 of Chalcedon the existence of deaconesses, as it were, is taken for granted; they ought to be forty years of age at ordination and committed to celibacy from then on; deaconesses are listed after the last (lowest) orders of men. Several *Novellae* of the Justinian Code, dated from 535 to 546, refer to deaconesses, leaving open whether they are considered clerics. The sources show that some deaconesses live in monastic communities, others alone or within their families. Ministry at baptism is mentioned repeatedly. It is interesting (perhaps significant?) that Epiphanius of Salamis (d. 403) shows himself quite well informed about deaconesses, but writes that he himself has never ordained any. Deaconesses are no topic for Pseudo-Dionysius, even though it should have interested him. The exegetes of Antioch simply do not say much in this regard.

Letters, biographies, inscriptions, and inspirational literature shed light on our topic from other angles. Inscriptions are found in larger cities, but are infrequent. (The author's desire for precision is shown in a lengthy note appended to chapter 6, containing further information on inscriptions, which he had obtained after the manuscript had gone to the printer; pp. 143–45.) Summing up we can say that the office of deaconess ratifies a life dedicated to God. Some deaconesses are active in works of charity. Quite a few belong to families of clerics.

Some documents, however, present as general practice what is contained in the Eastern Church Orders regarding baptismal ministry. According to the third *Novella* of Justinian (535), there were "only" forty deaconesses in Constantinople; no documentation can be found of deaconesses there, in the sixth century, engaged in baptismal ministry.

Since the end of the fourth century the custom spreads of deaconesses heading monasteries of nuns. Beginning in the fifth century, at least in the area of Edessa, women in monastic leadership are ordained deaconesses; they have the task to distribute Holy Communion when needed. The sources do not yield much on how the actual commissioning of deaconesses was done. The more ancient Church Orders give but scant descriptions of such rites. Only in the eighth century do we find a manuscript containing a complete ordination ritual of Byzantine origin. Ordination takes place after the Eucharistic Prayer, beginning with the formula Ἡ θεία χάρις (only these opening words are quoted). Then follow the laying on of hands, a first prayer, an "ektene" [litany], another prayer, and finally the Deacon's orarium (sort of a stole) is presented, which is worn by the deaconess in the fashion of the subdeacon. In everything else as well, also in many elements considered essential, ordination of deaconesses is differentiated from the ordinations of deacons and presbyters. The contents of the respective ordination prayers, too, indicate that the office of deaconess is substantially different from that of a deacon. Several documents about the Chaldean practice of installing deaconesses allow the assumption that it is primarily a monastic rite and that the main function of a deaconess is to direct a spiritual community of women.

From the tenth century on, it becomes increasingly clear that the Institution of Deaconesses has vanished.

Summing up, Martimort points out that the actual practice was more confined than what the abundance of documents may lead us to believe. Neither in Egypt nor among the Maronites (perhaps not even the

Georgians) could deaconesses ever be found. The Slavs, evangelized by Byzantium, never knew deaconesses, indicated also by the relatively late period. The office of deaconess takes various forms. In the easternmost regions, women are needed because of the strict separation of the sexes. Elsewhere deaconesses are ordained to acknowledge formally this new commitment. Eventually, leaders of monasteries are consecrated deaconesses. In such monastic communities, in the absence of priests and deacons, the deaconess gives Holy Communion and carries out certain functions at the Divine Office, in addition to the supporting ministry at baptisms. As soon as more convincing forms of installing an abbess are developed ordination of deaconesses ceases.

2.3: "Deaconesses and the Latin Church", is the title of the shorter Part Two (chapters 9–12). As in Egypt, there are no deaconesses in the West during the first five centuries, nor are they found in Rome, Africa, or Spain. Documents of the fourth and fifth centuries opposing the Institution of Deaconesses exist from Rome and Gaul. They are aware of the Eastern practice. Harsh criticism is advanced in an Ambrosian text. The much-traveled Jerome, significantly, remains silent. Gallic Councils (Nîmes 396, Canon 2; Orange 441, Canon 25) are strictly opposed: Could this indicate that such practices have crept up in their own country, prompting this attack? A Decretal of 494 by Gelasius I in no uncertain terms rejects any ministry of women at the altar.

Beginning in the sixth century, new developments appear. Deaconesses are mentioned in reference to the *consecratio/benedictio viduarum.* Apparently, the intention—in Gaul at first—is to imitate the custom of Constantinople: distinguished widows, as a privilege, may receive a *benedictio diaconalis.* The Council of Orléans in 533, canon 18, decidedly opposes this. The rite of *benedictio viduae* in Gallic Sacramentaries is probably a concession designed to reconcile such disagreements. Several sources since the sixth century call the wives of clerics *diaconissae, presbyterissae, episcopissae.* Regarding Italy, some attested texts of the seventh and eighth centuries speak of deaconesses. The Roman *Sacramentarium Gregorianum Hadrianum,* among its monastic rites, contains a short order, *oratio ad diaconam faciendam.* Such and similar occurrences derive from Eastern influences. This is shown in facts like this: In 753, just after a new archbishop had been chosen for Ravenna, his wife was ordained a deaconess. Documents from the early tenth century show abbesses in Rome and its environs receiving ordination as deaconesses. Carolingian Law, however, does not mention deaconesses. Commentaries of the ninth century on canon 15 of the Council of Chalcedon repeatedly identify deaconesses as abbesses. It should be noted that the *Pontificale Romano-Germanicum,* originating around 955 in Mainz, contains among monastic rites an Ordo, *ad diaconam faciendam.* The question of where this Ordo was in fact practiced, if at all, can hardly be answered by such manuscripts.

In Rome, this ritual in the Pontifical of Mainz soon becomes one of those parts which are eliminated. The Decree of Gratian contains, among others, canon 15 of the Council of Chalcedon. The glossarists then, in their commentaries, give the impression that this practice is, and was, unusual in itself and even more so in the West. The same position is taken by the theologians of the High Scholastic period.

A final Western variation of deaconesses appears sporadically during the fourteenth to the seventeenth centuries. Several liturgical manuscripts attest to the monastic custom of giving selected nuns a special blessing to allow them to proclaim the homilies and especially the gospel at Matins. This is an analogy to the commissioning of deacons to proclaim the gospel, *accipe potestatem legendi evangelium . . . ,* first attested in the early Middle Ages. Up to the *Pontificale Romanum* of 1595 (and therefore practically up to the present) the *consecratio virginum* concluded with an additional rite of commissioning for special duties at the Divine Office, a late vestige of the practice to ordain deaconesses.

3. In a final summary Martimort answers two fundamental questions, fully agreeing with outstanding liturgical theologians of the seventeenth century (see pp. 248f.): What was the meaning of this Ordo for deaconesses? And, does the sacrament of ordination apply to deaconesses in the same way as to deacons? According to Martimort, the name "deaconess" covers very diverse realities—diverse from one region to another, from one era to another. The pastoral conditions were so diverse that no continuity could develop. Only in regions at the farthest eastern border of the Roman Empire, and beyond, as the *Didascalia* shows, was a true ministry of women called for, simply because of the strict separation of the sexes and primarily only as long as adult baptism was the rule. The assumption of some modern authors that deaconesses, like deacons, were

part of the clergy, must be contradicted. Certain similarities at the
ordination should not let us lose sight of the differences. It is significant
that a deaconess was never allowed to minister at the altar. She never
acted as *minister calicis*. She was called to give Communion only in
monasteries and only when no priest or deacon was available. She served
as helper at baptisms of women and in the ministry of women only
where, and as long as, women were underprivileged in society. Never
have these women been allowed to preach publicly or teach in the
Church. According to Martimort, in a discussion of the actual practice,
this means that anybody who might try, in our own day, to invoke
historical realities in order to (re-)create an Institution of Deaconesses,
would only come up, after so many centuries, with another practice
which would have merely the name in common with things of the past.
M. B. von Stritzky, a speaker at the 1978 Paderborn Conference mentioned
at the beginning of this paper, had closed her talk with the call for an
"adequate correction of the historical section in the Synod's resolution"
on "The Pastoral Ministries in the Parish". The very subtle investigations
by A. G. Martimort confirm this evaluation in every respect.

IV

ON THE PRIESTHOOD OF WOMEN

9

HANS URS VON BALTHASAR

HOW WEIGHTY IS THE ARGUMENT FROM "UNINTERRUPTED TRADITION" TO JUSTIFY THE MALE PRIESTHOOD?

Translated by Lothar Krauth

I

The Declaration by the Congregation for the Doctrine of the Faith on the question of admitting women to the ordained priesthood [*Inter insigniores*] has carefully touched on all pertinent aspects of the problem. It did not shy away from pressing on into the depths of those mysteries which irradiate the most liberating, most convincing light for the true believer.

The main argumentation, though, to justify the Church's custom (chapters 2–4) relies on the normative practice of Christ, then of the apostles, and then of ecclesiastical tradition. This tradition, finally, is presented not as something "archaic, but as fidelity" to its author, and therefore possessing "normative character".

Only after this primarily historical argument does the Declaration (in chapter 5) proceed toward a profound reflection on the concept of *convenientia* according to St. Paul's "analogy of faith". But this concept must not be allowed to mislead us: in connection with mysteries of faith, *convenientia* often means something totally different from mere approximation, or purely human and even casual or relative appropriateness. Rather, it conveys the meaning of its root terms: the coming together, the inner harmony, say, of an organism whose various organs function in proper balance. The Declaration very explicitly insists that it is impossible to convert into purely rational insights the mysteries of faith, which include the sacraments, and so the institution of ordained ministry in the

Church. Those mysteries contain their own hermeneutics and self-interpretation, which become accessible and evident only to the believer who accepts being guided by the *Mysterium Christi* and its manifold interrelated aspects, into the depths of their inner harmony and plausibility. St. Anselm did not hesitate to ascribe a certain "necessity" to this inner harmony in God, despite all freedom of divine dispensation. For even though we might always assume that the Sovereign God could have acted differently from the way he actually deigned to act, we nevertheless are by no means licensed to relativize his logic—he being absolute Reason and *Logos* itself—by imagining other courses of action which he could have taken.

2

All this had to be stated before we could initiate any meaningful discussion of our question. For this is certainly clear from the start that the mere fact of an up-to-now uninterrupted practice in the Church cannot be taken as sufficient proof that this practice could not be altered in view of important insights or changed cultural conditions. If anything should be inferred from uninterrupted tradition, we have first to determine whether or not the matter in question belongs to the substance of the Church's structure as willed by Christ.

There are other elements which can claim significant reasons of *convenientia* while nevertheless being only "appropriate" and not "necessary" in the sense of St. Anselm. A case in point is priestly celibacy, which is supported by long and persistent tradition, but is much less embedded in the substance of the Church's Mystery; this is indicated in the Pastoral Epistles which mention married leaders of local churches; also in the Gospel when we hear of Peter's mother-in-law; and by Jesus' as well as Paul's recommendation of virginity, which is no more than a counsel.

The argument from "uninterrupted tradition" in the Church, therefore, must by necessity rest on a reality found within the substance of the Church's structure itself and her sacramental character. Such a reality has to be beyond the Church's power of disposal; for she cannot change herself at will but must accept herself the way she was born. Such a reality, however, would reveal to the faith the full substance of its logic only if considered in the context of the *analogia fidei* and the total Mystery of Faith. This context definitely includes the essential harmony between the order of creation and the order of salvation. The mystical relation of Christ and the Church in the order of salvation represents the overflowing perfection of the mystical relation of man and woman in the order of creation, according to St. Paul's insistence; so much so that the fundamental mystery of creation, in view of its perfection in the mystery of salvation, is called "great". The natural distinction between the sexes, as distinction, carries a supernatural weight of which it is ignorant. This may lead, outside the Christian Revelation, to various corruptions of that distinction; this can lead to a one-sided matriarchy or patriarchy, to the undervaluation of the woman, or eventually to the equalization of the sexes, which destroys all values of sexuality. The incorruptible distinction between Christ and his Church alone (prefigured, not yet incarnated, by the distinction between Yahweh and Israel) sheds a decisive light on the true interrelation of man and woman.

3

For two thousand years the ordained priesthood was invariably relegated to the man. The Declaration states that this clearly shows how much the Church considers this practice part of her original substance. Of particular importance, at this point, is the evidence found in the Eastern Church, which has never departed from the primitive tradition, even though "her Church Order allows considerable variations in many other areas." We see, clearly enough, that the deviations in the churches born out of the Reformation are the result of a changed and weakened view of the relationship between the congregation and the apostolic office. This relationship, by and large, is no longer based on the actual apostolic succession and thus on the structure of the apostolic Church but rather on the common priesthood of all believers. The Catholic as well as the Orthodox Church, however, considers the notion of apostolic succession as decisive. The early Church was clearly a structured community which gathered around the ministerial office which came from Christ to the believing congregation, with the authority to proclaim the word and administer the sacraments. Such she would remain throughout the centuries because that authority was always handed on in factual and personal succession. Continuity with the origins, in the Catholic and Orthodox view, resides, not just in the deposit of faith, but equally in the episcopal office, the agent responsible for the purity of that faith which comprises also belief in Christ's Real Presence in the Sacrament. This episcopal office had been prepared, at the least, by Christ before the existence of an actual congregation, when he called the Twelve and vested them with authority (see Mk 3:14f). For this "authority" was already christological: power to proclaim Christ's message in his name, and to subdue the antichristian spirits in the strength of the Holy Spirit. This means that here, apparently already near the beginning of his public ministry, Jesus granted others to participate in his specific messianic mission. And the mission of the Messiah, already in the expectation of the Old Testament, was to represent God and his definitive salvific action among his people. This foundation makes any apostolic office primarily a call—and so a responsibility—to represent God, or more specifically, Jesus Christ.

Representation, however, appears as a strange two-sided reality. At first it means something positive: the one representing has been authorized by the one he represents to make present some of the latter's superiority or dignity, yet without being able to claim any of this superiority or dignity for himself; and this is the negative side. This double aspect makes the notion of representation, and therefore the apostolic office, so vulnerable and so open to abuse.

In the natural order of the sexes, according to St. Paul, the one representing God and his glory [doxa] in creation is the man (I Cor 11:7). But it is impressed on him that he is only reflected glory, not glory itself: "For as woman was made from man (in Genesis), so man is now born of woman. And all things are from God" (v. 12). In the supernatural Christian order, which rests on the natural order as its foundation, the two-sided character comes out even more distinctly: The apostle as "God's steward" is exhibited "as last of all" precisely because he represents Christ; he is the servant of all, who deems it normal that "we are weak, but you are strong; you are held in honor, but we in disrepute" (I Cor 4:9f).

Catholic tradition with its conception of actual succession always kept the awareness, at the very least as an undercurrent, of that unbridgeable two-sidedness of priestly representation. True, because of sinful disregard, the positive aspect of such representation has often been unjustly accentuated in an arrogant clericalism, all the way to the exaltation of the priest as "another Christ"—something entirely impossible! And yet, there was always the reminder as well, coming from the saints but also from the Church's leaders, that the apostolic office is no more than service for and in the Church. And because this service requires specific qualifications, it is all the more only service: service, that is, of transmitting divine gifts which the priest in no way possesses by himself nor essentially in himself. Such gifts he transmits, as official minister, more readily if he makes himself totally into a simple instrument of transmission.

4

All this, however, becomes transparent only if we look at the subject for which the male apostolic service is to be exercised: the Church of Christ's faithful, always appearing as "female" in the New Testament—not to mention the Old Testament images of Israel as the "spouse" of Yahweh. In the Church's profound self-understanding, well founded in the New Testament, this feminine character of the Church is really as deeply rooted in tradition as the relegation of the apostolic office to the male. Patristic theology and Scholastic theology of the Middle Ages, even as late as the Baroque, saw the Church as the Mother of the Faithful and the Bride of Christ. Portals of cathedrals depict her as the exalted woman opposite the crushed synagogue. She is shown in countless miniatures as the only one standing under the cross, catching Christ's blood with the uplifted sacred chalice. Especially in Eastern theology, she appears as the definitive incarnation of the divine *Sophia* [Wisdom], the one who gathers and nurtures in her womb all the seeds of the *Logos* [Word] scattered throughout creation and the history of salvation.

At this point, I am compelled to mention two books by Louis Bouyer: the first, *Le Trône de la Sagesse* [Throne of Wisdom], is somewhat older (1957); the other, *Woman in the Church* (Ignatius, 1979), is more recent,

and explicitly deals with our topic. Bouyer's main intention is to elucidate the sexual and personal role of the woman, before even considering
the female character of the Church: the man as sexual being merely
represents what he is not and transmits what he does not really possess,
and so is simultaneously more, and less, than himself. The woman,
however, reposes in herself and is entirely her own being, namely, the
total reality of a created being facing God as his partner, receiving,
retaining, maturing, and nurturing his seed and his Spirit.

This thesis of Bouyer bears questioning, which we shall do elsewhere.
But to begin with we simply have to recognize its central content, all the
more because it represents the core of a certain tradition in the Church,
which is here purified of all marginal dross and confusion caused by
hellenistic antifeminism (which, in part, echoes through patristic and
medieval times).

It is simply unfortunate that this liberation and restoration of a great
tradition, a tradition that parallels the priestly office should occur at a
time when all the richness, which springs from the differentiation between
the specific properties of the two sexes, is more and more forgotten and
intentionally suppressed. Under the guise of equality and equalization of
the sexes, the goal is being pursued to masculinize the entire civilization,
which even now is marked by male technological rationality. By further
putting the sexual sphere at the disposal of every technological manipula-
tion, the person-centered height and depth of sexual differentiation is
lost. All "services" become equalized and therefore interchangeable; and
even though the man cannot conceive and give birth, why should this
keep the woman from assuming all those seemingly asexual "services" in
the Church, which are entrusted to the man?

A certain concept of masculinity which reduces the spirit to nothing
more than an object—and banishes all sexuality into a lower, mere
physiological region—is overvalued nowadays. More than anything else,
it is this overvaluing which stands in the way of an appreciation for the
Church's position as she clings to her tradition. Here, too, it is true that
gratia supponit naturam [grace builds on nature]. Restoring the harmony
of nature would bring to light—within the equality of both sexes in
essence and value—the profound difference which assigns to the woman,
not representation, but being; and to the man the task to represent,

making him more, and at the same time less, than himself. As far as he is more, he is the "head" of the woman, and in the Christian context he is mediator of God's gifts. As far as he is less, however, he is dependent on the woman as nurturing shelter and model of completion.

This is not the place to discuss in detail this difference within the equality of essence. First of all, the investigation would have to center on Christ as a male, in the context, however, of the Eucharist where he makes himself—complete as individual and beyond any sexual connotation—into God's seed which is given to the Church. Then the participation of the apostolic office in this all-sexuality-transcending male fertility should be considered, though this is very difficult to formulate. If this dimension could fully be brought to light, only then would the previously latent inferiority of the man in relation to the woman be somehow overcome. It must suffice here to have hinted at this concept.

5

It should fill a woman with elation to know that she is the privileged place where God is able and willing to be received into this world. The primary instance here is Mary, Virgin and Mother. But there exists an inner continuity between the singular Incarnation of God's Word in Mary, and his constantly renewed advent in the receiving Church. This, and only this, is the decisive Christian event; and as long as there are men in the Church, whether holding an office or not, they cannot escape being part of this all-embracing feminity of the Church modeled after Mary. Right from the beginning the Church, even Church in perfection, is realized in Mary, long before any apostolic office exists. Such office, in its representation, remains of secondary instrumentality precisely because its representatives are imperfect (see St. Peter!). Its reality is such that the grace it transmits is essentially not diminished by this imperfection. Whoever holds office has to aim at overcoming his deficiency as much as he can; but not by conforming more to Christ as far as he is Head of the Church, rather by learning to offer, in his own life, Mary's "Yes" more convincingly to the triune God.

The Church's tradition, then, as becomes evident from all this, has roots much deeper than a first glance would lead to believe. It reaches way down into depths which cannot be fully plumbed. And still, what little we are able to catch and form into stammering words, shows us that this tradition is justified and immune to the changes of time and opinion (including opinions about the proper role of the sexes).

10

HELMUT MOLL

"FAITHFUL TO HER LORD'S EXAMPLE"

ON THE MEANING OF THE MALE PRIESTHOOD IN THE CATHOLIC CHURCH

Translated by Maria Shrady

Whoever wishes to take a stand regarding the admission of women to the priesthood at the present point of Catholic theology and the Church, runs into manifold and diverse difficulties. A first obstacle arises from the outside, still external to the sphere of faith, insofar as more and more people in our modern society are raising demands for equality of the sexes, which they wish to see applied within the Church as well. Taking this highly charged idea of emancipation as its starting point, a new movement has arisen within the Faith and the Church, which may be summed up by the common concept of so-called feminist theology, which, however, at the present contains a wide variety of opinions. A further blockade has developed as a result of the alarming rise in the shortage of priests, and the call for the admission of women to the priesthood to make up for this shortage is becoming increasingly heard. Along with the pastoral-theological problems, the positions within the field of ecumenism confront each other: numerous church-communities which originated during the Reformation have decided in favor of admitting women to leading offices in the community and have thus broken the consensus within the churches. Beyond that, we are facing intra-ecclesiastical controversies of a dogmatic sort, according to which doubts as to the traditional argumentation have been raised, and new paths have been somewhat daringly blazed. By the same token, the insights of the human sciences combined with those of comparative religion are specifically invoked.[1]

In reading the following reflections, presented in the form of theses, these massive obstacles must be constantly kept in mind, together with the attempt to show that the exegetical, historical, dogma-historical, and dogmatic argumentation may provide an answer to the above mentioned obstacles.

I. OFFICIAL DOCUMENTS

Codex Iuris Canonici, Canon 1024 "Sacram ordinationem valide recipit solus vir baptizatus."

Pope Paul VI, Letter at the occasion of the elevation of St. Catherine of Siena and St. Teresa of Avila to doctors of the Church: AAS 62 (1970): 593.

Pope Paul VI, two letters to the Archbishop of Canterbury, Dr. Coogan: AAS 68 (1976): 599–601.

Pope Paul VI, Address to the members of the "Study Commission on the task of woman in society and Church" and to the "Committee for the International Year of Woman": AAS 67 (1975): 265.

Sacred Congregation for the Doctrine of the Faith, Concerning the Admission of Women to the Priesthood (*Inter Insigniores*): Gen. ed. Ecclesiastical Indicator for the Archdiocese of Cologne 117 (1977), no. 54. English edition published in *Vatican Council II: More Post-conciliar Documents,* by Austin Flannery, O.P. (Boston: St. Paul Editions,1982), pp. 331–45. (= I i).

Pope John Paul II, Sermon at the liturgy with the representatives of

---

[1] The main arguments are furnished by I. Bertinetti, *Women in the Religious Office: The theological problematic for the Evangelical-Lutheran view.* Theological Works 21 (Berlin, 1965); I. Raming, *The Exclusion of Woman from the Priestly Office. Tradition Willed by God or Discrimination?*) [Egalhistorical-dogmatic Inquiry into the Foundations of Canon 968, par. 1 of Codex Iuris Canonici (Cologne-Vienna, 1973); P. Hünermann, "Roma Locuta—Causa Finita? Concerning the Argumentation of the Vatican Declaration about the Ordination of Women", HKorr 31 (1977): 206–9; C. M. J. Halkes, *God Does Not Only Have Strong Sons. Fundamental Outlines of a Feminist Theology,* 2nd ed. (Gütersloh, 1980), especially 45, 68–72. The person who additionally consults H. van der Meer, *Priesthood of the Woman? A Theological-historical Inquiry* = QD 42 (Freiberg, 1969) should know that the author has meanwhile retracted his thesis.

priestly senates in Philadelphia on Oct. 4, 1979: Announcements of
the Holy See 13 (Bonn, 1980), 118.

Curial Cardinal B. Gantin. Papal legate to the Eucharistic World
Congress in Lourdes 1981: KNA, Jul. 21, 1981.

The German Bishops, Concerning Questions of Woman in Church
and Society, Sept. 21, 1981. Published by Secretariat of the German
Bishops' Conference (Bonn, 1981).

2. THE ATTITUDE OF JESUS CHRIST

The New Testament state of the question discloses the attitude of Jesus in
his messianic mission, his encounter with women, and the manner in
which he instituted his succession.

a. The Attitude of Jesus, Regarding Women and their Service

Contrary to general custom, Jesus speaks, to the astonishment of his own
disciples, in public to the Samaritan woman (Jn 4:27); he is not concerned
with the impurity (according to Jewish law) of the woman with hemor-
rhage (Mt 9:20–22); he allows himself to be touched by a sinner in the
house of Simon the Pharisee (Lk 7:37); he forgives the adulteress, showing that one must not apply stricter standards to women than to men (Jn
8:11); furthermore, he does not hesitate to distance himself from Mosaic
law by affirming the equality of rights and duties between man and
woman concerning the marriage bond (Mt 10:2–11; Mt 19:3–9).

In his itinerant ministry Jesus permits not only the Twelve to follow
him, but also a group of women: Mary, called Mary of Magdala, from
whom seven demons were cast out; Joanna, the wife of Chuza, a friend of
Herod's, Susanna, and many others. All of them ministered to him and the
disciples and took care of their temporal needs (Lk 8:2–3). In contrast to the
Jewish mentality, which did not allow for the witness of women, as testified
by Jewish law, it was nevertheless the women who were permitted to see
the Risen Christ first and who received the mission from Jesus to announce
to the apostles the first paschal message (Mt 28:7–10; Lk 24:9–10; Jn 20:11–18),
in order to prepare them for their future testimony to the Resurrection.

b. The Circle of the Twelve

"Jesus . . . , although he in particular exhibited a completely new attitude toward women, in comparison with the customs of his time, has not called them to the apostolic mission and testimony."[2] It is true that many women served him with their means, but "Jesue Christ did not call any woman to become part of the Twelve. If he acted in this way, it was not in order to conform to the customs of his time, for his attitude toward women was quite different from that of his milieu, and he deliberately and courageously broke with it" (Ii, 2).

At the choice of the Twelve, Jesus "called to him men of his own choosing" (Mk 3:13); "he appointed twelve that they might be with him and that he might send them forth to preach" (Mk 3:14). His choice therefore originated from his sovereign decision reminiscent of the twelve tribes of Israel, which found its symbolic expression in the twelve apostles. Since the tribes of Israel had been structured along male principles, the male symbolism was retained, as women and Samaritans could not have been represented.

Thus we find the Twelve gathered together at the institution of the Last Supper by Jesus, the Twelve with whom Christ inaugurated the New Covenant irrevocably in his blood (Mk 14:17–25; Mt 26:20–29; Lk 22:14–23; Jn 13:21–26). These, and exclusively these, are entrusted, during this sacred rite, with the authority to transmit his testament: "Do this in memory of me" (Lk 22:19). They were now authorized to perpetuate the Eucharist which was to remain a continual sign of the Lord's presence until his parousia.

c. Abba, Father

According to Holy Scripture, the incarnation of the Word had been effected in the masculine sex (Ii, 5). This fact is indissolubly joined with the economy of salvation. It is in accordance with God's universal plan as

---

[2] H.-J. Jaschke, *The Sacrament of Ordination: Encounter with Christ in the Sacraments.* Ed. H. Luthe, 2nd ed. (Kevelaer, 1982), 523; Similar, Joint Roman Catholic/Evangelical Lutheran Commission, *The Religious Office in the Church* (Paderborn and Frankfurt, 1981), 108.

revealed by himself, at the center of which resides the mystery of the covenant.

In the light of these interconnections with salvation history, the personal dialogue of Jesus with his Father, in which he addresses him with a unique intimacy and confidence, acquires a special significance. By calling him "Abba, Father" (Mk 14:36), the Son expresses himself to the Father without reservation, seeing in him the loving and gracious Father, who will also stand by him in the hour of temptation. Into this spiritual milieu the redeemed Christian enters when the Apostle of Nations proclaims: "And because you are sons, God has sent the spirit of his son into our hearts, crying 'Abba, Father'. So that he is no longer a slave but a son; and if a son, an heir also to God" (Gal 4:6–7). The heir, freed from the slavery of sin, may now enter into the spirit of intimacy shared by Jesus and his Father, crying: "Abba, Father" (Rom 8:15). In the symbolism of this prayerful attachment is again expressed the male structure of Jesus' relation to God, "for Christ himself was and remains a man" (Ii, 5).

d. The Attitude of the Apostles

Whatever was initiated by the Lord in his life and work is continued by the Twelve and by the successive Christian communities. "The apostolic community remained faithful to the attitude of Jesus toward women" (Ii, 3). The Jewish as well as the Gentile Christian communities, about to be founded, adopt the new attitude of Christ, and upgrade the status of women in the early Church, although the Greeks did not share the Jewish notions. These "facts manifest within the Apostolic Church a considerable evolution vis-à-vis the customs of Judaism. Nevertheless at no time was there a question of conferring ordination on these women" (Ii, 3).

3. THE UNBROKEN TRADITION OF THE CHURCH

a. The Catholic Church

It belongs to the most striking characteristics of the tradition of the priesthood that its doctrinal development has taken place uninterruptedly and unanimously since the days of the apostles, an overwhelming proof for the fidelity to the source.[3] "The Catholic Church has never felt that priestly or episcopal ordination can be validly conferred on women. A few heretical sects in the first centuries, especially Gnostic ones, entrusted the exercise of the priestly ministry to women: this innovation was immediately noted and condemned by the Fathers, who considered it as unacceptable in the Church" (Ii, 1). Such practices were expressly opposed by Bishop Irenaeus of Lyon (died c. 220), the African theologian Tertullian (died after 220), the great Alexandrian theologian Origen (died 253–54), Bishop Firmilian of Caesarea in Cappadocia (died c. 268), a pupil of Origen, as well as Bishop Epiphanius of Salamis (died 403). Admittedly numerous Church Fathers were not always free from prejudices against women, but the dominant factor regarding the priesthood of women was fidelity to the example of Jesus Christ. The Church attempted "to remain faithful to the type of ordained ministery willed by the Lord Jesus Christ and carefully maintained by the apostles" (Ii, 1). Testimonies to this may be found in the *Didascalia,* in the *Apostolic Constitutions,* and with the Bishop of Constantinople, John Chrysostom.

"The same conviction determines medieval theology, although scholastic theologians frequently try to elucidate the truths of faith by philosophical reason or by processes of thought modern thinking finds hard to accept, sometimes with a certain degree of justification. Since then, the question has not come up for discussion, because the practice in force has been willingly and generally agreed upon" (Ii, 1).

"The same conviction animates mediaeval theology, even if the Scholastic doctors, in their desire to clarify by reason the data of faith, often present arguments on this point that modern thought would have difficulty in admitting or would even rightly reject. Since that period and up to our own time, it can be said that the question has not been raised again, for the practice has enjoyed peaceful and universal acceptance" (Ii, 1).

[3] Cf. further H. U. von Balthasar, *What Importance Does the Unbroken Tradition of the Church Have in Reference to the Assignment of the Priesthood to Man?,* The Mission of Woman in the Church. The Declaration "Inter insigniores" of the Congregation for the Doctrine of the Faith, with commentary and theological studies (Kevelaer, 1978), 54–57.

b. The Eastern Church

"The same tradition has been loyally observed by the Eastern churches. Their unanimity in this respect is all the more remarkable as their ecclesiastical orders differ greatly in other questions. Their churches refuse to join the ranks of those who would like to open the priesthood to women (Ii, 1).

"The great ecclesiastical tradition does indeed speak against a female priesthood, also in its contemporary practice."[4] Both traditions, centuries old, constitute a unified front on the road to ecumenism, and cannot be divided by a short-term view of the present. . . . " It is hardly conceivable that the Catholic Church would decide in this question against the viewpoint of the Orthodox Church, and would alienate herself from these churches anew."[5]

c. The Lutheran Church

In the aftermath of the Reformation, different aspirations have been realized which distanced themselves from the tradition of the early Church. One of these is the admission of women to office. It can certainly be considered a historical fact that Martin Luther himself never wanted female priests.[6] The present situation of the Lutheran Church is defined by H. Legrand, O.P., and J. Vikström in "Joint Roman-Catholic and Evangelical-Lutheran Commission" about "the spiritual office of the Church" as follows:

> The Lutheran Churches do not present a unified viewpoint regarding the ordination of women. Although the majority of the member churches of the Lutheran World Confederation are in favor of it, some are not. Wherever the ordination of women had been introduced, one proceeds from the principle that Holy Scripture, interpreted in the light of the confession, not only does not impede it, but rather

[4] H.-J. Jaschke, op. cit., 522f.; more detailed: P. Evdokimov, *La Femme et le Salut du Monde* (Tourney, 1958).

[5] B. D. Dupuy, *Theology of Ecclesiastical Offices: Mysterium Salutis* IV/2 (Einsiedeln, 1973) 520.

[6] Cf. E. Zurhellen-Pfleiderer, *"Woman: III. in Christianity:"* RGG 2, Sp., 722 and H. van der Meer, op. cit., 111f.

warrants it. For it lends itself to serving the churches under new social
and cultural conditions and, besides, complies with justice, which is
expected of the churches in such questions.

Wherever there was an objection to the ordination of women,
biblical precedents and precepts have been referred to. These were
considered valid for all ages. In contrast to the argument in favor
of women's ordination, emphasizing the equality between man and
women, as it applies in connection with salvation, the opposing argument leans on the difference of man and woman according to their
creation.[7]

The Evangelical-Lutheran Church in Finland has not as yet admitted
women to the pastoral office because a church law proposed at a meeting
in Turku in the fall of 1976 has not come up with the required three-
quarter majority. In the evangelical county church of Schaumburg-Lippe
no woman is wearing the robe of office to the present date.

d. Anglican Church

After the break of the Church of England with Rome in the sixteenth
century, the Anglican Church went its own way as far as questions of
dogma and discipline were concerned. In respect to the ordination of
women, it has in the past favored the existing tradition. The highest
organ of the world-wide Anglican community, the Lambeth Conference,
could not, however, come to an agreement any more, when it met in
1968, and the question of admitting women to pastoral office has been
left to the individual provinces.[8] "The Anglican Church has not yet
decided in this matter, although a strong tendency in favor of admission
of women to the priestly office can be observed."[9] The net of common
tradition was torn when the Anglican bishop of Hong Kong ordained
three women to the priesthood between 1971 and 1973. During the last

[7] Joint-Commission 102–3; cf. with the whole 102–26.

[8] The starting points of this direction are to be found with M. E. Thrall, *The
Ordination of Women to the Priesthood* (London, 1958) and E. L. Mascall, *Woman and the
Priesthood of the Church* (London, 1960).

[9] B. D. Dupuy, op. cit., 520; see also the Report on the Status of the Anglican
Point of View, HKorr 30 (1976): 483.

few years women have also been ordained in the Anglican Church of North America and Canada, as well as New Zealand. Pope Paul VI had clearly stated in his letter to the late Archbishop of Canterbury, Dr. Coogan, that the Catholic Church would be faithful to the unbroken tradition, warning at the same time, that such contrary decisions would constitute a backward step in the ecumenical dialogue. Athenagoras of Thyateira, the Archbishop of the Orthodox Church in Great Britain, publicly protested against the action of the Anglican Church and censured it as a betrayal of the century-old common tradition. The present head of the Anglican Church, Archbishop of Canterbury Dr. Runcie, obviously wavers in his opinion, but has at the present moment clearly come out against the priesthood of women.[10]

e. The Old Catholic Church

An unambiguous position is held by the Old Catholic Church, which dates back to its founding after the First Vatican Council. In its teaching it understand itself to be in accordance with the councils and synods of an undivided Christendom, as Bishop P. J. Jans of Deventer, Netherlands, has clearly stated in his contribution "Man and Woman in Relation to Ecclesiastical Office".[11] As a result of the lasting controversies within the Anglican and Catholic positions, the Old Catholic Church felt compelled to issue the following resolution: "The international Old Catholic Bishops' Conference of the Utrecht Union cannot agree to the sacramental ordination of women to the Catholic-Apostolic office of deacon, presbyter, and bishop. It thus finds itself in accordance with the old, undivided Church. The Lord of the Church, Jesus Christ, has called, by the Holy Spirit, twelve men to the apostolic office in order to perpetuate his redemptive work for humanity. The Catholic Churches of the East and West have exclusively called men to the sacramental Catholic-Apostolic office. The question of ordaining women touches upon the fundamental order of the Church's mystery. Those churches which have retained the continuity of the old, undivided Church, together

[10] Accd. to *Rheinische Post*, no. 258 of Nov. 5, 1981.
[11] IKZ 52 (1962): 145–56.

with its Sacramental order of office, should jointly deliberate and consider seriously the possible consequences of unilateral decisions."[12] This declaration was signed by Archbishop Marinus Kok (Utrecht), Bishop Léon Gauthier (Bern), and Bishop Josef Brinkhues (Bonn).

4. DOGMATIC PERSPECTIVES

After having considered the exegetical and historical reflections, we may now turn to dogmatic theology. In this process a number of dogmatic perspectives will be proposed which shed light on the declaration of the Congregation for the Doctrine of the Faith, and point to the theological reasons for having decided on the retention of an exclusively male priesthood.

a. Christ as Permanent Example

The decisive argument, which determined the Congregation for the Doctrine of the Faith to adhere to the existing order, is contained in the following statement: "The Church, in fidelity to the example of the Lord, does not consider herself authorized to admit women to priestly ordination. The Sacred Congregation deems it opportune at the present juncture to explain this position of the Church. It is a position which will perhaps cause pain but whose positive value will become apparent in the long run, since it can be of help in deepening understanding of the respective roles of men and of women" (Ii, Introduction). Critics, before and after the publication of the document, repeatedly pointed to the fact that the practice of Jesus and of the apostles was conditioned by their culture and society, so that Jesus could not have acted otherwise.[13] In contrast, the Congregation responds: "An examination of the Gospels shows on the contrary that Jesus broke with the prejudices of his time, by

---

[12] According to *Rheinischer Merkur*, no. 7, Feb. 18, 1981.

[13] As example for many K. Rahner, *Priesthood of Woman?:* Notes to Theology XIV (Zürich, Einsiedeln, and Cologne 1980) 215–20; different is his pupil K. Lehmann, "Confirmation of the Traditional Practice: Concerning an Understanding of the Roman Declaration about the Admission of Women to the Priesthood", KNA Jan. 28, 1977.

widely contravening the discriminations practised with regard to women. One therefore cannot maintain that, by not calling women to enter the group of the apostles, Jesus was simply letting himself be guided by reasons of expediency. For all the more reason, social and cultural conditioning did not hold back the apostles working in the Greek milieu, where the same forms of discrimination did not exist" (Ii, 4).

According to B. D. Dupuy,[14] the majority of Catholic theologians today hold that the exclusive appointment of men does not originate in a temporary prejudice "but rather in an order which is deeply rooted in the physical and spiritual nature of human beings". More drastically formulated is the opinion of L. Bouyer:

> It is astonishing to hear people who believe themselves to be enlightened and free of prejudice come out unabashedly with such an enormity. In point of fact, from the earliest civilizations of the Fertile Crescent through the Greece and Rome of the early Christian era, the ancients had always been accustomed to female priests who were not in the least in an inferior position to male priests.[15]

What may appear arbitrary takes on constitutive importance deserving to be permanent and binding if seen from the standpoint of God's salvific intervention in human history. The Church, which arose under the law of a male priesthood, must be faithful to its own origin if it wishes to maintain its apostolic mission.

> This practice of the Church therefore has a normative character; in the fact of conferring priestly ordination only on men, it is a question of an unbroken tradition throughout the history of the Church, universal in the East and in the West, and alert to repress abuses immediately. This norm, based on Christ's example, has been and is still observed because it is considered to conform to God's plan for his Church (Ii, 4).

b. Sacraments—Given Beforehand to the Church

The argument of permanent fidelity to Christ as her example has already demonstrated how little latitude the Church has arbitrarily to change

---

[14] B. D. Dupuy, loc. cit., 520.
[15] L. Bouyer, *Woman in the Church* (San Francisco: Ignatius, 1979), 12.

divinely instituted signs in order to make them suit the demands of historical reality. The institution of the priesthood does not belong to those matters which may be manipulated by the institutional Church, but it rather sets a limit to her autonomy, within which the fundamental mission must be fidelity to what has been transmitted."[16] The priesthood, as well as the Church as a whole, cannot be arranged according to the norms of expedience and rationality, because they are given beforehand by God to man, and the Church must subject herself to them if she is to comply with the mission of her founder. "The priesthood is not simply a profession within the framework of the Church as 'institution', but it confronts her in a unique separateness and 'given-ness'."[17] If that is the case, then the Church's capacity to create new forms is merely a preliminary to what is central and essential, which is directly derived from her Lord. The Church develops new forms but only for what she has been given beforehand."[18] Seen from this angle, the frequently observed expression of the *right* of the individual to priesthood appears vulnerable and questionable because mission, and before that vocation, are the operative factors here, and they are unalterably withdrawn from the will of man.

The letter of the Congregation expresses the state of the matter thus:

> It has been noted, in our day especially, to what extent the Church is conscious of possessing a certain power over the sacraments, even though they were instituted by Christ. . . . As Pope Pius XII recalled: "The Church has no power over the substance of the sacraments, that is to say, over what Christ the Lord, as the sources of Revelation bear witness, determined should be maintained in the sacramental sign". This was already the teaching of the Council of Trent, which declared: "In the Church there has always existed this power, that in the administration of the sacraments, provided that their substance remains unaltered, she can lay down or modify what she considers more fitting either for the benefit of those who receive them or for respect towards those same sacraments, according to varying circumstances, times or places" (Ii, 4; cf. Ii, 6).

[16] J. Ratzinger, "The Priesthood of Man—an Offense against the Rights of Women?", Mission, 80.

[17] Ibid., 79.

[18] Ibid., 81.

c. Analogy of Faith

The sacrament of the priesthood must therefore be regarded in reference to the mystery of Christ. What is decisive is not a "demonstrative argument, but of clarifying this teaching by the analogy of faith" (Ii, 5). For the priest, in exercising his office,

> does not act in his own name, *in persona propria:* he represents Christ, who acts through him: "the priest truly acts in the place of Christ", as Saint Cyprian already wrote in the third century. It is this ability to represent Christ that Saint Paul considered as characteristic of his apostolic function (cf. 2 Cor 5:20; Gal 4:14). The supreme expression of this representation is found in the altogether special form it assumes in the celebration of the Eucharist, which is the source and centre of the Church's unity, the sacrificial meal in which the People of God are associated in the sacrifice of Christ (Ii, 5).

Within the symbolism and in the economy of faith, Jesus Christ and the male priest, who brings Christ before us, meet. For it is indeed "difficult to see the Christian office with its specific claim to be in the person of Jesus Christ the man, if a woman represent it, unless the special character of the Catholic priesthood were abandoned".[19]

Such a symbolism can also be recognized in the well-known Adam-Christ typology: what Adam had committed, and what has been lost in him, is restored in and through Christ, who himself lives on in the sacraments of the Church which are dispensed by priests (1 Cor 15:22, 45). E. Przywara, S.J.[20] expresses it thus: "The 'new Adam' is continued in the Church by a male priesthood, just as the creative receptiveness of the Christian woman continues in the 'new Eve'."

d. Mary, the Mother of God and the Priesthood

In the figure of Mary, Mother of God, the believing Christian can clearly observe how man and woman have received their own dignity from God, a dignity which cannot be transcended or even destroyed by the uniformity of egalitarianism. Man and woman do indeed

[19] H.-J. Jaschke, op. cit., 523.
[20] E. Przywara, *Deus Semper Maior: Theology of the Exercises,* I (Freiburg, 1938), 57.

share equal rights and equal dignity but in a distinct manner and form.

The Congregation for the Doctrine of the Faith has this commentary to make:

> Even his Mother, who was so closely associated with the mystery of her Son, and whose incomparable role is emphasized by the Gospels of Luke and John, was not invested with the apostolic ministry. This fact was to lead the Fathers to present her as the example of Christ's will in this domain; as Pope Innocent III repeated later, at the beginning of the thirteenth century, "Although the Blessed Virgin Mary surpassed in dignity and in excellence all the Apostles, nevertheless it was not to her but to them that the Lord entrusted the keys of the Kingdom of Heaven" (Ii, 2).

A comparable example is given by the choosing of the apostle Matthias by lot:

> Although Mary occupied a privileged place in the little circle of those gathered in the Upper Room after the Lord's Ascension (cf. Acts 1:14), it was not she who was called to enter the College of the Twelve at the time of the election that resulted in the choice of Matthias: those who were put forward were two disciples whom the Gospels do not even mention (Ii, 3).

To these lucid New Testament witnesses may be added another from our own time. Mother Teresa of Calcutta, when asked why women were not admitted to the priesthood, answered: because Mary was not. Mary, the Mother of God, is and remains a shining example for the Christian woman and mother throughout her life. Here exists a theological starting point which has been developed by the well-known French mariologist René Laurentin,[21] and on the German side, by Barbara Albrecht.[22]

---

[21] R. Laurentin, Marie, "l'Eglise et le Sacerdoce". *Etude Théologique* II (Paris, 1953) passim, especially 181ff.

[22] B. Albrecht, *Vom Dienst der Frau in der Kirche: Aktuelle Fragen und biblisch-spiituelle Grundlegeung* [On the ministry of woman in the Church: Contemporary questions and biblical spiritual basis] (Vallendar-Schönstatt: Patris Verlag, 1980).

e. Against the Danger of an Emancipation Ideology

It was *Gaudium et spes,* the Pastoral Constitution of the Second Vatican Council, which enumerated the forms of discrimination against basic rights of the person which will have to be overcome and relinquished because they stand in opposition to God's plan (no. 29). Among others, the discrimination against sex takes first place. Therefore it will be the task of the near and distant future gradually to diminish the still existing undervaluation of woman in professional and public life and to overcome it by a thoroughly Christian attitude. Although this tendency is to be welcomed, a development which, under the pretext of a true liberation of woman, has at its goal a total equalization of the sexes cannot be encouraged.[23] "The apparent victory which they would win in such circumstances, far from assuring them their hearts' desire, would be its veiled defeat."[24] The French theologian L. Bouyer analyzes the increasing loss of orientation and direction of woman by pointing out that both extremes would result in a loss of female identity: either she falls into complete dependence on man, or she is assimilated in him.[25]

Joseph Cardinal Ratzinger expresses his analysis of these tendencies as they presently emerge in different variations under the name of feminist theology, so-called, with the following words: "Behind the mask of emancipation, of the finally accomplished equality, hides total assimilation and the denial of the right to be a woman, and thus to be human ...; this is all the more threatening because what is perfectly justified can easily become the vehicle for what is destructive and untrue."[26]

The document of the Commission for the Faith is imbued with the fundamental idea of overcoming discrimination against woman, while at the same time emphasizing her true dignity against the background of our age. By thus striving to develop criteria from the order of creation and redemption, which correspond significantly and permanently to the

[23] L. Bouyer, op. cit., 23–24.

[24] Ibid., 24.

[25] Ibid. Cf. in continuation C. Meves, *The Folly of Egality—Misfortune of our Age: The Way to a Fulfilled Life, Orientation, and Aid*, vol 2 (Freiburg, 1981), 183–212.

[26] J. Ratzinger, op. cit., 82; also H. U. von Balthasar, "Woman Priests" *New Elucidations* (San Francisco: Ignatius Press, 1986), 187–98.

male and female manner of being, it hopes to have made a contribution
by which woman can recognize her own ideal. "The Church desires that
Christian women become fully aware of the magnitude of their mission.
Today their role is of the highest importance both for the renewal and
humanization of society, and for the rediscovery by believers of the true
face of the Church[27] (Ii, 6).

---

[27] After the conclusion of these reflections, the voluminous theological dissertation
by M. Hauke appeared: published in English as *Women in the Priesthood? A Systematic
Analysis in the Light of the Order of Creation and Redemption* (San Francisco: Ignatius,
1988).

II

JOSEPH D. FESSIO, S.J.

ADMITTANCE OF WOMEN TO SERVICE AT THE ALTAR AS ACOLYTES AND LECTORS

1. INTRODUCTION

In the discussions of the possible admission of women to the stable non-ordained ministries of acolyte and lector and also of the admission of women to the function of acolyte as altar servers, the impression has often been given that the main or only reasons against such admission are of a cultural, pastoral, or psychological nature. In particular, some have said there seem to be no intrinsic reasons of a doctrinal or theological character against such admission.

The purpose of this brief exposé is simply to outline some of the major philosophical and theological elements which many theologians consider relevant to this issue. There is, of course, an a priori presumption in favor of the existence of such theological arguments, since it is unlikely that a consistent two-thousand-year tradition of the Catholic Church across many ages and cultures would be based on merely contingent or culturally conditioned foundations. The intent of this exposé is neither to be complete and detailed nor persuasive in its argumentation. This would require much greater scope than the brief *outline* of relevant philosophical and theological elements presented here. Moreover, the limitation to such elements is not meant to neglect or deny the very many weighty arguments which can be brought to bear from the cultural, pastoral, and psychological perspectives. But the intent is to indicate that what may appear to be merely a matter of ecclesiastical discipline in fact involves principles derived from philosophical anthropology, trinitarian doctrine, christology, and ecclesiology.

2. THEOLOGICAL FOUNDATIONS

A. The Trinity

The source of all created being is the uncreated Divine Trinity: One same God in three radically distinct persons. This foundation of all created reality and the foundation of the Catholic Faith is a Being in which are found both total and complete unity and equal dignity in the most total and complete distinctiveness and diversity represented by the distinction of Divine Persons. We should therefore expect to find in created reality, especially in those levels whose perfection makes them closest to their Divine Source, a reflection of this unity in diversity, equal dignity in radical distinction.

B. The Incarnation

The doctrine of the Incarnation expresses the belief that the invisible and eternal God has made himself present and even united himself with the visible and the temporal. The hypostatic union of Divine and Human Natures in the One Divine Person expresses a radical union of the spiritual with the material, the uncreated with the created. This is a union in which the constitutive elements are both unconfused or unmixed and unseparated. The Incarnation is a divinely established safeguard against all dualisms which would divide the spiritual from the material, especially in the spiritual summit of material creation: mankind.

C. Creation/Grace (Redemption)

The order of grace is the order of divine life and infinitely superior to the order of God's initial creation although that created order itself is not only good but very good. According to Catholic belief the order of creation has not been destroyed by the original sin of Adam and Eve, nor by the actual sins of the human family. Man has been restored to the order of grace through Christ's sacrifice on the Cross and his glorious resurrection.

For human beings in their composite nature to understand and grasp the distinction between the two levels of creation and grace, it is necessary that the order of grace (and redemption) be made present in a symbolic way. From time immemorial all peoples have established sacred places, times, and persons to achieve this symbolic representation. To be sacred, i.e., to be set apart, does not remove the time, place, or person from the created order. Rather it makes present symbolically in the created order the invisible but infinitely exalted order of Divine Grace or of God himself. The setting-apart symbolizes the *otherness* of God.

Our Catholic belief mandates this distinction between grace and creation. Our human nature mandates its expression symbolically in sacred times, places, and persons. In Jesus Christ, however, this symbolic representation is raised to a level of reality which is the central Christian mystery: that created human nature has been hypostatically united with the Divine nature in Jesus Christ. Here creation not only represents the Divine but has become Divine.

D. The Man-Woman Relationship

In creating the material world and in particular in creating human beings male and female, God had in view both his ultimate intention of divinization or elevation of mankind and also his salvation of a fallen mankind through the Incarnation. Thus among the many meanings of the distinction of sexes, saints and theologians throughout the entire tradition of the Church have discerned an important symbolic or representative function which men and women fulfill in their very being.

Sexual differentiation is manifested in what biologists call the reproductive system. And although this difference extends into every cell in the human body, it is expressed most obviously and visibly in the physical differentiation between men and women. But it would be a lapse into metaphysical dualism to think that these differences were merely physical or biological. By the principle of the Incarnation, in which the invisible is intimately united with and expressive of the spiritual, these physiological differences are a manifestation of a mysterious but profound spiritual complementarity between men and women. Difficult as it is to describe this complementarity in adequate language, it may be seen from the vantage point of the marital act or the reproductive act, as characterized by equal dignity and equally active participation but diversity of role. The woman is active in receiving from outside of her that which comes from the man and nourishing within her the new life which is the fruit of their union. The man is active in giving what is interior to him into the womb of the woman. For this reason, even though both man and woman come from the creative act of a God who contains eminently all the perfections of all his creatures, woman has been created by God to represent what she and her male helpmate are by nature, i.e., creatures who receive all of their being from the creating God. And man has been created by God to represent what he and the woman are not: the creating God who gives being to nothingness, who speaks his word into the receiving void. He speaks and material creation (*materia* = *mater*) is.

This does not imply any difference in dignity between man and woman as creatures of God. But it does express a difference in roles intended by God so that the human composite which cannot live or communicate without material symbols, would have this symbolic representation drawn from the highest of God's creatures to help those creatures grasp in their proper form of knowledge the relationship between God and his creation.

E. Mediation of Mary—Church

In the act of redemption, this Creator-creation relationship is raised to a new order. That nothingness out of which all creation came is raised to the level of personality in Mary, whose virginity and whose "nothingness" express the perfection of all material creation raised to the personal. God speaks a second word—a word of grace and redemption—not this time into the void of non-being, but into the personal emptiness, the receptivity of the purest Virgin. Mary, who is the symbol of all creation, becomes at that moment the symbol of the Church as Bride of Christ. God becomes man, and specifically male, not arbitrarily but because God has so created the real-symbolic world of men and women precisely to provide for himself a language in which he can speak to us. The male Christ therefore represents and is the presence of God the Father (whose perfect image he is) in the midst of the maternal creation and maternal Church which is Mary.

3. APPLICATION

In the sacrament of Holy Orders, God, through the instrumentality of those whom he has authorized to speak in the name of his Son, confers upon the sacred ministers the power to act in the name of Christ and in certain sacramental acts to act in fact as extensions of the one mediator Christ. While the entire Church is feminine and maternal, the clerical ministry within the Church is by nature masculine and paternal. Because the bishop, the priest (and by participation the deacon) not only represent Christ but act as Christ in the Eucharistic Sacrifice of Sacrament and Word, only the masculine sex can represent sacramentally in an adequate way the male Christ who himself as male represents God facing creation and the Bridegroom facing his Bride the Church.

The Church only becomes the Body of Christ in the mystery of the two in one flesh by which, initially Bride, by being joined to her Groom she becomes one body with the head. The Eucharist, the center and summit of the sacraments, involves a sacred place, a sacred time, and a sacred person both symbolically setting apart the orders of grace and redemption from the order of creation and making really present the Divine Person of Christ in Word and Sacrament. For this reason, many theologians (e.g., de Lubac, von Balthasar, Bouyer) hold, in keeping with a long and unbroken ecclesiastical tradition, that there is an absolute prohibition of women as recipients of the sacrament of Holy Orders.

Do any of these philosophical and theological principles apply also to the question of admission of women to either the ministry of acolyte or lector or the exercise of these ministries? The following are some of the grounds for an affirmative response to this question.

The sanctuary, and in particular the altar, is the sacred place, the Eucharist is the sacred act, its celebration the sacred time, and the priest the sacred person in the most profound and mysterious center of the entire Christian religion. The acolyte participates in this most Holy of Holies—most holy of times, places, and persons—by being the immediate assistant at the altar of the priest acting *in persona Christi.* This he does especially by helping to prepare the sacrificial gifts. In this role as a helper or assistant of the priest he becomes as it were, the hands of the priest. For this reason, while it would not lead to the invalidity of the Sacrament for a woman to act as acolyte, it would be in serious disharmony with the very nature and character of the whole order of grace and redemption, the mediation of the priest, and the symbolic character of men and women. In addition, it would be a confusion of the role which is specifically that of the woman as representative of creation and the Church.

Although there has been a tendency during many periods of the Church's history to accentuate the sacredness of the Body and Blood of Christ and in relation thus to diminish the sense of sacredness surrounding the Word of God, the Second Vatican Council and much contemporary scholarship has emphasized the equal sacredness of God's Word in the Eucharistic Sacrifice. If this revalorization of the Sacred Word be thought through to its conclusion, it would raise questions about the appropriateness even of women exercising the role of lector.

4. CONCLUSION

As I said in the brief introduction, these philosophical and theological reflections are not meant to be conclusive or even persuasive as presented here. They are meant simply as evidence that "intrinsic" or doctrinal grounds do exist which argue against admission of women to the exercise of those ministries most directly connected with the Sacrifice of the Altar. At the very least, they would counsel caution and serious reflection and debate before a change is made which, though it might appear to be of small import, in fact may be of great significance. This is particularly true when we reflect that Western industrialized society might be particularly insensitive to the symbolic and representational character of creation and the created distinctiveness of the complementary roles of men and women, as well as having a much diminished sense of the sacred. With its bias toward uniformity, impersonality, anonymity, and egalitarianism, it might be wise to look toward the younger churches in less developed countries, not condescendingly as being more "primitive" and backward, but perhaps in this area as having retained a much more profound sense of the sacred and a keener sense for the intention of the Creator in preparing for the elevation to grace and the sending of a Redeemer.

PASTORAL REASONS FOR
NOT ADMITTING WOMEN TO THE ALTAR

1. There is a logical connection and progression from the altar boy, acolyte, and lector to the priesthood. If women are admitted to these offices, then it may give them the false hope of becoming priests. But women cannot now and never will be admitted to Holy Orders. Therefore allowing them on the altar is unfair to women because it can only end in frustration for them.

2. Altar boys are a major source of priests. If the Church allows altar girls, many young boys will not want to be altar boys. This will cause a decline in vocations to the priesthood.

3. Altar boys are symbols of the ordained priest. When girls are seen dressed in the garments of the priest, it causes an identity problem for the girl herself and for the faithful who see her on the altar vested as a priest.

4. Many bishops and priests now allow altar girls, contrary to the discipline of the Church. In some countries this is another step in a conscious tactic: force change by violating Church discipline and then agitating for official approval of a fait accompli. If the Pope gives in on this point, the inevitable perception will be that the "first step" toward women's ordination has been achieved. The feminists will increase their demands for more concessions and there will be further violations of Church discipline at the "next step". Now is the time to say NO.

5. Allowing altar girls is divisive in the Catholic community because of the negative influence it will have on the majority of Catholic women who support the Church's teaching on the roles for men and women.

6. Orthodox, faithful Catholics defended the Pope in maintaining the then prevailing discipline on Communion in the hand—and lost. They likewise defended the Pope on the then prevailing discipline of Communion under one species on Sunday—and lost. If the Pope gives in on altar girls it will be another defeat for those who are trying to support the Pope and the Magisterium, and further demoralization of the faithful laity and priests will result.

7. The ultimate goal of the feminists is to eliminate all sex-based distinction of roles between men and women, including motherhood and the priesthood. They seek a society that is essentially gender-neutral.

They want to eliminate the idea of God as our Father—in the Bible and in the "Our Father". Getting approval of altar girls and women acolytes and lectors is only one aspect of the larger strategy. For now, they will settle for altar girls. Giving in on that point will be seen by the feminists, and rightly, as a sign of weakness on the part of the Pope and the Catholic church. It will be seen as appeasement that will only increase their demands. Therefore the Pope and the Synod should say NO to altar girls, and women acolytes and lectors.

8. If the Synod Fathers vote favorably on a proposition to admit women to the service of the altar, even though this is done under the seal of secrecy, it is inevitable that the world press will become aware of this vote. This will be given worldwide dissemination and will create widely publicized expectations for change in Church discipline. This will place enormous pressure on the Holy Father and it will be all the more difficult for him to uphold the dignity and unique role of women in the Church. The Synod Fathers would create a situation similar to that which Pope Paul VI faced before issuing *Humanae Vitae*.

12

BARBARA ALBRECHT

ON WOMEN PRIESTS

Translated by Maria Shrady

INTRODUCTION

"Incline my heart to your decrees and not to covetousness!" So prays the author of Psalm 119 (v. 36). It may seem absurd that we should wish to build a bridge with his words, linked to our theme "Women Priests". And yet it seems to me that this verse provides food for thought. Indeed, it provokes one to ask a number of questions.

"Incline my heart to *your decrees.*" "Decrees?" Nowadays some people see red at the sound of these words. Decrees: that sounds like oppression! Our battle cry in the world and in the Church is "liberation!" Whoever dares to speak of "decrees of God" belongs to the last century. Such a person is conservative, traditionalist, pre-conciliar, dated, finished! And who would dare be stuck with an image like that? The attention to the decrees of God has, moreover, been unmasked by progressive female and male theologians as a cover-up for a patriarchially structured Church whose priests certainly do a lot of talking about social, economic, and political equality of woman, but run a mile when it comes to professional equality in the Church. Apart from this: who says that women are not allowed to be priestesses? Anyway, are there really "decrees of God"? Is there something like an eternally valid order? Does not all human order, even in the Church, consist of sociologically and culturally conditioned arrangements which keep changing according to circumstances? And what has changed more profoundly than the image and stature of woman? All that talk about "the eternal woman"; isn't it just "mythology" which may be allowed in a poet like Gertrud von LeFort, but is useless for life on earth?

"Incline my *heart* to your decrees. . . . " How is that? Decrees one accepts with one's mind, at best with gritted teeth. But to consent with one's heart, even to the decrees of God—that goes a bit too far. That is romanticism pure and simple, useless for life as we know it!

"Incline my heart to your decrees, and not to *covetousness!*" Surely covetousness aims first at material possessions. But this vice also refers to other goods not in one's possession: office, professional status, power, fame, and much else. "Wanting to have" at any price by negating all limits! Hence the call for egality, equality for all. Once it is achieved—so thought the fathers of the French Revolution and even more so those of Communism—we will have arrived at the peaceable kingdom on earth.

What has all this to do with our subject? Well, the Catholic priesthood is the last professional bastion which women have not yet conquered. Yet, whoever can lead a nation in this world as president should surely be equally able to lead the people of God as priestesses or female bishops or even as Pope. In the future the episcopal office will have to be accessible to woman if she is qualified by the Spirit of God and if she possesses the proper requirements for the task.[1]

Equality for all! That is the demand of those who aspire to the female priesthood. They believe it to be a test case for the sincerity of the Catholic Church regarding woman—and beyond that a test case for authentic womanhood, the equalization with man, which is "woman's right".[2] Whoever does not "possess" the entire range of professional options, is not of full value but a victim of discrimination. Hence the pressure from below, which will be effective in the long run. For there is no doubt in the mind of the psychoanalyst E. Fromm that the women's revolution and the sexual one count among the triumphant revolutions of our century, "although they are still in their initial stage. Their demands, however, have already been accepted by the consciousness of the majority and the old ideologies are becoming daily more ridiculous."[3]

A connection of our theme with the battle cry "freedom and egality",

[1] J. Willig, "On the Question of Women Having a Share in Clerical Positions within the Church", *Signum,* 3 (1973), 69.

[2] A. Röper, *"Is God a Man? A Conversation with K. Rahner"* (Düsseldorf, 1979), p. 81.

[3] E. Fromm, *To Have or to Be,* 7th ed. (Stuttgart, 1978), p. 79.

with revolutionary liberation theology and contemporary egalitarianizing tendencies is clearly visible. Perhaps a number of preliminary remarks may be sufficient for the moment.

1. A REPORT ON THE STATE OF THE MATTER

Let us look at some single factors.[4] Already in the early 1920s there were female theology students here and there who had the courage to attend theological lectures. Their goal was the *Missio Canonica*, which entailed teaching at schools. And that way it remained until the close of the 1950s. The first German woman who obtained a doctorate in Canon Law at a theological faculty (Munich) was G. Redick, with a dissertation on "The Hierarchical Structure of Marriage", a thesis which she has since retracted. Among this group of graduate female theologians, a few got married (e.g., E. Gössmann, V. Ranke-Heinemann, and others). They continued working partly at specialized institutes (as did their unmarried colleagues), in education departments in universities, and in publishing houses. Some worked in schools or in special adult education programs in the theological-spiritual sector.

Since the middle 1960s and the beginning of the 1970s, the picture has changed. Thousands of women are now studying theology and acquiring degrees or doctorates to become pastoral counselors, and not a few of them are waiting for the final nod from the Church, which will enable them to be ordained deacons or priests. As early as 1964, a small group of German Catholic women theologians, together with a Swiss woman lawyer, published a votum with the title "We Shall Be Silent No Longer."[5] It was directed to the Council Fathers, and it energetically advocated the priesthood for women. This publication became an instant international success.

One of the authors, I. Raming, received her doctorate in 1972 at the Catholic theological faculty in Münster. Her dissertation was entitled

---

[4] For more detail see M. T. van Lunen-Chenu, "Feminism and the Church", *Concilium* (Jan. 1976), pp. 63ff.

[5] G. Heinzelmann, ed., *We Will Be Silent No Longer!* (Zürich, 1964).

"The Exclusion of Woman from the Priestly Office—Tradition Willed by God or Discrimination?" Meanwhile, this discrimination had become a subject for discussion on an international scale, outside of Germany mostly in Holland, Belgium, and the United States. This discussion is promoted by the representatives of so-called feminist theology, whose center is the University of Nymwegen; with *Concilium*, which welcomed its contributions (January 1967; May 1978; April 1980), feminist theology has acquired an important organ with strong public relations to boot.

E. Schüssler-Fiorenza (a German woman theologian, married to an American lay theologian at Notre Dame University in Indiana) justifies feminist theology with the "necessity of creating an institutional basis which would enable women to take charge of their own theological education and seek alternate forms of ecclesiastical service and theological work".[6] For one cannot allow "clerical women" to be assigned to second-rate ecclesiastical institutions "after they have finished their theological studies. It would restrict them to sexually stereotyped fields like ministry to women and children" (288). This is, according to M. T. van Lunen-Chenu, typical of a Church which "uses" women by "underclericalizing" them.[7] Hence it is not merely a question of "promoting" women, but rather of emancipating and "liberating" them. "We want the kind of Church in which we and all those who are excluded may find meaning and, as a result, status. The goal is in the distant future; it is political, economical, and cultural; it presupposes such drastic and sweeping reforms that it can rightly be called radical and revolutionary."[8]

The immediate goal of feminist theology is (according to E. Schüssler) full participation of women in the academic community. That, however, is possible only "if the patriarchal and sexist structures of academic institutions are changed" (289). For this reason feminist theology insists "that the affiliation of academic professions and academic theology with

[6] E. Schüssler-Fiorenza, "For a Liberal and Liberating Theology—Women in Theology and Feminist Theology in the USA", *Concilium* (May 1978), pp. 287ff.

[7] Van Lunen-Chenu: op. cit., p. 66.

[8] Ibid., p. 67.

the male sex must be underrepresented and dissolved" (290). The sexism of many Catholic theologians—that is, the rejection and oppression of women—is said to be not only a personal failure but "a structural evil which corrupts and destroys theological science as well as the Christian message. Insofar as feminist theology analyzes myths, mechanisms, systems, and institutions which oppress women it has the same goals as critical theology and adds depth to it" (291). It thus participates in the goals of liberation theology, but it is considerably more universal and radical in its essence. "The full participation of woman in academic theological science has as its basis and consequence not only the reform of academic institutions and the conversion of male theologians but also the fundamental change of theology as a scientific discipline, its content and methods" (291). Beyond that the issue is one of changing theological language and its androcentrism as a whole.

The representatives of feminist theology maintain that the language of God the Father and the Son prevents "a genuine Christian self-understanding of woman" and suggests "an understanding of divine and ecclesial reality which excludes women as complete human beings and Christians. Such androcentric language of God not only hinders the ego-development of woman but also legitimizes the cultural mythology of the eternal feminine, which results in the Christian subordination and second-rate position of woman in the Church" (292). The central mysteries of the Christian faith have "no room for woman" (292). E. Schüssler-Fiorenza ends by saying this: "Only if female theologians collaborate in different countries in order to create new structures and take the offensive in respect to liberation and reform of theology, will we be able to effect basic changes in the present theological and ecclesial theory and practice" (293). Change of ecclesial practice in the direction of a female priesthood—that is the unequivocal final goal of feminist theology. Therefore: Female theologians of all countries unite!

A number of other facts ought to be mentioned here. First, the *ecumenical aspect:* "In 1972 the situation in other churches was as follows: in 270 member-churches belonging to the Ecumenical Council of Churches (ÖRK), 72 women have been ordained and 143 refused. The rest had not given the matter any thought. Since then the number of churches ordaining women is on the increase. Since this question is taking up more and more space, the ÖRK has established a new subdivision: 'Woman in Church and Society'."[9]

Meanwhile women are being ordained in the Anglican Church of North America and Canada as well. In the Church of England a resolution in this respect failed at the General Synod in 1978, because it was opposed by the clergy. But it did so by a hair's breadth.[10] Apparently tides there cannot be stemmed, particularly because the Lambeth Conference in August 1978 left the choice to the local churches. As a result the sacramental communion between Anglicans and Old-Catholics became severely endangered, not to mention the new burden imposed on the ecumenical dialogue between the Anglican Church on the one hand, and the Catholic and Orthodox Churches on the other. The Anglicans fully realized this, as stated in a letter by Archbishop Coggan to Pope Paul VI on July 9, 1975. Coggan wrote: "We bear in mind all this when we write this letter to inform Your Holiness that the conviction has slowly but steadily grown within the Anglican Community that there exist no serious impediments to the ordination of women. We are at the same time aware that a step in this direction could present an obstacle to the unity of the Church as willed by Christ." Therefore, the Archbishop continues, contacts regarding this issue have been sought with the Roman Secretariat for Unity. "Beyond that we expect joint discussions on this issue at a future date."[11] The Pope's answer on November 30, 1975, read as follows:

> Your Grace is, of course, familiar with the standpoint of the Catholic Church regarding this question. It adheres to its position that women cannot be admitted to the ordained priesthood for reasons of immense importance. These reasons include: The example, laid down in Holy Scripture, of Christ, who chose exclusively men for his apostles; the unbroken practice of the Church, which (in imitation of Christ), has chosen only men; and the actual doctrine of the Church which has consistently viewed the exclusion of women from the priesthood in accordance with God's plan for his Church. . . . We must regrettably

[9] I. Schüllner, "Review and Perspectives on the State of the Development of the Feminine Diaconate", in *Diakonia XP,* published by the Secretariat of the International Diaconate Center, Freiburg, *Documentation* (Apr. 1978), p. 25.

[10] Herder's Correspondence (Dec. 1978), p. 645.

[11] KNA (Ökumene) *Documentation,* no. 13 *(Sept. 1, 1976).*

state that the new path which the Anglican Community has taken by admitting women to the ordination of the priesthood has allowed grave difficulties to enter the dialogue, which those who conduct it must seriously consider. However, obstacles do not destroy the present obligation to strive for reconciliation."[12]

The above mentioned reasons are treated in detail in the document by the Congregation for the Doctrine of the Faith *Inter insigniores* (Ii, October 15, 1976, published January 27, 1977). The issue is the admission of women to the priesthood. As could be expected, the declaration ran into strong opposition.[13] We must now carefully inspect it, for it contains the most serious arguments which prevent Catholics, Orthodox, and the majority of other Christian Churches from introducing a female priesthood.

At the outset it may be in order to examine a number of other facts which throw some light on the situation. In Germany, the "Action Community of Responsible Collaboration for Woman in the Church" (AFK) has for years spoken for "The Rights of Woman in the Church" and thus also for the "right" to the priesthood, by making requests to the Bishops Conference. Among other things, their argument runs as follows: "A certain presence of [woman] should be achieved in the ecclesiastical office, so that a fully human form of the office is rendered possible."[14] In April 1979 the Union of Catholic Women's Organizations of Germany (KFD) joined its almost one million members to these aspirations concerning the deaconate and the priesthood of women. This took place in Mainz, on the Anniversary Celebration of their community.

Finally another look at the United States. From the Second Conference regarding the Ordination of Woman in the Catholic Church (November 1978 in Baltimore) we get the following report:

As an expression of their disappointment about the Vatican announcement, which expressed opposition to the ordination of woman, 2,000

[12] Ibid.

[13] German edition: *Die Sendung der Frau in der Kirche,* [The mission of women in the church]: The Declaration *Inter insigniores* of the Congregation for the Doctrine of the Faith with commentary and theological studies, published by the German-language editorial staff of the *Osservatore Romano* (Kevelaer, 1978).

[14] Schüllner, loc. cit., p. 27.

members, fettered by symbolic chains, marched across town to the city center, where the conference took place. 60% of the participants were sisters; 30%, laywomen. ... The presence of delegates from Canada, South America, Europe, Asia, India, and Africa illustrated the universal interest in this cause. ... It must be said, that these women theologians differ widely in their opinions. Elisabeth Schüssler-Fiorenza ... gave a comprehensive report concerning differences which emerge when discussing the question of the priesthood of woman. There are those who believe in a complementary part in the priesthood within the state of its present structure. Others maintain that a change in structure is of the essence and that it is not possible for women to execute their office together with men until the patriarchal system on which the priesthood is built be reformed, and that all men and women who have accepted this state of affairs in the past must publicly confess their mistakes. Another group holds that there is no hope that men will change their attitudes and that there remains only one thing for women to do: to seek a mandate of a community and to go ahead without much fanfare, so that the accomplished fact may perhaps be accepted and the exclusion of woman from the priesthood may be declared outdated."[15]

The theological discussion should thus be overtaken by practice. Among numerous resolutions which were voted on in conference, one was unanimously passed, namely, that a group of delegates should present a petition in Rome in order to discuss the issue of the female priesthood with the Pope.[16]

2. POSITIONS ON THE ROMAN DECLARATION "CONCERNING THE ADMISSION OF WOMEN TO THE PRIESTHOOD"

The Declaration of the Congregation for the Doctrine of the Faith, approved by Pope Paul VI firmly rejects the admission of women to the priesthood. These are the reasons cited:

[15] "Information in Reference to the Ministry and Diaconate for Women", published by the Secretariat of the International Diaconate Center, Freiburg, no. 1 (1979), pp. 3f.
[16] Ibid., p. 3.

1. The weight of the Christian tradition, nearly 2,000 years old, and never contested;
2. The practice of the Lord;
3. The practice of the apostles;
4. The permanent value of the practice of Jesus and the apostles;
5. The mystery of the Catholic priesthood within the mystery of Christ.
6. The mystery of the Catholic priesthood within the mystery of the Church.

Counterarguments

K. Rahner, in his essay "Priesthood of Woman?",[17] first refers to the theological qualification of the declaration. We are dealing, he says, with an authentic, but basically reformable announcement: "in which case an error cannot be excluded from the first" (17). As a theologian, he respects the declaration. Nevertheless, it did not take long till he published his critical counterarguments.

According to Rahner, this is the decisive point:

> In the cultural and social situation of the time, Jesus and the early Church could not have considered choosing women to preside over the Eucharistic Celebration. Judaism at the time of Jesus was based on such a self-evident patriarchal system (still very noticeable in St. Paul) that he and the apostles would and could not have abolished this male preponderance in the communities, in spite of the emerging break-through, more basic and general, of the equal dignity and right of woman in the religious—and inchoately—in the profane-social dimension. . . . If, then, in every case cultural and social reasons are cited for the non-use of women as administrators of the communities, one would have to prove unequivocally that these reasons are insufficient to demonstrate the conduct of Jesus and the apostles. This has not been demonstrated by the declaration (24ff).

[17] K. Rahner, "Feminine Priesthood?" *Stimmen der Zeit* 195 (1977): pp. 291ff.; incorporated by A. Röper in *"Ist Gott ein Mann?"* [Is God a man?] A Conversation with K. Rahner" (Düsseldorf, 1979). Subsequent numbers in parenthesis refer to this publication.

Jesus and the apostles were bound to act in this manner at that time, "which does not signify that their actions possess normative meaning for all times" (28). Behind this fact hides the essential problem: it is theologically not known "in what manner a 'divine' tradition can be basically distinguished from a long-lasting 'human' tradition" (31).

A second argument of Rahner's is this: no insight has accrued, that "a person who acts at the mandate of Christ, and to this extent (but not otherwise) 'in persona Christi', would have to represent him in the male sex" (26f). Hence, Rahner recommends further study.

> Carefully, and in mutual respect, critical of bad arguments, which exist on both sides, critical of emotionalism, which is out of place and which is at work expressly or disguisedly on both sides, but also with the courage to effect a historical change: such a courage is part of the fidelity the Church owes her Lord (33).

I would like to agree with these words, but alter them somewhat at the end: the discussion must continue with the courage to effect a historical change, wherever such a change is confirmed in a manner required by the Church; let us also have the courage to persevere in an existing order, as far as it is sufficiently validated by the authority of the Church. The courage to be obedient to the will and the practice of Jesus Christ and his apostles also belongs to "fidelity" which the Church owes her Lord. It may indeed take first place.

Supporting Arguments

Yes, it takes courage nowadays, in the midst of the general trend, to publicly assent to Rome's firm "No" on the female priesthood. And not only because of the perhaps oldest slogan: *Roma locuta, causa finita,* but because of personal conviction. I have won this conviction partly from the argumentation of the Roman declaration and partly from other reflections. A few of them may be briefly sketched.

1. The Weight of Tradition

I believe that the weight of tradition plays a decisive role and increases in importance the more we lose our historical consciousness, both in and outside the Church. The longevity of an institution is today considered an argument against it, and frequently "the defender of a tradition finds himself a priori, and unjustly, the defendant. Thus one confuses the issue of the priestesses with the old war for woman's rights, and the new war between the progressives and the conservatives in the Church."[18] Many, also within in the Church, agree with the motto: "Everything flows, only change is constant!" The change referred to here is, of course, a manmade one, which is within our control. Whoever, in our century, attempts to translate this motto into action with a certain amount of flair, will be easily recognizable.

That the Catholic Church, the Orthodox churches, and the Old Catholics adhere to the tradition of a male priesthood—and that the majority of churches and communions whose origin stems from the Reformation reject ordained women in office by appealing to the intention and practice of Jesus Christ and the apostles—demonstrates, in my opinion, the weight of fidelity to the example of the Lord of the Church as it has been transmitted to us in the Bible. It seems absurd to interpret the honest efforts to gain understanding and obedience to the Lord's will by saying that the existing unity of the majority of Christendom rests solely, in this respect, on the "conspiracy of men",[19] namely, the patriarchal structure of the churches. Moreover, one must keep in mind that the present way of formulating the question did not even exist two thousand years ago, hence there was nothing these priestly conspirators had to unite against.

To risk the still existing unity—unfortunately broken in other respects— after two thousand years (as the Anglicans are doing now with full knowledge in some of their local churches) seems deeply to injure the will of the Lord in respect to unity. After all, this will to unity should have become a matter of conscience in our ecumenical age. The ecumenical witness of adherence to every existing unity is, I believe, incomparably greater, both in weight and in rank, than the contemporary trend toward women priests—no matter how strident the voices of possible millions of women and those who supply the movement with its theoretical tools

[18] I. F. Görres, "On the Ordination of Women", in *Bedenkliches* (Donauwörth, 1966), pp. 75f.

[19] E. Schüssler-Fiorenza, op. cit., p. 289.

are to get the applause of the masses. Let us remember the prayer of the Psalmist: Incline my heart to your decrees!

2. The Conduct of the Lord

The declaration refers to the fact that Jesus has not summoned a woman to the group of the Twelve, although his conduct toward women was quite different from that of his milieu, with which he deliberately and courageously broke. "Not even his mother, who was so closely associated with his mystery" and who—one would have to add to the Roman declaration—could have had the right like no other human being to continue the Eucharistic office of her Son by saying "This is my body"—not even his mother did he entrust with the mandate of the Twelve.

Likewise, the argument that Jesus could not help but call twelve men to the apostolic office because of the socio-cultural environment—all temporal and historical considerations—appears highly unlikely to me. Jesus did not adapt himself and his sovereign freedom much to existing conditions, as is shown by his conduct regarding the command of the Sabbath, etc. I can perceive something else here, something the Roman declaration only refers to in its Sixth Section: the phenomenon of vocation.

Chosen by the Lord

The Catholic priesthood is placed under the words of the synoptic Gospels: "He called to him those of his own choosing" (Mk 3:13). The same thought emerges later in the Johannine Gospel: "You have not chosen me, but I have chosen you" (Jn 15:16). It is exactly this point which is unbearable to people of the late twentieth century. Nevertheless, the Church adheres to it, whether it is convenient or inconvenient: the priesthood as such is fundamentally different from any other profession in the world. It therefore is removed from any legal demand, be it from women or from men. The priesthood in the Church is neither a fundamental right, rooted in God's creative order nor is it a "human right" determined by men. "It has nothing whatsoever to do with any supernatural equality of opportunity vis-à-vis our ultimate purpose."[20] The choice, vocation, and mission of a priest of Jesus Christ is purely due to grace. Hence it eludes a priori any discussion as to prestige of "equality of rights". Such an equality can operate only in the worldly order, not, however in the order of grace, exclusively at God's disposal. The declaration reads: "The priestly office cannot become the goal of social advancement; no merely human progress of society or of the individual can of itself give access to it; it is of another order."[21] Here the "reality of the supernatural", so often touched upon by J. Kentenich, can be detected, a truth which is indeed "concrete".

This point clearly emerges when the Roman declaration refers to women who feel that they have a vocation to the priesthood. Vocation is an occurrence which involves dialogue, similar to a vocation to marriage or to the monastic life. It takes two. The intention to be married must be pronounced by both partners or no marriage will come about, no matter how strongly one party may believe himself to be called to it. The ordination to the priesthood or the taking of a monastic vow cannot be effected unless the Church or the Abbot gives consent. That is the way it has always been. St. Mark tells us of a man with a burning desire to "remain" with Jesus and to follow him, as did the apostles. After his healing and conversion he apparently felt an urgent vocation. Hence his insistent entreaties. We nevertheless read in Mark 5:19: Jesus "did not allow him but said to him: 'Go home to your relatives, and tell them all that the Lord has done for you.'" This constitutes a call to testify, similar in many ways to that which the women received from the Risen Lord. But neither of them belonged to those who have been called to office. Such is the will of the Lord.

Is this man who was sent back or are the women who brought the news of the Resurrection or is Mary, who was not included in the circle of the Twelve, therefore "less"? Something inferior, entitling them to be offended? Certainly not. For nobody may assert that Mary's service in the redemptive work of her Son was "less" than that of the apostles, their

---

[20] J. Ratzinger, "The Male Priesthood — A Violation of Women's Rights?" in *Die Sendung der Frau in der Kirche*, p. 79.

[21] *Inter insigniores*, no. 6.

coworkers and successors, who were men. The tasks and functions, then, differ, and this difference eludes all comparisons. The same is stated in the declaration: "The roles are distinct, and must not be confused; they do not favor the superiority of some vis-à-vis the others, nor do they provide an excuse for jealously.... The Church desires that Christian women should become fully aware of the greatness of their mission."[22]

Let us remember the "burning desire for justice" (I. F. Görres), and all the laments about underclericalization, oppression, and deprivation of women who have but one goal before their eyes: the priesthood, that last bastion denied to them, which therefore has to be conquered for their liberation's sake. They earnestly ask the question: "Will woman have to conquer the fathers in order to obtain her place before God—or will her brothers be able to accept her as sisters in a new age of the Spirit, after centuries of misogyny?"[23]

"Incline my heart to your decrees, and not to covetousness." It is depressing to observe how much precious energy is wasted by women because of this, energy which the world and the Church urgently need, so that this earth may regain some "warmth".

What is it, though, that hides behind those laments and accusations? "It is difficult not to contribute it to a huge inferiority complex, which creates problems of precedence wherever possible ... irreconcilably insisting on unrealizable demands which cannot be placated."[24]

The reasoning becomes recognizable by the language alone. It is quite apparent that this emancipation, as far as it seeks the Catholic priesthood, is a case in point of the "global power of envy", and of that rebellion against all limits and differentiations which is on the rise everywhere, by no means exclusively among women. It has a silent and overwhelming effect. This "global power of envy" can be found in different variants: envy of him who is different, of that which is different, of what one person "has", and the other has not. "Envy as root of rigorous egalitarian aspirations."[25] "You must be equal!" Beneath this battle cry, which

[22] Ibid.

[23] J. Arnold, "Maria—Motherhood and Woman", *Concilium* (Jan. 1976), p. 28.

[24] Görres, loc. cit., p. 84.

[25] C. Meves, "The Loss of Human Happiness Due to the Principles of Egality", in *Does Equality Lead to Happiness?*, HB 682: 132.

sounds so socially conscious, just, and Christian, lurks—if equality is
equated with uniformity—precisely the opposite of justice, a basic injustice.
C. Meves, I. F. Görres, E. Fromm,[26] and others confirm this.

I. F. Görres, however, in her inconvenient sincerity, takes one further
step, and I completely agree with it: she points at the "concave side" of
this global power of envy: "the global power of bad conscience, which is
its response."[27]

"Whoever is still in a position to represent dignity and authority, be
it . . . rank, position, or refinement, exercises it with uneasiness, embarrassment, almost shame: parents with children, managers with workers,
professors with students, superiors with members of their religious
communities . . . also some men with women. . . . This attitude is almost
generally found with priests vis-à-vis the laity. It is intensified where the
laity are women who behave as champions for the restoration of the
rights of the oppressed and the deprived. . . . Instead of a firm and clear
"No", one encounters a more or less embarrassed silence, sometimes a
shy support, an "indirect promotion", and, recently, not shy but open
sympathy.

> Because of all this upgrading of the laity and of its universal priesthood,
> those who are in possession of an inalienable, undeniable dignity,
> hardly dare to take notice of it, let alone express it. Many [priests]
> would prefer to slip it off, like a coat that has become too heavy, and
> willingly offer it to the laity. Thus the pendulum swings from one
> extreme to the other.[28]

The Representation of the Lord

Within the discussion of the priesthood of woman, the most contestable
point seems to be the argumentation which circles around the *representatio
Christi.* According to Catholic understanding, he who holds office represents the Lord. Christ acts through the priest: not in his own person, but
in *persona Christi,* the priest celebrates the sacrament which is at the core
of the Church, and effects the transsubstantiation. The same is true of the

---

[26] Fromm, *To Have or to Be,* loc. cit.

[27] Görres, loc. cit., pp. 74f.

[28] Görres, loc. cit., p. 79.

sacrament of reconciliation, the office of preaching and presiding over
the community: "On behalf of Christ, therefore, we are acting as
ambassadors, God, as it were, appealing through us. We exhort you in
Christ's stead, be reconciled to God" (2 Cor 5:20). This self-understanding
of the Apostle Paul corresponds totally with the pre-paschal words
of Jesus to the disciples, whom he sends out to preach the gospel of
the Kingdom of God in his name: "He who hears you, hears me"
(Lk 10:16).

The one who says this is the incarnate Son of God, who has become
like to us in all things but sin (Heb 4:15). "In all things"—that includes
that the Son of God has also submitted as man to the order of creation,
hence also to the order of sex. The Son of God was purely and simply a
man, and that surely not by accident. There are no accidents in the
Incarnation of God. The Incarnation of the Word "has been effected in
the male sex. This, of course, is an issue of fact; this fact, however, is
indissolubly united with the economy of salvation, without in the least
denoting a presumed natural superiority of man over woman."[29] Since
the priest represents the Lord not in his Godhead, but as the One who is
incarnate, crucified, resurrected, and ascended to the Father in Heaven,
the logical conclusion is that the priest, too, must be a man.

The champions of the female priesthood reject this argumentation.
This clearly emerges in a book by A. Röper (1979) entitled "Is God a
Man?" which includes a conversation between the author and K. Rahner,
as well as two other articles. What concerns us is Rahner's assertion
that the maleness of Jesus was nothing but a presupposition for accom-
plishing his task, "without real significance to salvation" (74), and indifferent as far as God's self-disclosure is concerned (77), indifferent
for mankind altogether. Rahner thinks that woman "should not forget
that she is called to add to Christ . . . , what he could not realize in the
narrowness of his own existence" (78), "what was absent in his maleness", and A. Röper concludes: "that which can only be rendered by a
woman" (85).

It follows, then, that it is up to woman to complete what is missing in
the priesthood as a whole, "wherever it is exercised only by men", and

[29] *Inter Insigniores*, no. 5.

that is "the feminine". "The service at the altar [is] not tied to being a man. Even more important, as a purely male function, lacking the female side, it is not wholly human and therefore remains incomplete" (88). So much for a woman who, strangely enough, considers the male sex imperfect but clearly "the sex preferred by God and men" (66). This is because, she says—and this takes one's breath away—woman has the "disadvantage" of having to give birth (51), and A. Röper continues: "As long as this is the case, equal rights remain a utopia that is not realized." This shows, in my opinion, in the most shattering way, that "the Catholic woman of today is less and less the Catholic woman of yesterday".[30] This, however, not because of a positively raised consciousness, but because of a diminished one, and as a result also a diminished feeling of self-worth. Theologically, something of the old heresy of Manichaeism is perceptible here, a heresy which despises the body and the creative order and is hostile to the deepest Christian mystery, the Incarnation.

3. Sexual Distinctions in the Order of Creation and Redemption

In my opinion, this raises the question whether the "self-disclosure of God" in Jesus of Nazareth the man, and consequently the representation of Christ by a male priest, should not be viewed and interpreted in a more profound manner. I am thinking of a fundamental priority of events, preceding even the redemptive order, and eternally irreversible. One must remember what is metaphysically named "ontology", and theologically, "order of creation". In this ontology, the *ordo essendi*, God's will, "his precepts" are engraved, as it were, indelibly imbued, like a watermark. So are the sexual distinctions. "Incline my heart to your decrees, and not to covetousness!"

The order of being and of creation must point the direction. It is not annulled in the redemptive order but is rather lifted up, elevated, assumed into the action of the Lord and his Church, and remains valid until the

---

[30] H. Strätling-Tölle, "Emancipation of Women in the Church—The Changing Position of Women in Society and the Effect on the Church", in *Documentation Institute of Orders* (INS), Frankfurt, Serie Referate, 110 (1973): p. 6.

end of time. The same applies to the context and sphere of salvation history: God created MAN as man and woman: both equal in dignity, both images of God, both fully human, both fully redeemed, yet not identical, but both in every smallest cell (far transcending biology), in every expression of spirit and bearing, distinct, though equal in their humanity. This fundamental distinctness may, of course, be stronger or weaker in some individuals, and thus we find feminine characteristics in men and masculine ones in women. What counts is the dominant characteristic, which, I believe, is not as "absolutely dark and indeterminate" as Rahner thinks.[31] What belongs to this difference is, as described in biblical imagery (Eph 1:22f; 5:21ff), the "being head" of man, and the being "helpmate" and "body" of woman. Neither can claim for itself any superiority over the other.

"To be head" is an image which nevertheless (without making any evaluations) attempts to express something characteristic of man: his power to guide and rule, to engage in purposeful reflection, to plan a project rationally and objectively; his aptitude for looking ahead and translating a plan into action, his being an "arrow", his ability to define ideas, the ability to abstract and speculate.[32]

"Being body", on the other hand, is an image that describes the woman as virgin, spouse, and mother, her closeness to receiving and giving life, her closeness to nature, to "mother" earth.

"Helpmate" refers to the fact that it is characteristic of woman to help. This is not something second-rate, which offends against the principle of equality before God and man. It is rather something precious, something indispensable to humanity, which forms part of the dignity of woman. In it is reflected the entire wealth of her psychological sensibility, the power of her thinking as related to persons, her planning, her acting, her intuitive gifts, the ability to understand people and situations sympathetically, her sense of the concrete. Without the effective complementarity of woman, man cannot live, just as the head cannot live without the body, or vice versa. Parallel to what St. Paul has expressed in his images of foot and eye and limbs (1 Cor 12), it is necessary that the head accept its

[31] Röper, op. cit., p. 49.
[32] J. Kentenich, *Marian Education* (Vallendar-Schönstatt, 1971), pp. 200f.

function of being head, as does the body, and that woman thus accept her specific role as helper without wanting to be head. These roles can in no way be interchanged.

The order of being has a built-in tension, an "elliptical" character which is valid for the redemptive order as well. On this insight—and on its spiritual, educational, psychological, and even sociological consequences— rests P. Kentenich's entire opus. His argumentation had always been "radical", from the roots. The elliptical nature of the Order of Being[33] guarantees the organic correlation between God and man, primary and secondary cause, man and woman, Christ and Mary, Christ and the Church, head and body. This fundamental reality is related to the Catholic understanding of the priesthood as well.

In opposition to this, it has been said that there have always been highly respected priestesses in the old religions, so why not also in the Church of Jesus Christ? It should be remembered that these women of the ancient nature religions, within the Greek-hellenistic area, served as priestesses to divinities of nature (Artemis, Athena, Demeter, and others).[34] In this Pantheon, which was designed from the earth upward, priestesses presented no problem. The situation changed radically with the advent of the Christian religion, whose revelation descends from above, namely, from the absolutely supernatural self-revelation of the triune God in the Incarnate Son, the Shepherd of the people of God, the Head of his Body, which is the Church. The fact that neither Jesus nor the apostles took over the institution of a female priesthood, which was well-known to the pagans of the time and highly regarded by them, refers to the fundamentally different starting-point of Christianity and the consequences which followed from it.

In the New Testament, the Church too is described as standing in a certain distinct relationship to its officeholders. The priest represents Christ the Head, who as Lord gives himself completely in his body and blood. To this image corresponds the other one of the temple, the house of God, the tent, into which he is received and in which he dwells. The

---

[33] Ibid., p. 200.

[34] O. Simmel, "Faulty Arguments: The Church and the Feminine Priesthood in the Hellenic Mystery Cults", in *Rheinischer Merkur* (Jan. 28, 1977), p. 21.

Church is also designated as the bride of the bridegroom Christ, and here she is altogether feminine, "marian", Virgin and Mother. In all these double images, the elliptical nature of the creative order (man and woman) is expressed. So is the Order of Redemption and Grace (Christ and the Church, head and body), which is founded upon it, penetrating and perfecting it. Polarity is an archphenomenon, indispensable to our question of the priesthood of woman. Both poles refer to each other; they are, nevertheless, not interchangeable, neither in being or function, in distinctness nor in dignity. "The desire women feel to hold ecclesiastical office can therefore only be the result of a mistaken notion of their dignity within the Church (as Church)." It is a "misconception to level and cancel out the mystery of sex, instead of unfolding and fulfilling its tensions by carrying them to a fruitful conclusion."[35] Such a misunderstood equality attenuates the creativity and effectiveness of the Church's role in the world. This cannot be in the sense of the Lord.

CONCLUSION

If the official Church rejects the priesthood of women, we must have demonstrated that in the end this rejection stems from consideration for woman, not against her. The Church upholds the right of woman to be "herself", namely, a woman, and that means "to be human in the highest way".[36]

For us women, the Roman declaration presents an abundance of tasks:

1. "Joyously self-assured" (C. Meves), we should again remember our worth and our "nobility" (J. Kentenich), without becoming resigned, embittered, or aggressive, hankering after what we are not and what we cannot have.

2. It is urgently necessary to the Church that we should become aware of our identity and recover a self-image oriented toward the order of being.

---

[35] H. U. von Balthasar, "The Marian Features of the Church", in *Honor Mary Today*, ed. W. Beinert (Freiburg, 1977), p. 276.

[36] J. Ratzinger, op. cit., p. 82.

3. Egalitarian tendencies and practices should be discouraged within the Church, in its educational system, its liturgy, and its preaching. What C. Meves has to say about the situation of woman in the world applies equally to the woman in the Church. A lot more energy should be spent to let us women become and be real women.

> The true psychological-spiritual emancipation has not yet begun; for it would presuppose that woman develop a consciousness of her own specific attributes; that she would recognize that assimilation to man, in whatever form, will never liberate her from "slavery," whereas a concept which will help to unfold her potentialities will. Only in this way, by becoming increasingly aware of her self-worth, and by realizing that there exists no future for humanity without her psychological and spiritual contribution, ways to her emancipation could be found. It would then clearly emerge that women have to take different educational paths than men, and that their realization should be sought in special educational institutions.[37]

4. In order to see the controversial subject "priesthood of woman" in the proper light, the self-understanding of the Church should be oriented anew toward Mary. There could hardly be anything of greater urgency for the Church and the world.

The great spiritual changes of our century, above all the Schönstatt Movement and the Focolarini, have recognized this concern. Particularly P. Kentenich, a metaphysician, theologian, educator, and psychologist, has presented the Church with an image of man, deeply rooted in the order of being. At the same time he has demonstrated how to educate men to become genuine men and fathers, women to become genuine women, virginal persons, and mothers, and finally, priests to become genuine priests.

That this concern for the dignity and future of humanity is also of immense importance for the future of the Church of Jesus Christ is demonstrated to the world—conveniently or not—by the Holy Father, Pope John Paul II. His image of mankind, oriented toward the creative and redemptive order, his completely marian image of woman, his

---

[37] C. Meves, "Emancipation in the Cause of Suffering", in *Freedom has to be Practiced*, HB 517, p. 103.

understanding of the priesthood and the Church, and finally his charis-matic personality all show a deep affinity with the personality and work of P. Kentenich. May the Church discover these interconnections soon, not for the sake of the person, but for the realization of what is truly Christian: for the salvation, joy, and hope of humanity.

13

MONSIGNOR DESMOND CONNELL

WOMEN PRIESTS: WHY NOT?

Why not indeed if every baptized person shares in the priestly, kingly, and prophetic dignities of Christ?[1]

But, it will be said, this common priesthood of all the faithful is not what we normally mean by priesthood, and it is not the question at issue. That is true. But if the question at issue is taken without reference to this common priesthood, the impression will inevitably be conveyed that the common priesthood is devoid of truly priestly significance, and the consequent isolation of women from the priesthood will then appear so absolute as to seem to reduce them to total passivity with respect to the Christian ministry.

---

[1] As the Declaration of the Sacred Congregation for the Doctrine of the Faith of October 15, 1976, *Inter insigniores* makes clear, the Catholic Church finds the answer to the question in the title of this paper in the unbroken tradition throughout her entire history both in the East and in the West of calling only men to ordination: "This practice of the Church therefore has a normative character: in the fact of conferring priestly ordination only on men, it is a question of an unbroken tradition throughout the history of the Church, universal in the East and in the West, and alert to repress abuses immediately. This norm, based on Christ's example, has been and is still observed because it is considered to conform to God's plan for his Church" (*Inter insigniores,* sect. IV, p. 11; English translation as published by the Congregation for the Doctrine of the Faith). The first four sections have developed this essential and fundamental consideration. At the beginning of section V we read: "Having recalled the Church's norm and the basis thereof, it seems useful and opportune to illustrate this norm by showing the profound fittingness that theological reflection discovers between the proper nature of the sacrament of Order, with its specific reference to the mystery of Christ, and the fact that only men have been called to receive priestly ordination. It is not a question here of bringing forward a demonstrative argument, but of clarifying this teaching by the analogy of faith" (ibid., p. 12). The reflections presented in this paper are to be understood in precisely this sense.

We may indeed experience difficulty in presenting the meaning of the common priesthood, and we have need of great care when we do so. But that is no excuse for neglecting it. It may perhaps be providential that the Second Vatican Council gave it prominence at a time when the controversy about the ordination of women was about to develop. I have heard it said, and by no mean theologian, that this common priesthood is mere metaphor. That is a mistake. It is intrinsic to the profound and mysterious reality of Christian being, and, abiding within that reality, it abides in the kingly and prophetic dignities as one of a trinity that abide in one another. And so the Council tells us that "the faithful join in the offering of the Eucharist by virtue of their royal priesthood. They likewise exercise that priesthood by receiving the sacraments, by prayer and thanksgiving, by the witness of a holy life, and by self-denial and active charity."[2] Of the prophetic office we are told: "The holy people of God shares also in Christ's prophetic office. It spreads abroad a living witness to him, especially by a life of faith and charity and by offering to God a sacrifice of praise, the fruit of lips which give honour to his name."[3] If we reflect on these texts we shall see that the priestly office is both kingly and prophetic.

COMMON PRIESTHOOD OF THE FAITHFUL

Certainly the common priesthood empowers and summons Christ's faithful, without distinction of sex, to participate in a great variety of ministry, which we can call ministry in the wide sense, as distinct from the special ministry that takes its origin from the sacrament of orders. I have heard this special ministry described as sacramental, as if ministry in the wide sense could be nonsacramental. It is, however, not just sacramental but priestly as well, because it takes its origin from the sacrament of baptism. Have we not just heard the Council describe active charity as an exercise of the common priesthood?

Given that all the faithful really and truly share in Christ's priestly

---

[2] *Lumen Gentium,* chap. II, no. 10.
[3] Ibid., no. 12.

dignity, that they are called to exercise a variety of priestly activity, the question surely arises as to why there should be a distinct sacrament to confer on some of the faithful an essentially different share in that same dignity. What can be meant by the difference in kind, stressed by the Council, between the common priesthood and the ordained, or ministerial, priesthood?[4] Clearly if that difference did not exist all ministry would take its origin from baptism, and all the baptized, without reference to sexual difference, would be equally eligible to be called by the Church to exercise whatever ministry she required. Because some Protestant churches find no basis for the difference between two kinds of ministry they have no difficulty about entrusting their entire ministry to women equally with men. The Catholic and Orthodox churches, on the other hand, recognize the sacrament of orders as a distinct sacrament and reserve it exclusively to men. The Anglican Church, in broad conformity with differences within it about the nature of orders, is divided on the question regarding the ordination of women.[5]

---

[4] "Though they differ essentially and not only in degree, the common priesthood of the faithful and the ministerial or hierarchical priesthood are none the less ordered one to another; each in its own proper way shares in the one priesthood of Christ" (*Lumen Gentium,* chap. I, no. 10).

[5] These remarks are in no way intended to anticipate the outcome of the ARCIC–I *Final Report.* In the recent correspondence between the Archbishop of Canterbury and Cardinal Willebrands, Cardinal Willebrands had this to say in response to the theological argument advanced by Archbishop Runcie in justification of the ordination of women within his Communion: "My first observation would be to note that the language used in this argumentation is the language of priesthood and sacrament. This makes it clear that what is at issue is precisely the question of sacramental ordination of women to the ministerial priesthood. It is important to draw attention to this, so as to make clear that this discussion is directly relevant only to those Christians who share this understanding of Christian ministry. For our two communions, the stimulus to our present correspondence is the *Final Report* of the Anglican-Roman Catholic International Commission (ARCIC–I). That commission claimed to have reached substantial agreement on the doctrine of ministry. In addressing this issue now, I write as one for whom the sacramental understanding of the ministry is part of the faith of the Church. The issue then, is the ordination of women to the priesthood and, that being so, it is clear that the question of who can or cannot be ordained may not be separated from its appropriate context of sacramental theology and ecclesiology. The practice of only ordaining men to the priesthood has to be seen in the context of an ecclesiology

At the source of these differences between the churches is a difference in the interpretation of the Eucharist: the difference between the reduction of the Eucharist to a sacred meal and the recognition of the Eucharist as a sacrificial meal in which Christ's own priestly offering is sacramentally represented and thereby made present. The celebration of the Eucharist is not just the celebration by the Christian community of a meal made sacred by the memory of Christ. More profoundly, it is a meal made sacred by the sacramental representation of Christ's unique act of sacrifice on Calvary. That sacramental representation is effected in the elements of the meal, the bread and wine as representative of his body and blood; and it is effected by one who has been made sacramentally one with him so as to be able to say in all sacramental truth: this is my body, this is my blood. Perhaps I could go so far as to say that whereas baptism enables the faithful to exercise the priesthood of the Church, which she exercises in so far as she unites herself with Christ's offering, it is ordination that enables the priest to exercise the priesthood of Christ in so far as it is the source and exemplar of the priesthood of the Church, transcending it and making it possible. As Christ's priesthood excels the priesthood of the Church, so the priesthood of the ordained priest excels the common priesthood of the faithful. It is a fundamental aspect of the mystery of the Eucharist that the Church's offering can be one with Christ's offering only in so far as she is enabled by the sacrament of orders so to transcend herself in the ordained priest as to represent Christ's own unique offering in a sacramental action that makes it present in her midst. Only on this condition can the unity of the Christian sacrifice be maintained. And it is in this way, I believe, that we can see a fundamental aspect of the difference between the common priesthood and the ordained priesthood.

---

in which the priesthood is an integral and essential aspect of the reality of the Church. It is in and through the ministry of priests that the once-for-all sacrifice of Christ is present reality. So there is real continuity between the redemptive work of Christ and the priestly office exercised both by those in the episcopal order and by their collaborators in the order of presbyters." (Cardinal Willebrands to the Archbishop of Canterbury in *L'Osservatore Romano,* English language edition, July 7, 1986, p. 12.)

SACRAMENTS OF BAPTISM AND MARRIAGE

It seems to me that what I have been saying is implicit in a key sentence of the Declaration, *Inter insigniores*. The Declaration has been considering the objection that the priest acts not only *in persona Christi* but also *in persona Ecclesiae;* and that since there can be no difficulty against a woman's acting *in persona Ecclesiae* there can be no difficulty against her being ordained. The Declaration answers: "It is true that the priest represents the Church, which is the Body of Christ. But if he does so, it is precisely because he first represents Christ himself, who is the Head and Shepherd of the Church. The Second Vatican Council used this phrase to make more precise and to complete the expression *in persona Christi.*"[6] The Declaration here affirms that although the Church as *Corpus Christi* is one with Christ, he as *caput et pastor Ecclesiae* nevertheless transcends the Church; that within the unity between Christ and the Church there is a distinction involving an order of priority and posteriority; and that in celebrating the Eucharist the ordained priest must in the first place, *in primis,* represent Christ in his very priority. This is what I had in mind in saying that the Church must transcend herself in the ordained priest. The reason why a woman cannot be ordained has essentially to do with that priority, which enters into the symbolism, the sacramental mode of signification, of the Eucharist. It is also worth noting the suggestion of a certain ambiguity in the term *in persona Christi,* which, taken on its own, is insufficiently precise and complete to express the sacramental identification between the ordained priest and Christ. And so, although a woman certainly acts *in persona Christi* when she administers the sacraments of baptism and marriage, this does not of itself justify the conclusion that she can act *in persona Christi* in the sense required by the sacramental representation constitutive of the Eucharist and orders, which is the precise sense at issue in this special instance.[7]

---

[6] *Inter insigniores,* sect. V, p. 15.

[7] I feel that the late Father Eric Doyle did not appreciate the ambiguity in the phrase *in persona Christi.* He wrote: "Now it may be objected that I am evading the issue by comparing the ministers of various sacraments instead of considering the necessary conditions in the recipient of orders. I would reply to that, however, with the general

SEXUAL DIFFERENCE AND
SACRAMENTAL SYMBOLISM

I must now try to develop that point by sketching briefly the symbolism of the Eucharist and of the ordained priesthood because sexual difference is profoundly involved in the sacramental symbolism.[8] A brief sketch is all I can attempt within the limits of my time. A full treatment would require a consideration of the natural symbolism of the sexual difference and of the manner in which that natural symbolism has been made, through the historical unfolding of Revelation, the bearer of divine signification, to become in Christ the theme of sacramental representation. I am well aware of the distortion that brevity makes inevitable when consideration of this symbolism is directed toward the negative end of showing that a woman cannot be ordained. A comprehensive view would rather bring out the richness of the symbolic significance of

---

principle that the minister of the sacraments always acts *in persona Christi*. Hence it cannot be that because the priest acts *in persona Christi* at the Eucharist that the recipient of orders must be male. We have seen that women act *in persona Christi* and natural resemblance does not mean physical likeness." ("The Question of Women Priests and the Argument *In Persona Christi*", *The Irish Theological Quarterly*, vol. 50 (1983–84), p. 219).

[8] "The sacraments of the New Testament, instituted by Christ the Lord and entrusted to the Church, as they are the actions of Christ and the Church, stand out as the signs and means by which the faith is expressed and strengthened, worship is rendered to God and the sanctification of humankind is effected, and they thus contribute in the highest degree to the establishment, strengthening and manifestation of ecclesial communion; therefore both the sacred ministers and the rest of the Christian faithful must employ the greatest reverence and the necessary diligence in their celebration" (*Codex Iuris Canonici*, c. 840; English translation by Canon Law Society of America). In speaking of the sacramental symbolism I am referring to the essentially representational character of the sacraments expressed in this definition by the words "stand out as the signs". My preferred source for this aspect of theological teaching is Abbot Anscar Vonier's fine presentation of St. Thomas's teaching in *A Key to the Doctrine of the Eucharist* in *The Complete Works of Abbot Vonier*, 3 vols. (London: Burns and Oates, 1952), vol. 2, bk 3, pp. 227–360. Although Vonier came too early for some of the developments with which we have been made familiar by the Second Vatican Council, his presentation, as far as it goes, has lost neither its validity nor its depth of penetration.

womanhood and show that there is no affront to the dignity of women in their exclusion from the ordained priesthood. On the contrary, since woman as virgin, bride, and mother is symbol of the Church, and since the ordained priesthood exists for the sake of the holiness of the Church, what woman symbolizes gives its final fulfillment to the ordained priesthood. As Christ's earthly mission was for the sake of the Pentecostal gift of the Spirit, so is the ordained priesthood for the sake of the perfection of the Church. Thus, even though the ordained priesthood has a certain excellence—a sublime excellence indeed—in one respect, it would be a mistake to conclude that it excels all other Christian dignity absolutely. The calculating mentality is here out of place, for we are in a realm of qualitative difference in so far as it serves by divinely inspired analogies, presented to faith through the concrete context of historical Revelation, to convey to our sense-bound experience the mysteries accomplished by Christ in his Body, the Church. Sacramental symbolism expresses and effects a mystery accomplished in freedom, the freedom of God's generous purposes in grace and the freedom of our openness to him in faith. It is not perhaps by accident that the controversy about the ordination of women has developed against the background of a scientific technological culture. For science establishes a realm from which difference is removed by univocal abstraction, a realm of impersonal necessity, and, in accordance with its quantitative method, it measures, calculates, and reduces to uniformity, A scientific technological culture favors a particular kind of egalitarian vision that remains blind to the symbolic significance of the difference between the sexes.

SYMBOLISM OF MARRIAGE AND THE EUCHARIST

It is especially when we consider the sacraments that we must be attentive to the symbolism employed by Revelation. The sacraments are essentially symbolic or representational realities: they represent and thereby proclaim to our faith the gift of God, and through this representation they confer by the power of Christ's Spirit the gift they proclaim.[9] Now there are two sacraments that represent in a special way the union between Christ and the Church: marriage and the Eucharist. Marriage is the sacrament of sexual union between a man and a woman; but if it is a sacrament it is precisely because it symbolizes the union between Christ and the Church.[10] It is significant that although the bride equally with the bridegroom administers the sacrament, and so acts *in persona Christi,* sacramentally she represents not Christ but the Church, and this in virtue of her sex.[11] She can no more be a sacramental representation of Christ here than she can be bridegroom. Thus Christ's union with the Church is symbolized by the nuptial union, in accordance with a recurrent theme of sacred Scripture. And this same symbolism enters into the signification of the Eu-

[9] "St. Thomas lays it down as an axiom that a sacrament is always an object of the senses. A merely spiritual thing, an act of our intellect or will could never fulfil that role of signification which is so essential to the sacrament. The sign, on the contrary, is an external manifestation of the process of thought and volition: St. Thomas quotes from St. Augustine a very succinct definition: 'A sign is that which, besides the impression it makes on the senses, puts one in mind of something else'. When I see the baptismal water poured on the head of the catechumen, and when I hear the words of the priest who does the christening, if I am a man of faith, my mind, roused by these external rites and signs, travels a long way back. I go back to the Jordan, where Christ is being baptized; I go back to Calvary, where blood and water issue from the side of Christ; my mind leaps forward to that people who stand before the Throne of God in white robes which have been washed in the Blood of the Lamb; and, more audacious still, my mind gazes right into the innermost soul of the catechumen and distinguishes that soul from all non-baptized souls, through that spiritual seal which makes it a member of Christ. The sacramental sign is pregnant with all that spiritual vision of my faith." (A. Vonier, op. cit., p. 240). "The wonderful signs we call sacraments are not only powerful in reminding us of the things of God, they have power to make them live again. They are instruments of the almighty power of God; they are tools in the hands of Christ, 'who worketh until now'. This is the profound Thomistic concept of the sacraments, that they are the *instrumenta Dei* for bringing about supernatural effects, so that they may be truly called containers of grace" (ibid., p. 242).

[10] "Finally, in virtue of the sacrament of Matrimony by which they signify and share (cf. Eph 5:32) the mystery of the unity and faithful love between Christ and the Church, Christian married couples help one another to attain holiness in their married life and in the rearing of their children. Hence by reason of their state in life and of their position they have their own gifts in the People of God (cf. 1 Cor 7:7)" (*Lumen Gentium,* chap. II, no. 11).

[11] Cf. Eph 5:22–23.

charist, the sacrament *par excellence* of Christ's union with the Church.[12]

The eucharistic union is not, of course, a sexual union, but the union effected through participation in a symbolic meal, that is, by the sacramental eating of the flesh which is food indeed and drinking of the blood which is drink indeed.[13] This meal, precisely as a meal, already has a nuptial significance in so far as it looks forward to the heavenly feast, to its final fulfillment in "the marriage supper of the Lamb".[14] It is not, however, just a sacred meal through which Christ's union with the Church is brought to perfection, but a meal that represents sacramentally the sacrificial act in which he gave himself totally in loving obedience to the Father in order that he might purify the Church and thus prepare for himself a spotless bride.[15] It is the meal in which the Church responds to his love by making his sacrificial act her own. Thus Christ and the Church return to the Father in a sacrificial worship that expresses their union as Bridegroom and bride. The Eucharist is Christ's bridal gift to the Church: it expresses and effects the perfection of his union with the Church in the sacrifice of his Body and Blood.

Congar views the nuptial theme in the light of the great texts of the Apocalypse that present the Church as the bride. He continues:

> According to the Bible, the truth of all things is found at the end, but it is envisaged at the beginning. What is seen as fulfilled in the last chapters of the last book in this final "unveiling" or "Apocalypse" was already in mind in the first chapters of the first book, the book of "beginnings" or "Genesis".

He then quotes Genesis on the creation of the man and the woman, and he goes on to say:

---

[12] "Taking part in the eucharistic sacrifice, the source and summit of the Christian life, they offer the divine victim to God and themselves along with it. And so it is that, both in the offering and in Holy Communion, each in his own way, though not of course indiscriminately, has his own part to play in the liturgical action. Then, strengthened by the body of Christ in the eucharistic communion, they manifest in a concrete way that unity of the People of God which this holy sacrament aptly signifies and admirably realizes" (*Lumen Gentium,* chap. II, no. 11).

[13] Jn 6:55.

[14] Rev 19:6–8.

[15] Cf. Eph 5:25–27.

From the time of Tertullian onward at least, the Fathers of the Church and the early Christian writers have been unanimous in seeing this as a prophetic announcement of the wedding between Christ, the new Adam, and the Church, the new Eve, when from the pierced side of Jesus, fallen into the deep sleep of death, came water and blood, the sacraments, baptism and the Eucharist, which built up the Church: the marriage of the Cross and the marriage of the Lamb.[16]

We can see then that sexual difference enters profoundly into the symbolic representation of the relation between Christ and the Church and that this symbolism is present in the eucharistic celebration.

CELEBRATION OF CHRIST'S VICTORY OVER SIN

Before turning to the sacrament of orders perhaps I might say a word about the sacrifice of Christ and about the mode of its eucharistic representation. Taking a hint from Congar's reference to Genesis and the tradition of which he speaks, and bearing in mind the teaching of the Letter to the Romans, where Christ's sacrifice is revealed as the obedience by which the original disobedience is reversed and its consequences overcome, one may describe his sacrifice as his confession of the truth that Adam rejected when he believed the word of the tempter: "you will not die" and determined to seek life in opposition to God.[17] Although he was the Son of God, the Savior was seen in our midst not in the form of his Godhead but in the form in which he was sent to redeem us, bearing in his sinless body the burden of sin as a burden of vulnerability to suffering and death.[18] He who is the truth of the living God yielded himself up to death to proclaim from within our fallen race the truth made known from the beginning that death is the outcome of sin, that in obedience to God alone is the fullness of life. Such was the sacrifice acceptable to the Father which inaugurates our restoration in holiness and truth. In his merciful love he gave us his Son without reserve, not

---

[16] Y. Congar, *I Believe in the Holy Spirit*, trans. by D. Smith, 3 vols (London: Geoffrey Chapman; New York: Seabury Press, 1983), vol. II, pp. 56–57.

[17] Cf. Gen 3:1–6; Rom 5:12–21.

[18] Cf. Phil 2:5–8.

sparing him even the abasement of the death by which, in humble submission, he could confess on our behalf the truth to which he came to bear witness.[19] This is the return to the Father that we could never accomplish on our own because the truth denied by the first head of our race, that we continue to deny with every sin, which had originally been bestowed as the gift of God's love and the bond of his friendship, could never be ours again except by a covenant of God's mercy and as a gift restored. It is now restored in the very place of our shame—in the dark pit of death—and it is restored by the blood of the new and eternal covenant in the person of him who came to us as the Father's gift, who consecrated himself that we might be consecrated in truth.[20] And so the Father's love raised his stricken Son as the faithful witness to the truth of that love in the imperishable life of his resurrection.[21] This is the victory over Satan and sin and death which annihilates our guilt, restores us to life and holiness, and remakes us in the truth. The Eucharist is the celebration of that victory and the distribution of its spoils.

The eucharistic sacrifice, then, is celebrated in the Church, and God's people, gathered together in the Holy Spirit, are made one with Christ in confessing the truth to which he bore witness in his paschal mystery: that in God alone and in his love is the source of life. "Father, you are holy indeed and all creation rightly gives you praise. All life, all holiness comes from you through your Son, Jesus Christ, by the working of the

---

[19] "For this I was born, and for this I have come into the world, to bear witness to the truth", Jn 18:37. Cf. 1 Tim 6:11–16. Before making "the good confession in his testimony before Pontius Pilate" (ibid., v. 13), Christ had, with clear reference to Genesis, related his sacrificial death and his witness to truth: "I know that you are descended from Abraham; but in spite of that you want to kill me because nothing I say has penetrated into you . . . you put into action the lessons learnt from your father . . . If you were Abraham's children you would do as Abraham did. As it is you want to kill me when I tell you the truth . . . What you are doing is what your father does . . . The devil is your father and you prefer to do what your father wants. He was a murderer from the start; he was never grounded in the truth; there is no truth in him at all: when he lies he is drawing on his own store, because he is a liar, and the father of lies. But as for me, I speak the truth and for that very reason you do not believe me", Jn 8:37–45. On the Father's total gift of his Son, cf. Rom 8:32.

[20] Jn 17:19.

[21] Cf. Rev 1:5.

Holy Spirit."[22] This confession is the worship in spirit and truth of which Christ spoke when he told the Samaritan woman: "The hour will come—in fact it is here already—when the true worshippers will worship the Father in spirit and truth: this is the kind of worshipper the Father wants."[23]

THE COVENANT TRUTH PROCLAIMED BY CHRIST

This is the covenant truth, revealed in the body which is given for us and the blood which is poured out for us, the truth to which the Spirit opens our hearts in repentance and faith. Confessing it we return through Christ to the Father to be renewed and embraced in the holy covenant intimacy expressed in the words: "I will be their God, and they shall be my people."[24] The eucharistic bread and wine, consecrated in the manner first enacted by Christ himself at the Supper, recall the memory of his paschal sacrifice by renewing sacramentally its presence in our midst with a view to our return to the Father in the confession of the covenant truth. We are to confess it, not just with our lips, but out of the deepest depths of our hearts, into which God's love has been poured through the Holy Spirit, so that it may possess and command our entire being.[25] That is how it possessed and commanded the heart of Christ, as

[22] *The Roman Missal,* Eucharistic Prayer III.

[23] Jn 4:23.

[24] Jer 31:33. The nuptial theme is present in the passage when God reminds his people that under the Sinai covenant he was their husband (ibid., v. 32). Cf. Rev 21:2–3. In speaking of the covenant truth I am, of course, taking the term *truth* in its biblical sense. "The Christian meaning of *truth,* therefore, is not the boundless area of being which we must conquer by the powers of the mind. It is the truth of the Gospel, the revealing Word of the Father, present in Jesus Christ and illuminated by the Spirit, which we must welcome in faith, so that it may transform our lives." (I. de la Potterie, "Truth" [trans. by D.F. Brezine] in X. Léon-Dufour [ed.], *Dictionary of Biblical Theology,* 2nd ed. revised and enlarged [London: Geoffrey Chapman, 1973 in paperback ed. 1982], p. 621). God's truth is not just the revelation of what is so but also the power whereby his saving designs are accomplished. And so St. Paul can say of the Gospel that "it is the power of God for salvation to every one who has faith", Rom 1:16.

[25] Cf. Rom 5:5.

our faith discovers when it contemplates the sacramental signs of the body and blood in which he confessed it as our Saviour and our Head. As the consecrated bread and wine show forth and thereby make present the body and blood of the Lamb who was slain, so the body and blood show forth and make present the covenant truth they proclaim through the sacramental representation of the state to which they were reduced in his sacrificial death.[26]

The covenant truth was first proclaimed by Christ in his body and blood on Calvary, when, having fulfilled in loving obedience all that the Father had laid upon him, he delivered his spirit into the Father's hands and bowed his head in death. By his death he entered the sanctuary of the living God to receive the abundance of life so that, gloriously risen from death, he might be the faithful witness to the truth that God is life, not just for himself alone, but for all whom the Father has given him by the covenant established in his blood.[27] In his body and blood he confessed the truth on our behalf and bore its light into the dark abyss of our death; in his body and blood death was transformed to become the womb of life, of the life to which we are reborn in the likeness of his rising from death; in his body and blood is the outpouring of life from the divine abundance in the gift of the Holy Spirit to the Church; in his body and blood the truth of God's life is revealed and proclaimed as the covenant truth that henceforth he is life for us. The all-powerful mystery of God's generous mercy is held in the hands of the priest when he says the words: "This is my body, this is my blood."

The sacrament of Christ's body and blood is his own offering of the covenant sacrifice now become the sacrifice of the Church. When the ordained priest pronounces the words of consecration over the bread and wine in the person of Christ he places Christ's offering in the hands of the Church. In the beginning Eve placed in Adam's hands the fruit that signified their shared determination to seek life in defiance of God's truth.[28] Now, by the ministry of the priest, Christ places the life-giving

---

[26] Readers will recognize here the influence of A. Vonier, *A Key to the Doctrine of the Eucharist,* especially pp. 281–87. Vonier does not emphasize the aspect of covenant truth as I have done.

[27] Heb 9:11–14; Jn 17:24.

[28] Cf. Gen 3:6.

fruit of his body and blood in the hands of his bride the Church to that
she may return with him to the Father in a sacrificial worship that
expresses their union in the confession of the covenant truth.

SACRAMENTAL REPRESENTATION OF
CHRIST'S SACRIFICE

Turning now to the sacrament of orders, we must consider how it
constitutes the recipient as the one who brings about the Eucharist in the
Church, and that, not just as minister, but in a representational role that
is integral to the eucharistic symbolism itself.

It is essential here to note that this does not mean that what Christ
offered on Calvary to the Father—his body and his blood—is first made
present in the sacrament and then offered in her turn by the Church.
Rather, the very sacramental representation of Christ's sacrifice, the very
bringing about of the Eucharist, is identically the offering of the sacrifice.
If we were to suppose that what Christ offered on Calvary—his body
and his blood—had first to be made present and then offered in her turn
by the Church, we should fall into the error of thinking that the Church
offers in the present what Christ offered in the past, with the result that
the Church would now be the principal offerer in a new offering distinct
from that of Christ. But the Church can never be the principal offerer;
she becomes offerer only through her being united with Christ's own
unique and all-sufficient offering. For that very reason Christ's own very
offering must be represented and thereby made present sacramentally in
the celebration of the Eucharist.[29] That is why the ordained priest, in
and by the very act in which he brings about the eucharistic sacrament,
makes present Christ's own priestly act of offering. This he can do only
in so far as he is sacramentally one with Christ; that is, in so far as he is, in

---

[29] In the second chapter of the decree, *Doctrina de sacrificio Missae,* the Council of
Trent (*Sessio* XXII) teaches that it is Christ who offers the sacrifice by the ministry of
priests: "Una enim eademque est hostia, idem nunc offerens sacerdotum ministerio, qui
se ipsum tunc in cruce obtulit, sola offerendi ratione diversa", DS 1743. Cf. the words of
Cardinal Willebrands in note 5 above: "It is in and through the ministry of priests that
the once-for-all sacrifice of Christ is present reality".

the act he performs in virtue of his ordination, the sacramental representation of Christ himself as prior to the Church. Just as Christ, the new Adam, offered his sacrifice on Calvary, and Mary, the new Eve and figure of the Church, united herself with his offering, so in the Eucharist the ordained priest makes Christ's offering present and the Church throughout history continues to unite herself with that offering.[30]

In his treatment of the Eucharist, St. Thomas considers an objection against the identity between the Eucharist and Calvary that may help us to grasp this fundamental point. On Calvary, the objection goes, Christ was both priest and victim: in the Eucharist, though Christ is victim, the priest is not Christ but the ordained minister. Consequently the Eucharist cannot be the same sacrifice as that of Calvary. St. Thomas answers that in the Eucharist Christ is indeed both priest and victim because the ordained priest is the sacramental sign of Christ.[31] In other words, it is of the essence of the sacrament of orders that it constitute the ordained minister as representation of Christ in Christ's act of offering. And when we take into account that Christ offered his sacrifice as the new Adam, as Head and Savior of the new race symbolized as the new Eve, we can see, in the light of the analogy of faith, that there are solid grounds for holding that only a man can be ordained.

The objection has been made that if a woman cannot represent Christ because he was male, we shall have to say that a twentieth-century non-Jew cannot represent him because he was a first-century Palestinian Jew.[32] This is to miss the point and to descend to the level of the frivolous. I do not say that a woman cannot represent Christ: every baptized person, man or woman, is *alter Christus.* What I do say, however, is that a woman cannot be the sacramental image of Christ in the act that is proper to him precisely as the new Adam. The symbolism of the new Adam and the new Eve expresses the relation between Christ and the Church which is profoundly involved in the Eucharistic celebration. Now the distinction between Adam and Eve is the sexual difference

---

[30] Cf. Jn 19:25.

[31] "Per eandem rationem, etiam sacerdos gerit imaginem Christi, in cuius persona et virtute verba pronuntiat ad consecrandum, ut ex supra dictis patet. Et ita quodammodo idem est sacerdos et hostia" (*Summa theologiae,* III, q. 83, a. 1, ad 3).

[32] Cf. E. Doyle, op. cit., pp. 217–18.

between man and woman, the primordial distinction universally present wherever human beings are to be found.

It may, of course, appear that I am attributing disproportionate importance to Christ's role as the new Adam, but I do not believe that that is so. We have heard Congar on this theme in the text I quoted above. The figure of Adam is of capital importance theologically, as St. Paul makes clear in the Letter to the Romans, by reason of its implications for the absolute universality of the redemption accomplished by Christ's sacrifice.[33] As the whole race was affected by Adam's sin, so the whole race is redeemed and renewed by Christ's sacrifice. Christ died, not as a Jew for Jews, but as the new Adam for the sake of all, so that all might be incorporated in him as all are descended from Adam.

REPRESENTATIVE OR SACRAMENTAL REPRESENTATION

And yet we must also say that in celebrating the Eucharist the ordained priest does what the Church does, that he represents the Church and acts *in persona Ecclesiae*.[34] But if the Church is the new Eve, and if a woman cannot represent the new Adam, how is a man to represent the new Eve? Here I would suggest that it is important to distinguish between acting as a representative and acting as a representation. A couple of examples will illustrate what I mean. We know that an unbaptized person can validly confer baptism.[35] Now in baptizing he acts as Christ's minister, and consequently *in persona Christi*.[36] Thus he acts as Christ's representative, but he is in no sense the sacramental representation of Christ, because he has himself received no sacrament. Again, in marriage the bride administers the sacrament, and in this sense she acts as Christ's representative, but

---

[33] Cf. Rom 5:12–21.

[34] Cf. *Inter insigniores,* n. V, p. 15.

[35] Cf. Council of Florence, *Decretum pro Armenis,* DS 1315.

[36] "It is common sacramental doctrine that the minister of the sacraments acts as vicar of Christ. With regard to the validity of baptism, it is the explicit teaching of the Church that anyone with the use of reason, having the right intention and employing due matter and form, may be minister of this sacrament and the minister, male or female, acts *in persona Christi.*" E. Doyle, op. cit., p. 215.

she does not act as sacramental representation of Christ, because this is distinctive of the bridegroom.[37] In celebrating the Eucharist, then, we can say that although the ordained priest acts as the Church's representative, he does not act as sacramental representation of the Church, but rather as sacramental representation of Christ.

If the priest does what the Church does and acts as the Church's representative, it is because the Eucharist is a sacrament, and consequently it is an act of the Church that she performs when the priest ministers as her representative. In that sense the Church acts in and through the priest. But because the Eucharist is the sacrament of Christ's sacrifice, the priest must act as sacramental image of Christ. In other words, the priest must represent Christ sacramentally as prior to the Church if the Church's own act is to be the sacrifice of Christ. In representing Christ as prior to the Church he is able to perform the action which is Christ's offering become the offering of the Church, the offering of the Head become the offering of the Body. Because the priest acts as sacramental representation of Christ it is Christ's sacrifice; because he acts as the Church's representative the Church offers the sacrifice of Christ. This, it seems to me, is what the Declaration intends when it says: "It is true that the priest represents the Church, which is the Body of Christ. But if he does so, it is precisely because he first represents Christ himself, who is the Head and Shepherd of the Church." It is what I meant above when I said that in the Eucharist the Church has to transcend herself in the priesthood of her minister in order that the very identical offering of Christ be her offering. The priest is one with the Church, because the sacraments of the Eucharist and orders are ecclesial realities, and at the same time he is representationally prior to the Church as image of Christ in order that Christ's offering be hers. From what we have seen of the symbolism involved in the Eucharist it seems to me to be confirmed that only a man can be the priest through whom Christ's offering is made the offering of the Church. And if it is proper to a woman to be sacramental representation not of Christ but of the Church, does it not follow that she could not represent any offering other than an offering of the Church? In that case she would represent the Church as

[37] Cf. Eph 5:22–33.

principal offerer in an offering distinct from that of Christ. If that is correct it is clear that the very validity of ordination is at stake in the decision on the question of the ordination of women.

St. Thomas has been justly criticized for saying that women cannot be ordained by reason of their inferiority to men.[38] In giving that as a reason he is quite mistaken. It is not at all that woman is inferior to man. But because the Head of the race is a man she cannot represent sacramentally the Head of the race in the action that is proper to him in that role. This does not imply woman's inferiority. It merely implies that the dignity of woman is different, that the role proper to her is different from the role that is proper to man.[39]

In this context I prefer to speak of difference than to speak of inferiority and superiority; but if one insists in speaking in that way I am prepared to argue that what woman symbolizes is in a profound way superior to what is symbolized by man. From the point of view of the natural symbolism of the sexual difference it seems to me that, precisely in the exercise of his sexuality, man's role is characterized by efficiency, exteriority, and transitoriness, whereas the role of woman is characterized by finality, interiority, and by the abiding fruitfulness that alone can raise man's sexuality beyond its episodic transitoriness.

Man's masculinity, then, endowed with its greater muscular strength, symbolizes exteriority and efficiency. He moves about in his environment to tame it and bring it under control. He is worldbuilder, a hunter, a warrior, aggressive and masterful, constantly on the move in his impatience to conquer and subdue.[40] Exteriority and efficiency likewise characterize technology. A world dominated by technology loses its sense of the interiority of nature, of being, in the untrammelled effi-

---

[38] Cf. E. Doyle, op. cit., pp. 218–19.

[39] Louis Bouyer has an excellent study of this subject: *Woman in the Church*, trans. by M. Teichert (San Francisco: Ignatius Press, 1979).

[40] Do not some women exhibit such qualities? Certainly, just as there are men who exhibit qualities that we regard as feminine. In the order of natural realities, although the symbol is expressive of typical natural characteristics, in the case of the individual the reality may conflict with the symbol. This can never happen in the case of the sacraments because they are essentially signs: the reality they contain and effect is precisely the reality they signify. On the difference between the natural order and the sacramental order, cf. A. Vonier, *A Key to the Doctrine of the Eucharist*, pp. 241–45.

ciency of its aggression against nature: it is not without reason that we speak of the rape of the environment. Perhaps its greatest perversion is the estrangement of woman, who, accepting the ideals of exteriority and efficiency for herself in forgetfulness of her femininity, aspires not just to be equal to man but to be indistinguishable from him.[41] The substitution of test-tubes and incubators for the womb would be the final achievement of this tendency.

But woman has a higher vocation and destiny. Her sex symbolizes the finality of human existence: what it is for. Here we encounter the symbol of dwelling, so powerfully developed by Heidegger—but long before him as a basic symbol in sacred Scripture.[42] It is a symbol of the interiority which alone makes it possible to be at home in the world, to savour proximity to the mystery of life and of its hidden purposes. Deprived of the interiority symbolized by woman, our being in the world is rootless, deprived of its inner center, without depth, without dwelling, without purpose, without heart. The only interiority it possesses is the inner emptiness that forms the theme of so much contemporary literature and philosophy. Created nature has nothing more eloquent of its mystery than a woman's love. In this love we glimpse a strength greater than the strength that transforms the world, because love is the strength that created it, the strength that maintains it in the depths of its being, the strength that guides it toward its end.

In the Church, symbolized by woman, we find the three qualities to which I have referred. The first is interiority. The Church indeed has an outward and visible aspect as a visible community gathered together by the Holy Spirit through the instrumentality of the priestly ministry; but more profoundly she is a mystery of inner life in virtue of the presence

[41] Cf. Joseph Cardinal Ratzinger with V. Messori, *The Ratzinger Report. An Exclusive Interview on the State of the Church,* trans. by S. Attanasio and G. Harrison (San Francisco: Ignatius Press, 1985), pp. 96–99.

[42] Cf. W. J. Richardson, *Heidegger. Through Phenomenology to Thought* (Martinus Nijhoff, The Hague, 1963), pp. 583–84. Richardson is here commenting on the lecture "Bauen, Wohnen, Denken"; the theme is all-pervasive as expressive of the fundamental structure of *Dasein: in-de-Welt-sein.* For the theme in sacred Scripture, cf. the article "Temple" by Francois Amiot (trans. by J. P. Langan) in X. Léon-Dufour (ed.) *Dictionary of Biblical Theology,* pp. 594–97.

within her of the same Spirit.[43] She is the dwelling of God with men where they can be at home with God.[44] She is the place of intimacy, as the Holy Spirit is the dwelling of Father and Son. The Church's unity is participation in the unity of the Holy Spirit, the unity in which, as the Church's prayer puts it, Father and Son live and reign forever.[45] In the Church, filled with the Spirit, Father and Son live and reign forever with the redeemed. Is not this the meaning of Christ's prayer at the Supper?

The second quality is finality. As man's sexuality is for the sake of what is accomplished in and through a woman, so the incarnation of the Word and Christ's redemptive mission on earth are for the sake of what is accomplished in and through the Church: *Propter nos homines et propter nostram salutem descendit de caelis.* Insofar as the Word became flesh he was, precisely as man and sent by the Father to accomplish a mission amongst men in human history, ordered toward the Church; because he is Word, of course, the Church, like the whole of creation, is ordered toward the glory which is his with the Father in the unity of the Holy Spirit. Moreover, that glory, withheld from him in his humanity during the course of his earthly life, is now his in the splendor of his resurrection and as Head of the Church. The Church is, indeed, the consummation of God's plans; the Church finally transfigured in the glory of her Head is that for the sake of which the whole work of redemption was undertaken, so that reflecting his glory she might be ever to the glory of God.

---

[43] "The one mediator, Christ, established and ever sustains here on earth his holy Church, the community of faith, hope and charity, as a visible organization through which he communicates truth and grace to all men. But, the society structured with hierarchical organs and the mystical body of Christ, the visible society and the spiritual community, the earthly Church and the Church endowed with heavenly riches, are not to be thought of as two realities. On the contrary, they form one complex reality which comes together from a human and a divine element. For this reason the Church is compared, not without significance, to the mystery of the incarnate Word. As the assumed nature, inseparably united to him, serves the divine Word as a living organ of salvation, so, in a somewhat similar way, does the social structure of the Church serve the Spirit of Christ who vivifies it, in the building up of the body (cf. Eph 4:16)." (*Lumen Gentium,* chap. I, no. 8.)

[44] Cf. Rev 21:2–3.

[45] The translation in the *Roman Missal:* "who lives and reigns with you and the Holy Spirit" completely misses the meaning of the Latin "in unitate Spiritus Sancti".

Lastly there is fruitfulness. Like Mary, the Church is the fruitful virgin, the virgin whose fruitfulness derives not from man's sexuality but from the gift of the Holy Spirit.[46] She is blessed because she believes that there will be a fulfillment of what was spoken to her by the Lord.[47] Open to God through this virginal faith, she receives from the Holy Spirit the fruitfulness that makes her mother of all the living. In her they are born not to a perishable life but to everlasting life. And the abiding fullness of that life is charity. It was in the call to that charity that the virgin, Thérèse of Lisieux, found a vocation that embraced and surpassed all other ministry.[48]

[46] I have developed this theme in "The Fruitful Virginity of Mary", *The Way* (Supplement 51, Autumn, 1984), pp. 44–52.

[47] Cf. Lk 1:45.

[48] Cf. the Office for the feast of St. Thérèse (October 1) in *The Divine Office*.

14

HELMUT MOLL

REFLECTIONS ON A RECENT THEOLOGICAL STUDY REGARDING WOMEN PRIESTS

Translated by Lothar Krauth

Manfred Hauke, *"Die Problematik um das Frauenpriestertum vor dem Hintergrund der Schöpfungs- und Erlösungsordnung"* [The problem of women priests related to the order of creation and salvation]. Konfessionskundliche und kontroverstheologische Studien 46, 2nd ed. Paderborn: Bonifatius Druckerei, 1986, 496 pp. English edition: *Women in the Priesthood? A Systematic Analysis in the Light of the Order of Creation and Redemption* (San Francisco: Ignatius Press, 1988), 497 pp.

Many of us have been waiting for such a study for years! Here now comes this doctoral thesis, directed by Professor Scheffczyk (Munich) and approved in 1981. It is *comprehensive* in several respects, and includes in its research an anthropology of the sexes; a vast spectrum of religious ideas from several millennia; considerations based on the Old and the New Testament, the Church's history, dogmatics, and liturgy—always "accompanied by an ecumenical concern" (p. 19). Various statements scattered in the documents of the Second Vatican Council prompted renewed discussions about the role of women in the Church. The true context of this highly-charged topic, however, is to be seen elsewhere: developments in society at large have irreversibly leveled the gender differences, emptying them of their richness and significance—in effect causing a masculine preponderance to become now all-pervasive. Such a development was fostered, first, by the teachings of socialism as found in today's orthodox Marxism and its revisionist varieties, stating that any difference in the behavior of the sexes is caused by social conditions (pp. 30–32). Then, certain currents of liberalism (clearly evident in Simone de Beauvoir) rejected all notions of inborn differentiation, saying, "One does not arrive in the world a woman, but one becomes a woman" (p. 34). Contemporary feminism, especially active in the U.S.A., grows out of these roots (pp. 36–39). In the religious arena, the Lutheran Church in Sweden was the first to adopt and adapt such teachings, but other Protestant Churches soon followed (pp. 46–54).

In Part One, Hauke develops some basic insights from a theology of creation, reflecting on the position of man and woman in the order of creation. Generally, he affirms that each of the two sexes is endowed with specific characteristics and potentials, in opposition to a so-called "androgynous utopianism" which, now as then, attempts to deny such specific differentiation. The genes already decide a person's sex and determine the evolving sexual differentiation (pp. 85 ff.). The physical appearances of men and women, defined by primary and secondary sexual characteristics, show substantial differences, many similarities notwithstanding. The biological reality progressively unfolds in specific developments which are then described by psychology and sociology. Decisive in this is the intimate interrelation between body and soul, the root spiritual powers of intellect and will, and the different way each gender experiences body-awareness and self-awareness. The internalized nature of the woman and the externalized nature of the man will determine different consequences for each. In philosophical thought, "there is a tendency to interpret the polarity of the sexes as an elemental *human* phenomenon" (p. 111), and "the male nature is explained as expressing a more creative, assertive principle, the female nature a more receptive, formative principle" (p. 110).

The findings of comparative religion are dealt with extensively (pp. 121–94). In contrast to a mere pragmatic approach, Hauke emphasizes the importance of symbols which allow access to the realm of mystery. He states, "The image of God in the theistic religions of revelation has more masculine than feminine traits" (p. 196). Consequently, "men [only] are chosen as his priestly representatives" (p. 196), who represent a reality which lies beyond themselves. Women, on the other hand, "not only represent creation but belong to it themselves; the symbolism in them is more strongly realized" (196).

Part One culminates logically in an interpretation of the Genesis accounts. The priestly author as well as the Yahwist hold that "the sexual differentiation of mankind is willed by God" (p. 198), while their being created in God's image and likeness establishes the fundamental equality of man and woman (p. 196).

Part Two deals with "the question of women in the priesthood against the background of the order of salvation" (pp. 205ff.). The contemporary discussion about the true definition of a Christian woman's dignity reveals how far we have moved away from Gertrud von Le Fort's positive view as expressed in her immortal work *Die ewige Frau* [The eternal woman]: "Catholic dogmatics has proclaimed the most powerful teachings on women ever. All other philosophical attempts to interpret a woman's reality pale in comparison; they offer nothing more than counterfeit theology, or else their content and meaning are spiritually insignificant" (p. 13). Instead, more and more women seem determined to discover in the Church's teaching an attitude of discrimination, even oppression, and respond with aggressive defiance. This already begins with Holy Scripture where, in this view, all biblical symbols are mere expressions of a patriarchal society (p. 216). Hauke, however, follows G. von Rad who declared that Yahweh is "beyond the polarity of the sexual" (p. 216), and then analyzes the exact details of God's image in the Old Testament. The symbol of "Father" pervades and dominates all Scripture; it bridges the distance between Creator and creature without interfering with God's transcendence. At the same time, we find traces of maternal symbolism (Is 49:14–15; 66:13; Dt 32:18) which, according to Hauke, "has no independent value, but is . . . a component part of the father symbol" (p. 239).

The title question, "Christ's maleness: a situationally conditioned coincidence or an essential aspect of revelation?" (p. 249) leads to Hauke's demonstration that Christ's mission cannot be separated from his male nature. This also refutes the androgynous conception of Christ, which originated under neoplatonic and gnostic influences. The Bible's male symbolism as applied to God the Father and God the Son is unambiguously clear, in contrast to symbols for the Holy Spirit. Here, the textual interpretation gathers concepts like Wisdom, Immanence, Relationship, and the specific condition of the recipient—concepts which are not readily compatible with each other. Many of these concepts could be stretched in interpretation and applied either to Christ or to Mary. However, further studies are needed to shed light on the connection between God the Spirit and any female symbolism.

Whenever the Blessed Mother is considered within the order of salvation, it leads to a fruitful blossoming of Christian spirituality. "Mary: Archetype and Mother of the Church" (p. 297), occupies an important position in salvation history. "If the masculinity of Christ is essential to his redemptive mission, then so, too, is the femininity of Mary to representation of the Church, which opens herself to that work" (p. 298). A Christian woman should recognize Mary as her model; "because, within [Mary's] concrete life-circumstances, she rendered obedience, unconditionally and conscientiously, to the will of God" (p. 313).

The most important clue to an understanding of Christ's actions is offered in his call of the twelve apostles. True, a first meaning of this event can be seen in its relation to the Old Testament, insofar as the apostles typify the twelve tribes of Israel. But beyond that, it shows that Christ did not call any women to be his apostles and witnesses, in spite of the fact that he dealt with women in a radically new way, compared to the attitude of his time.

Hauke then carefully identifies St. Paul's teaching within its cultural and theological context, interpreting 1 Cor 11 and 1 Cor 14:33b–38, and relating these texts to Gal 3:28 and 1 Cor 12, all of which show a unified view: "For Paul, both men and women are, through the Holy Spirit, children of God. Within this fundamental equality, however, allowances are made for the differences between the sexes, that are grounded in creation and that are also expressed within the divine service according to ecclesiastically regulated order" (p. 357).

Hauke's thorough knowledge of Church history is evident in the chapter on the question of women priests during the time of the Church. For two thousand years, the practice of the apostolic Church and the teaching on this subject have remained unchanged. Against the early heresies of Gnosticism and Montanism stand numerous patristic testimonies, affirming fidelity to the Founder. It is certainly true that the teachings regarding the male priesthood were influenced over the years by changing social and cultural conditions; and yet, as Hauke points out, the unchanging and decisive point of reference has always been obedience to Christ's will (pp. 435–38).

Sketching the medieval world of ideas, however, especially as expressed by St. Thomas Aquinas, Hauke is compelled to acknowledge there certain androcentric attitudes. Balancing this view is the reverence accorded to women in sources selected from songs of courtly love, bridal mysticism, and marian devotion.

What conclusion does this study offer? First of all, Hauke denies that a history of undervaluation lies at the root of the exclusion of women from the priesthood. This is amply evidenced by almost two thousand years of devotion to the Blessed Mother (pp. 469–70). Wherever the will of the Creator is disregarded, wherever the richness of the female nature is forgotten or actively discarded, there the symbolic reality of the sexes will wither, and all will be the poorer for it. Whoever acknowledges God's order of creation, whoever accepts creation's fulfillment in the order of salvation, will find the Church's position confirmed by the various arguments based on the structure of these two orders. Whoever reads the New Testament and in spite of clear evidence only finds the message *non liquet* [still undecided], should remember the history of the Church and the so-called "argument from prescription" which states: "If it is not known with absolute certainty whether the behavior of Jesus is binding or not, then there is but one possibility, namely, to remain with Tradition" (p. 473). This tradition, indeed, is clear beyond any doubt. Hauke further quotes one of the Lord's pronouncements as found in St. Paul and there described as "a command of the Lord" (1 Cor 14:37), claiming due authority (pp. 474–79). Based on these conclusions, Hauke feels entitled to repeat Barbara Albrecht's position stated in her book of 1980, *Vom Dienst der Frau in der Kirche* [The Ministry of Women in the Church]: "Official priesthood for women is contradictory to binding Church doctrine and to the nature of woman" (p. 481). The exclusion of women from the ordained priesthood, therefore, is not based on discrimination. "The No to priesthood for women and the Yes to the worth of women are, to a certain extent, two sides of the same coin" (p. 482).

Our present time is "marked by the 'masculine' belief in the 'manipulatability' of all things and a rationalism that is tearing itself away from the roots of life" (p. 482). We are, therefore, charged with the task "of discovering once again the value of woman" (p. 482).

This book deserves particular attention, not least because of its survey of the pertinent contemporary currents. Of course, sympathizers will praise it, while opponents will find fault with it. Nevertheless, from now on anybody claiming to have anything to say about our subject cannot afford to disregard this study.

V

THE CHALLENGE OF FEMINISM

15

JUTTA BURGGRAF

THE MOTHER OF THE CHURCH AND THE WOMAN IN THE CHURCH

A CORRECTION OF FEMINIST THEOLOGY GONE ASTRAY

Translated by Maria Shrady

The feminist movement has for a long time been considered a trendy current, barely worthy of consideration. Today, however, it has grown into an issue in our public life. To its justification, the sense or nonsense of its goals, hardly a serious thought is given. But now this has become all the more necessary, since it has also penetrated the realm of theology, faith, and the Church. What Lutz von Padberg has pointed out several years ago has gradually become clear: feminism does not constitute a peripheral movement within our pluralistic society, but rather a counter culture which demands the attention of all society.[1] A quick glance at the history of its development will be sufficient to elucidate this point.

DEVELOPMENT AND EXPANSION OF FEMINIST THEOLOGY

Within the last one hundred fifty years, the life of woman has profoundly changed. Industrialization, the shift from large to small families,

[1] Cf. Lutz von Padberg, "Der Feminismus. Historische Entwicklung—ideologische Hintergründe—kulturrevolutionäre Ziele" [Feminism: historical development—ideological background—cultural and revolutionary goals], in Peter Beyerhaus, ed., *Frauen im theologischen Aufstand. Eine Orientierungshilfe zur "Feministischen Theologie"* [Women in theological revolt: an orientation aid to "feminist theology"] (Newhausen and Stuttgart, 1983), p. 72.

increasing professional activity outside the home, are important reasons for this. The women's movement of the nineteenth and early twentieth century attempted to deal with these evolving problems. Its roots were in the theology of the Enlightenment, and it understood itself to be a continuation of the demand for human rights, which should not be exclusively affirmed of men. Accordingly, it aimed at improved education for women to allow for a free development of their personality, their compatible political voting rights, and working conditions commensurable with the dignity of the human person. It is true that excesses existed within the movement, but seen within the context of the entire societal development, it presented a positive step. The goals were achieved and for all intents and purposes, the movement dissolved.[2]

Today's feminism has little in common with the women's movement of that time. It does *not* start from the same premises but aims far beyond its original objectives. Contemporary feminism does not concern itself with the legal and social equality of women but rather with the total equalization of the sexes, or even the elevation of women above men. Sexuality, motherhood, marriage, and family are definitively rejected. Free abortion is advocated, and after the education of children is transferred to men and society, the substitution of pregnancy by test-tube breeding is envisaged.[3] The long-term objective is the radical change of human beings as they exist in traditionally structured society, the achievement of a "new" (androgynous) man in a "new world".

The relationship between socialism, Marxism, and the feminist movement has been frequently pointed out.[4] All of these movements, in

---

[2] Cf. H. Schenk, *Die feministische Herausforderung. 150 Jahre Frauenbewegung in Deutschland* [The feminist challenge: 150 years of the woman's movement in Germany], 2nd ed. (Munich, 1981), p. 57ff. Also of interest is the study about the founding and development of Catholic women's associations in the 19th century by Alfred Kall, *Katholische Frauenbewegung in Deutschland* [Catholic woman's movement in Germany] (Paderborn, 1983).

[3] Cf. Ferdinand Menne, *Kirchliche Sexualethik und Geschlechterrollen in der Kirche* [The sexual ethic in the Church and the roles of the sexes], in Bernadette Brooten and Norbert Greinacher, eds., *Frauen in der Männerkirche* [Women in a church of men] (Munich, 1982), p. 32ff.

[4] Cf. Helmut Moll, "Feminist Theology—a Challenge", in *Munich Theological Journal,* 34 (1983), vol. 2, p. 120, see pp. 259–73, below; also cf. August Bebel: "Woman and Socialism", in *Internationale Bibliothek,* vol. 9 (Berlin, Bonn, Bad Godesberg), p. 376.

their extreme manifestations, hold present society with its values and traditions in low esteem. Catharina Halkes, one of the leading feminists, believes that feminism and socialism need each other, if we are to attain a new freedom for all. She thinks these two parallel tendencies possess a common dynamism.[5]

Feminism may even be considered the climax of contemporary anti-Christian revolutions: the French Revolution of 1789, for instance, had abandoned the Three Estates; the Bolshevik Revolution of 1917, private production. Now, however, an immediate work of *God* is to be abolished, namely, the polar sexuality of man, the psychological and biological nature of man and woman.[6] Hence Marcuse is perfectly justified when he calls this "possibly the most important and potentially radical movement of contemporary life".[7]

Significantly, feminism made its first onslaught in Germany during the student revolts of the 1960s. It received powerful impulses from the United States where it expanded particularly during the 1970s. In order to provide a metaphysical base for its ideas, the so-called "feminist theology" was developed. It is pursued by numerous groups both large and small, within which are found a diversity of opinions; the spectrum ranges from moderate to radical circles.

According to its own statements, "feminist theology" is closely interwoven with "liberation theology" and so-called "black theology".[8]

[5] Cf. Catharina Halkes, "Feministische Theologie. Eine Zwischenbilanz" [Feminist theology: an interim statement], in Bernadette Brooten and Norbert Greinacher, eds., *Frauen in der Männerkirche*, p. 163; *Gott hat nicht nur starke Söhne. Grundzüge einer feministischen Theologie* [God does not only have strong sons: outline of a feminist theology], 3rd ed. (Gütersloh, 1982), p. 117.

[6] Cf. "An Aid to Orientation by the Theological Convent of Confessing Communities: What is our answer to 'Feminist Theology'?" in Beyerhaus, *Frauen im theologischen Aufstand*, p. 56.

[7] Herbert Marcuse, "Marxismus und Feminismus", in *Jahrbuch Politik* 6 (Berlin, 1974), p. 86.

[8] Cf. J. L. P. van Nieuwenhove, "The Theology of Liberation: The Faith of the Oppressed", in Catharina Halkes and Daan Buddingh, eds., *Wenn Frauen ans Wort kommen. Stimmen zur feministischen Theologie* [When women speak their turn: The voices of feminist theology] (Gelnhausen, 1979), pp. 116–25; Jacquelyn Grant, "Black Theology and the Black Woman", in Brooten and Greinacher, *Frauen in der Männerkirche*, pp. 212–34.

What all of these trendy theologies have in common is the desire to liberate a certain group of the population—be it the poor, those of color, or women, from their presumed enslavement. How to go about this becomes the focal point of the entire program. God is furnished with the characteristics of the "oppressed", and presented as their special advocate. In this connotation one may frequently hear the provocative sentence: "God is a she and black."[9]

Feminists frequently object that women do not hold ecclesiastical office.[10] By claiming a revolutionary reform program, they infiltrate Church and theology, where they are acquiring a growing influence. There are more and more Church services with a theme, courses and workshops, Church work for women, educational institutions, Church academies, and even universities stamped by feminist ideologies.

The first theological publications appeared during the middle 1970s in the United States. The titles alone clearly express their intention. To quote a few:

Beyond God the Father: Toward a Philosophy of Women's Liberation, by Mary Daly, (Boston: Beacon Press, 1973). Mary Daly is described as "foster mother" of almost all European feminists. She demands the "exorcism" of God the Father, who puts a psychological burden upon woman.[11]

Gottes neue Eva—Freiheit, Gleichheit—Schwesterlichkeit, by Elisabeth

[9] Halkes, "Feministische Theologie. Eine Zwischenbilanz", p. 116; cf. also Ingeborg Hauschildt, "Die Verunsicherung der Gemeinden durch die 'Feministische Theologie' " [The threat to the security of parishes from "feminist theology"], in Beyerhaus, *Frauen im theologischen Aufstand,* p. 17.

[10] In her anniversary lecture at the occasion of the 75th year anniversary of the World Union of Catholic Women's Organizations (WUCWO) in Spring, 1985, Halkes formulated once more her viewpoint: "God has not become man so that men may be in the Church, as if women were not worthy to transmit what is holy." Press Office of the Archbishop of Cologne, Article and reportage, no. 244, May 4, 1985, p. 2. Also cf. James Hitchcock, "Self-idolization: A Spotlight on the Spiritual State of Catholic Religions in the U.S.", in *National Catholic Register,* March 1984, p. 4; Hans Küng, "Für die Frau in der Kirche. 16 Thesen zur Stellung der Frau in Kirche und Gesellschaft" [For the woman in the Church: 16 theses regarding the position of woman in the Church and society], in Brooten and Greinacher, *Frauen in der Männerkirche,* pp. 186–90.

[11] Cf. Mary Daly, *Jenseits von Gott Vater, Sohn und Co.* p. 5ff.; English edition: *Beyond God the Father* (Boston: Beacon Press, 1973).

Moltmann-Wendel, Munich, 1977. English Edition: *Liberty, Equality, Sisterhood: On the Emancipation of Women in Church and Society* (BKS Demand, UMI). Moltmann-Wendel is known to be the leading feminist theologian in Germany.

Gott hat nicht nur starke Söhne [God does not only have strong sons] by Catherina Halkes, Gütersloh, 1980, 4th ed., 1985. Since 1977 Halkes has been a lecturer on feminism and Christianity at the Theological Faculty of Nijmwegen (Netherlands).

METHODS AND PRINCIPAL THEMES OF THEOFANTASY

The systematic underpinnings and methods of "feminist theology" are not easily grasped, for feminists refuse to bind themselves to a single line. They move outside scientific theology, which for them is characterized by rigid concepts and structured systems. To do theology in such a way is typically masculine. All the great theologians to this day are rejected for being "patriarchically one-sided". They are considered an obstacle to women who wish to experience the vitality of their faith.

Feminists reject theo-*logy* in favor of "theo-*fantasy*", which seeks to discover new ways of experiencing in a playful way, exalting them as the measure of all things. This claim is fortified and sustained by the conviction that women are, due to their nature, in closer harmony with the universe and hence also nearer to God.[12]

What is hiding behind the expression "theofantasy" is intellectually not new: we detect similar features in the Romantic Movement and in the poetic ideal of "Sturm und Drang". Naomi Goldenberg, however, who has coined the expression, does not refer to these tendencies but to those of C. G. Jung who describes dreams as sources of revelation.[13]

---

[12] Cf. "An Orientation Manual of the Theological Convent of Confessing Communities", p. 41.

[13] Cf. Naomi R. Goldenberg, "Träume und Phantasien als Offenbarungsquellen: eine feministische Aneignun von C. G. Jung" [Dreams and fantasies as source of revelations: a feminist appropriation of C. G. Jung], in Brooten and Greinacher, eds., *Frauen in der Männerkirche*, pp. 235–44.

Nature and feminine modes of experiencing thus become the highest criterion. Hence practically everything may be embraced uncritically, everything that people in every culture and religion have ever experienced, thought, and expressed. As a result syncretism is the characteristic mark of "feminist theology". By way of nature-enthusiasm one arrives at Eastern mysticism and beyond that at witchcraft, astrology, and the occult; evolutionary theories and depth-psychology are included along the way. Witch dances are performed, "Mother Earth" is worshiped in Indian style, modern group dynamics are employed, and one dreams of the restoration of ancient matriarchal cultures with their celebrations and rituals. How correct Beyerhaus is when he points out that pagan nature worship has entered the Church by way of the feminist movement.[14]

Holy Scripture plays an ambivalent role in this "feminist theology". Some of its supporters question its so-called "androcentric" world view and plainly reject it.[15] So, for instance, Catharina Halkes calls the Bible "a nasty book for women".[16] Other feminists wish to reinterpret it or even write it anew.[17] The texts are to be evaluated "as to their intentional meaning".[18] The women of the Old and New Testament (e.g., Judith, Esther, Deborah, Magdalen, Martha, and Mary) become symbols of a misunderstood revolution.[19]

[14] Cf. Beyerhaus, *Frauen im theologischen Aufstand,* Preface, p. 10.

[15] Cf. Dieter Bauer, "Die Bibel aus der Sicht der Frauen" [The Bible from woman's point of view], in *Bible und Kirche* [Bible and Church], ed. by Kath. Bibelwerk, 4/4, (Stuttgart, 1984), p. 141.

[16] Cf. Halkes, *Gott hat nitch nur starke Söhne,* p. 55.

[17] Cf. Herlinde Pissarek-Hudelist, "Religionspädagogische Konsequenzen aus einer feministischen Bibelauslegung" [Consequences of feminine exegesis for pedagogy in religion], in *Bible und Kirche,* p. 167; Marga Monheim-Geffert and Renate Rieger, *Feministische Bibelauslegung im Kontext der Feministischen Theologie* [Feminist exegesis of the Bible in context with feminist theology], ibid., pp. 142–48.

[18] Paul Schmidt, *Maria, Modell der neuen Frau. Perspektiven zur zeigemässen Mariologie* [Mary as model of the new woman: perspectives for a contemporary mariology] (Kevalaer, 1974), p. 57.

[19] Cf. René Laurentin, *Jesus und die Frauen. Eine verkannte Revolution?* [Jesus and women: a misunderstood revolution?] in Brooten and Greinacher, *Frauen in der Männerkirche,* p. 94ff; Karl Lehmann, "Die Stellung der Frau als Problem der theologischen Anthropologie" [The status of woman as problem of theological anthropology], in International Catholic Journal *Communio,* vol. 11 (4/82) (Paderborn), p. 315; Bernadette

The feminists question not only the methods but also the content of Catholic theology: they take offense at the image of God in Christianity. Within the traditional doctrine of the Church we are dealing—according to Christa Mulack—"with a masculine God, who has been created by men for men".[20] Catharina Halkes continues in a similar vein: for women these masculine, patriarchal images are offensive.[21]

Numerous divine names and attributes are repudiated as "obsolete", as in the case of "creator", "ruler", "king", and "shepherd".[22] Because woman wants to be like God and God is not a woman, she creates her own God, within feminist theology. One speaks only of "God-Mother" and "God-Daughter". In reference to the Old Testament in which the word spirit (*ruach* in Hebrew) is feminine,[23] the Third Person of the Godhead is designated as feminine (*Heilige Geistin*).[24]

Theological feminism is constantly seeking new names and attributes for God, or else it leaves these images consciously in a state of suspension. Thus it takes its place near so-called negative theology: many feminists believe that one may speak of God only by negating human attributes or in general terms.

J. Brooten, "Mehodenfrage zur Rekonstruktion der frühchristlichen Frauengeschichte" [Questions of method concerning the reconstruction of early Christian history of women], in *Bibel und Kirche,* pp. 157–64; Rodney Venberg, "Das Problem der Bibelübersetzung in einem weiblich geprägten Gottesbild" [The problem of biblical translation in a woman-oriented image of God], ibid., pp. 174–75.

[20] Christa Mulack, *Maria und die Weiblichkeit Gottes. Ein Beitrag feministischer Theologie* [Mary and the femininity of God: a contribution to feminist theology], in Wolfgang Beinert, et al., *Maria, eine ökumenische Herausforderung* [Mary, an ecumenical challenge] (Regensburg, 1984), p. 144.

[21] Cf. Halkes, "Feministische Theologie. Eine Zwischenbilanz", p. 166.

[22] Cf. Elisabeth Moltmann-Wendel, "Menschwerden in einer neuen Gesellschaft von Frauen und Männern" [To become human in a new society of men and women], in *Die Zeichen der Zeit* [The signs of time] (9/82) (Berlin), p. 233; Kurt Lüthi, *Gottes neue Eva* [God's new Eve] (Stuttgart, 1978), p. 202; Dorothee Solee, "Vater, Macht und Barbarei. Feministische Anfragen an autoritäre Religion" [Father, power, and barbarism: feminist questions to authoritarian religion], in Brooten and Greinacher, eds., *Frauen in der Männerkirche,* p. 149ff.

[23] Cf. Mulack, *Maria und die Weiblichkeit Gottes* [Mary and the femininity of God], p. 143.

[24] Cf. Halkes, "Feministische Theologie", loc cit., p. 158f.

God should—so they say—not be spoken of as belonging to a definite "sex", but rather conceived as a neutral being, as impersonal ground of being. Mary Daly, for one, wishes to understand him as "Life-energy in process";[25] Catharina Halkes sees in him a "source of unrest and creative chaos", which summons us to "recreate what exists".[26] At this point one can recognize the attempt to provide Marxism with a "theological" foundation.

According to feminists, a woman can set herself free from anything that may impede her development; she is capable of realizing all her potentialities if she only wills to do so.[27] Her liberation is entirely up to her. To her are attributed almost unlimited powers; her essence is seen as being in total harmony with the universe. There is no room for alienation or sin. Hence there exists no necessity for a redeemer. Christ's death on the Cross as expiation for our guilt is rejected. Thus "feminist theology" presents itself as a doctrine of modern self-redemption which exhibits clear anti-Christian features. Jesus—also called "Jesa Christa"—is not the savior but the archetype of the "new man".[28]

[25] Cf. Mary Daly, *Kirche, Frau und Sexus* [Church, woman, and sex] (Olten, 1970), p. 186f. Mary Daly asks the provocative question: "Why must God really be a substantive? Why not a verb—the most active and dynamic of all word forms? Has the naming of God by a noun not been a murder of this dynamic verb?" *Jenseits von Gott Vater*, p. 49. Cf. also Magdalena Bussman, "Anliegen und Ansatz feministischer Theologie" [Concerns and roots of feminist theology], in Gerhard Dautzenberg et al., ed., *Die Frau im Urchristentum* [The woman in early Christianity] (Freiburg, 1983), p. 344f.

[26] Cf. Halkes, "Feministische Theologie. Eine Zwischenbilanz", p. 167. Sheila Collins mentions a conference in 1972, in which God has been presented as "fulcrum" rather than "authoritarian apex" of reality. In another image, God is compared to an electric power plant, "the grid of being", the energy source of all Being. Cf. *A Different Heaven and Earth: A Feminist Perspective on Religion* (Valley Forge, 1974), p. 219f.

[27] Cf. "Die Thesen zur Emanzipation der Frau in Kirche und Gesellschaft" [The emancipation theses on woman in society and church] by Catharina Halkes, *Freiheit, Gleichheit, Schwesterlichkeit* [Freedom, egality, sisterhood], pp. 70–72.

[28] Cf. Maria de Groot, "Sprache und Bild" [Speech and image], in Halkes and Buddingh, ed., *Wenn Frauen ans Wort kommen*, p. 62.

The Mother of Christ is also fundamentally reinterpreted. These interpretations, however, are not always consistent. They only agree in rejecting the traditional image of Mary. The uniqueness of Mary is eschewed by excluding the marian archprinciple of her motherhood of God: this would establish a one-sided picture of woman as mother and nurturer.

The fact that Mary was "the obedient handmaid of the Lord", arouses indignation among feminists. They consider it to be the invention of theologians who in the past have influenced the religious and social image of woman in a negative way. For by describing Mary as a woman who voluntarily submitted to the "patriarchal Man-God", Christian women have been encouraged to do the same. Mary predominantly served as a model for a Christian ethic and an anthropology, which emphasized such "passive" tendencies as serving, receiving, and obeying as specific feminine ideals. Thus, as Paul Smith formulates it, "a one-sided and disturbed relationship of the Christian to the world"[29] has been encouraged. Catharina Halkes observes, not without irony: "for us girls and women there was only a single model: that of the lowly and pure Virgin Mary. Over and over again we were led to believe that for us, too—humble, chaste, modest and self-effacing—there was a task pleasing to God."[30]

As a result of this mariology, woman was "debased". This state of affairs is also not changed—so feminists believe—by the presumed upgrading of Mary through her assumption into Heaven; for her passive "assumption" contrasts with the active "ascension", the ascension of her divine son into Heaven, superior in value to her own.[31]

A number of feminists discard mariology altogether due to its "unfortunate consequences".[32] They hold that the prevailing image of Mary always corresponds to the role of woman in the Church, and that in inverse proportion: the more woman is debased, the more

[29] Schmidt, *Maria, Modell der neuen Frau,* p. 8.
[30] Halkes, *Gott hat nicht nur starke Söhne,* p. 93.
[31] Cf. Mulack, *Maria und die Weiblichkeit Gottes,* p. 152.
[32] Cf. Schmidt, *Maria, Modell der neuen Frau,* p. 56.

Mary is exalted.[33] For this reason marian piety ought to be avoided altogether.

There are some feminists who try to achieve a "woman-friendly evaluation"[34] of Mary's image by pressing their own idiosyncratic interpretations. They would like to transform the biblical context completely by adding extra-Christian elements of their own. The Magnificat for instance, seen through their eyes, appears as a political hymn of protest with an emancipating effect.[35] Catharina Halkes calls it "the battle hymn against injustice in the world",[36] and concludes:

> It is a song filled with gratitude and praise, but at the same time a critical and prophetic one . . . , Mary continues the sharp social criticism of the prophetic tradition, joining the political criticism with a messianic vision of social justice . . . . The Magnificat exhibits a radical option for the poor, the disinherited, and the oppressed.[37]

The image of Mary which we see emerging from this becomes the prototype of feminine emancipation, a model of a spontaneous and radical person, turning the status quo upside-down. The Mother of Jesus is pictured as advocate of the oppressed, particularly of oppressed women.[38] One does not venerate her as Queen of Heaven, but as a

[33] Cf. Magdalena Bussmann, "Maria und die Frauen in der Kirche heute" [Mary and women in the Church today], Oct. 2–3, 1982 lecture at a meeting in Franz-Hitze Haus (Münster) with the theme: "Die Frau in Kirche und Gesellschaft" [Woman in Church and society] (1982), p. 153.

[34] Mulack, *Maria und die Weiblichkeit Gottes*, p. 153.

[35] Cf. Schmidt, *Maria, Modell der neuen Frau*, p. 47; Marianne Dirks, "Königin, Magd oder Schwester im Glauben?" [Queen, handmaid, or sister in the faith?], in Wolfgang Beinert et al., *Maria, eine ökumenische Herausforderung*, p. 184; Luise Schrotoff, "Nicht-viele Mächtige: Annäherungen on eine Soziologie des Urchristentums [Not many powerful], approaches to a sociology of primitive Christianity, in *Bibel und Kirche*, pamphlet 1/1 (1985) (Stuttgart), p. 5; Ernesto Cardenal, *Das Evangelium der Bauern von Solentiname* [The Gospel of the peasants from Solentiname], vol. 2 (Wuppertal, 1967), p. 32f.

[36] Halkes, *Gott has nicht nur starke Söhne*, p. 57.

[37] Ibid., p. 43.

[38] Cf. Waltraud Wagner-König, "Der Streik der Madonnen, oder: Die Legende von der Erdenfahrt Mariens" [The dispute of the madonnas, or the legend of Mary's descent to earth", in *Frau und Mutter*. Members journal of the Catholic Women's Association in Germany (5/84), pp. 22–24.

strong woman, who herself has experienced poverty and suffering, as well as contempt and banishment.[39]

This veneration, however, does not attach itself predominantly to her. Other women surrounding Jesus, Mary Magdalen, for instance, and Mary of Bethany, are viewed as possessing even stronger profiles and more independent features than she. They may become the impulse, according to some authors, for superseding the traditional image of woman. It is even suggested that the historical facts be dispensed with entirely and that "Maria" should be understood as a collective name for all outstanding biblical women. Thus the path to making Mary a merely outward symbol finally leads to her being only a myth.[40]

There exists, however, still another current in feminism. It consists not in an undervaluation but in an overvaluation of the Mother of Jesus. With Catharina Halkes, for example, there appears a divinization of the figure of Mary, which becomes the subject of adoration, or "feminine-mystical self-immersion". According to Leonardo Boff, "The feminine is to be divinized in Mary, just as the masculine is divinized in Jesus".[41] In her, he says, the Third Person of the Trinity has become "pneumatized", as, in a similar way, the Second Person became incarnate in Christ.[42] Mary was seized by the Holy Spirit so that the maternal face of God might become visible.[43]

Accordingly, for Christa Mulack, the Virgin-Mother with the Son on her knees, represents the most sacred expression of the polar unity of the feminine and the masculine, the highest form of love. Christa Mulack continues: "The fact that the masculine is here always pictured smaller than the feminine, expresses the fact that love can be expressed only

---

[39] Cf. Horst Goldstein, "Anwältin der Befreiung. Mariologische Neuansätze in Lateinamerika" [Woman-advocate of liberation: Mariological points of departure in Latin America], in *Diakonia* (Nov. 1981), p. 398.

[40] Cf. Leo Scheffczyk, "Maria—die neue Frau und vollkommene Christin" [Mary —the new woman and perfect Christian], in *Christliche Innerlichkeit* [Christian Interiority], 18, no. 5 (Mariazell, Sept.–Oct. 1987), p. 218.

[41] Cf. Leonardo Boff, *Ave Maria. Das Weibliche und der Heilige Geist,* p. 94.

[42] Ibid., 94.

[43] Cf. ibid., p. 99.

where the feminine elements are dominant, where the feminine retains its independence and thus can enfold freely, dispensing its love."[44]

These characteristic religious views held by feminism may suffice. What we see here is a pathological fantasy rather than a sane doctrine. It has little in common with genuine Christianity.

THE GOD-IMAGE IN REVELATION

In the presence of fabricated God-images, one must quite simply be reminded of the First Commandment, which constitutes not a limitation of our freedom but a clear expression of our natural finiteness. We may not conceive of God as we see fit. His being surpasses all human imagination. Attempts to conceive of God from our own point of view are necessarily quite inadequate. If we wish to come to know something about him, we do well to listen to revelation, which is contained in Holy Scripture and Tradition and has been entrusted to the Magisterium of the Church in order to be authentically interpreted.[45] Revelation presents an inexhaustible source which brings us closer to truth than any of our own efforts.

The immediate subject of revelation are the divine names. Through them the ineffable God reveals himself. These names stand for God himself. It is true that led by the light of faith, we may seek a deeper understanding of these names; they may not, however, be changed. Friedebert Hohmeier has some pertinent remarks on the subject: "If our human name is an expression of a unique person . . . what right have we to permit ourselves the change of names regarding the Most High God? Do we believe that God's being may be comprehended better by these names, than by the name in which he has revealed himself?"[46]

---

[44] Mulack, *Maria und die Weiblichkeit Gottes*, p. 162.

[45] Cf. Conc. Vat I, const. dogm. *Dei Filius de fide catholica*, c. 2 DS 1787 f. conc. Vat II const. dogm. *"Dei verbum,* cc 2–3.

[46] Friedebert Hohmeier, "Der Theologische Feminismus im Spiegel seines Bibel-gebrauchs" [Theological feminism as reflected in the use of the Bible], in Peter Beyerhaus, ed., *Frauen im theologischen Aufstand,* p. 103.

In his salvific decree, God was pleased to reveal himself by masculine names. They stand in contrast to the feminine God-images of pagan nature-religions, against which the chosen people had to prevail in battle. If feminism wishes to re-introduce the veneration of female goddesses, the result will be a relapse into pagan nature worship.

We invoke God as our Father because he is the father of Christ.[47] Repeated attempts to explain the Divine names from a trinitarian viewpoint have shown that God the Father, who begets the Son eternally, can by no means be addressed with equal right as "eternal Mother".[48] In the end we must, of course, confess that we are incapable of explaining any of God's names.

God stands beyond the sexes. In his essence he is completely simple, in the Trinity of Persons neither masculine nor feminine.[49] This is equally true of the Holy Spirit—who, incidentally, is spoken of in the New Testament grammatically as masculine and neuter—who cannot be grasped by these creaturely categories.

On the other hand, all perfections of creatures, be they paternity or maternity, are caused by and contained in God. Holy Scripture exhibits in fact maternal features of God as well, as he comforts his child,[50] which he never forgets,[51] which he lovingly lifts to his cheeks,[52] and, who, at the end of history, finally wipes away all tears.[53] Clement of Alexandria declares: "God is love . . . and the inexpressible in him is Father, the Compassionate, Mother."[54]

In a certain sense one may say that within God there is contained "masculinity" as well as "femininity", but not in a humanization according to a pagan manner, but in an analogous, archetypal-ideal, exemplary and eminent way.

---

[47] Cf. Mt 11:25–27.

[48] Cf. Hans Urs von Balthasar, "Die Würde der Frau", in International Catholic Journal "Communio", p. 351.

[49] Cf. Claudia Lavaud, *Personsein oberhalf von Geschlecht,* ibid., pp. 339–45.

[50] Cf. Is 66:13.

[51] Cf. Is 49:15.

[52] Cf. Hos 11:4.

[53] Cf. Rev 21:4.

[54] Clement of Alexandria, *Quis dives salvetur?,* 37, 2f.; PG 9, 642f.

God releases, as it were, the original possibilities of the masculine and feminine. He creates man and woman in his likeness.[55] "The" man, therefore, does not really exist, instead there exists man and woman, both possessing the same ground of being.[56] Both are in possession of a final immediacy in relation to God, an inviolable freedom and superior dignity.

Christian anthropology had always defended equality of dignity and worth without, however, paying homage to the feminist ideal of egalitarianism. Men and women, in their essence, are equal in worth, but this essence manifests itself in different manners.

Woman is a person in the specific manner of being woman. She is no less of a person than man, but she is that in *her* manner. For her, sexuality is not merely a condition which she might possibly lack. It is rather a reality which fundamentally contains her essence and determines her conduct; she cannot dispose of it arbitrarily. It is God himself who determines in his creative act what indeed feminine vocation is, not the woman's own willfulness.

It is of the essence of woman, once her equality is granted, to have a creatively different mission and task than man. As a result she is, in a manner of speaking, turned toward man, a fact which is expressed in marriage and family life.[57] Just as a hierarchic order is present as a fundamental principle in the universe, so also in the relation of the sexes to each other. Viewed from a temporal perspective, the division of labor between man and woman may make the works of woman appear "subordinated". This "subordination", however, is in no way to be understood as absolute. For woman is not created toward man but toward God. Nevertheless, it is the man's obligation to hold a certain precedence within the marriage community. This position of his is a provisional one and will pass away. At the end of time there will reign a

---

[55] Cf. Gen 1:27.

[56] Cf. Joseph Cardinal Hoffman, "Von der Würde und dem Dienst der Frau, Zeitfragen Heft" [About the dignity and the service of woman, problems of our time], Pamphlet II, Press office of the Archdiocese of Cologne (1982), p. 4.

[57] Cf. I Cor 11:3; Col 3:18.

hierarchy determined, not by sex (nor by any other creaturely categories), but by the holiness of each individual alone.

The relation between man and woman had originally been one of harmony. They pointed to the voluntary "self-renunciation"[58] of the Son of God, who subordinated himself as man to the Father, although he is one with him in essence. It was through the Fall that man separated himself from God and rebelled against his creation. This necessarily caused a disorder in the relationship of the sexes to each other. The consequences are visible in many cultures and civilizations: men debase women and deprive them of their rights, and they in turn resist the tutelage of men.[59]

Even within the thought-forms of late Judaism woman is by no means apprehended as equal to man. Werner Neuer observes that "in religious, juridical, and moral respects, woman was not as highly regarded as man, which in its turn led to religious and social oppression."[60]

The position of woman was radically altered with the advent of Jesus. Jesus reconciled men with God and with each other anew. He demon-

---

[58] Phil 2:7.

[59] Edith Stein explains that the vocation of man and woman is not precisely the same according to the primeval order, the order of fallen nature and the order of redemption: "Originally both were entrusted with resemblances or likeness to God, the rule over the earth and reproduction of mankind. A sovereignty of man, which appears to be expressed by his earlier creation, is not yet elucidated. As a result of the Fall, their relationship to each other changed from one of pure love to one of lordship and subordination which now was defaced by concupiscence. Redemption is to restore the original order. The precedence of man is revealed by the fact that the Redeemer was born a man. Redemption is to restore the original order. The female sex is enabled by the birth of the Redeemer from a human mother", *Frauenbildung und Frauenberufe* [Women's education and profession] (March 2, 1951), p. 152f.

[60] Werner Neuer, *Mann und Frau in christlicher Sicht* [Man and woman from a Christian vision] (Giessen, 1981), p. 85. Informative in this respect are also the points Georg Siegmunds makes in reference to the situation of women in Israel: "In the home woman's place is not next to the man, but next to the children and slaves. A prayer has been handed down to us repeatedly, in which the Jew should ask daily: 'Praised be God, who has not created me a hero! Praised be God, who has not created me a woman!' Thus the study of the Torah was the privilege of men . . . , Rabbi Eliezer, a contemporary of John the Apostle, even observed: 'It would be better if the Torah were burned than if it were entrusted to woman' ", *Die Stellung der Frau in der Welt von Heute* [The status of woman today] (Stein on the Rhine, 1981), p. 54.

strated in his dealings with women great freedom as against the prejudices and conventions of a male-dominated society. His acceptance of
woman as a person of equal value differed radically from that of his
milieu. Women were his faithful companions from the beginning until
the end at the Cross; and it was the women, whose courage surpassed
that of the disciples, who were permitted to be the first witnesses of the
Resurrection.[61]

Despite this fact, Jesus, in appointing the Twelve, whom he made the
foundation of his Church,[62] did not commission a woman, but only
men. These again transferred the care and guidance of the early Christian
communities to other men.[63] Thus the order of creation was being
realized: just as man presides over the family, so a number of men, called
by God, preside over the great family of the Church. The acceptance of
their decisions must nevertheless take place in freedom and not by
coercion; in full consciousness of their equal worth. In that sense St. Paul
remarks: "There is neither Jew nor Greek, there is neither slave nor
freeman; there is neither male nor female; For you are all one in Christ
Jesus."[64]

THE "NEW" WOMAN

Voluntary submission to the will of God is the secret that leads to the
restoration of the disturbed order. A creature who was fully aware of this
and whom God called into salvation history in a unique way, was Mary.
She made a complete and perfect surrender to the Lord, which was never

[61] Cf. Mt 28:9–10. Alicia Craig Faxon has this to say: "Birth came to be through
a woman; rebirth was proclaimed by a woman. Thus Jesus made women responsible for
bearing witness to him, recognizing that he had loved them, trusted them, and that he
considered them full citizens in the new Kingdom of the Risen Lord", *Frauen im Neuen
Testament. Vom Umgang mit Frauen* [Women in the New Testament: about the conduct
with women] (Munich, 1979), p. 85f.

[62] Cf. Eph 2:20.

[63] Cf. Acts 6:3; 14:23; Tit 1:5f.; 1 Tim 4:14. Cf. also, Communications of the
Apostolic See, no. 3; Declarations of the Congregation of the Doctrine of the Faith,
"Concerning the Admission of Women to the Priesthood", Oct. 15, 1976.

[64] Gal 3:28.

diminished by any aberration or faithlessness. The litany of Loreto calls her *"virgo fidelis"*.

The perpetual virginity of Mary signifies her bridal state as well as the overshadowing by the Holy Spirit. The Third Person of the Blessed Trinity did not, as Boff believes, become "incarnate" within her,[65] but works in her through extraordinary graces. The proof of this is her holiness, which according to Suarez is greater than that of all the angels and saints,[66] and also her virginal integrity. Mary is entirely claimed by God for the purpose of our redemption and she responds without reservation. Her physical virginity is both expression and sign of a profound inward state. The Church Fathers are indeed right when they say that Mary first conceived in her spirit and only then in her body. Her entire soul and spiritual strength is commended to God. There is no doublemindedness: her surrender is complete.

By this obedience Mary conquered the pride of Eve. Hence she is also called the "new" woman.

Scheffczyk explains that the "new" in biblical-Christian thought designates that which has never been, the unique, definitive. The "newness" of Mary does not signify that her image should be redesigned from a modern point of view. She is not to be grasped within a socio-political context. "Newness" in the framework of salvation history is rather "that which remains *forever* new in the midst of the worn and old. Thus its fullness can never be exhausted. It is the presence of the definitive and supra-temporal, which therefore may not be claimed by any one age."[67] It is that which remains, from which all generations can draw.

Mary is the "new" woman, the perfected human being. In her is recognizable what being Christian really means: not an ideological or spiritual stance in the manner of other religions, but communion with Christ, taking hold of us and transforming the whole of physical and spiritual life. Being Christian is a continuation of God's incarnation within the Church and its members, as it was first realized in Mary.

The reality which Mary personifies is much too revolutionary and

[65] Cf. Leonardo Boff, *Ave Maria*, p. 81.

[66] Cf. F. Suarez, "De mysteriis vitae Christi", Disp. 18, sec. 4, no. 14, in *Opera Omnie*, ed. L. Vivès, Paris 1856–61, Tom. 19.

[67] Scheffczyk, "Maria—die neue Frau und vollkommene Christin", p. 213.

radical to be limited to a political concept. The revolutionizing of what is human, which took place within her with full consent, must, however, grow from the roots. She brings liberation from sin, change of heart and transformation of the innermost human core. Such a process cannot come about by a merely external revolution.[68]

Mary completely accepts God's plans and makes them her own. Her attitude is sometimes disdainfully described as "passive". One should always remember that such virtues as surrender, humility, obedience, and the ability to serve and sacrifice presuppose a high degree of spiritual activity, enabling one to ignore one's own selfish demands. Mary is never servile but free and responsible.

In the light of faith, passivity is not always a merely negative trait, as it was, for instance, in ancient philosophy. In a sense it is a condition for Christian life as such. Only those who abandon themselves to God can be filled with his grace. This is the only way to the highest self-realization: the "handmaid of the Lord" is also the "Queen of Heaven".

Mary is therefore the archetype of what it means to be Christian, Virgin of virgins and Queen of Heaven. Above all, however, she is Mother. In her motherhood the dignity of woman is revealed. More than any feminism, it endows woman with worth and recognition.

It was in her capacity as woman that Mary cooperated with our redemption. As woman she was the first to receive it, to preserve it, and to become the mediator of grace. Within her feminine nature, surrender to God and to humanity was internalized. She went the way of silence, selflessness, and service. As helper in need, as refuge of the afflicted, and as heavenly advocate, she points toward the mercy of God. Her femininity affords a sublime supplement to man's task in salvation.

Mary is Mother, not priest. Her specific tasks are situated in the realm of maternal care and love, not in that of hierarchy. She never stood in front of or beside her Son, always behind him. Even after his death, she stood not before or next to the apostles but behind them. For the mother never fulfills herself in the mother, but in the child.

Here Mary's mission within the Church touches the deepest vein: for

[68] Cf. ibid., p. 221ff.

the Church too, regarded as mother, is a cooperating principle. The one who works in her is Christ.

MARY AS MODEL FOR CONTEMPORARY WOMAN

Mary symbolizes humanity in the Church, as it receives its salvation. Her trusting acceptance becomes the model and example for every Christian, also for men. Women, however, may learn from her attitudes in a special way.

The fulfillment of feminine existence lies not in an exact copy of the masculine. All attempts to measure woman with the measurements of man, distort her image more than they show its true worth. They misunderstand the special mission and endowments of woman. She can achieve fulfillment, not by convulsively breaking all ties, but by accepting completely the creative order from which her nature unfolds. Here Mary points the way.

It is precisely the maternal essence of Mary which is felt as immensely beneficial by an age which is permeated by selfishness and vainglory. Gertrud von Le Fort observed some years ago, "Nothing is as portentous and tragic in the contemporary condition than this absence of a maternal sensibility."[69]

In order to imitate Mary one must renounce all forms of ambition and self-dramatization. Self-realization comes from forgetting oneself and turning to others so that one may become their refuge by exercising patience, goodness, and forbearance. Characteristic of the maternal woman is the ability to wait and to be silent. In that manner she becomes the complementary part of man. Now and then she may have the privilege to overlook an injustice or a weakness in order to soothe and calm. According to Gertrud von Le Fort, one of the most disastrous errors of the modern world is its contentiousness, its mission, as it believes, to uncover every injustice and pass judgment on it.[70] The maternal woman understands how to alleviate the difficulties of life by her attentiveness

[69] Gertrud von Le Fort, *Die ewige Frau* [The eternal woman] (Munich, 1950), p. 128.

[70] Cf. ibid., p. 118.

and understanding. She is the great conqueror of everyday life. Every day she conquers by making it bearable. Her greatest moment of conquest arrives when it is barely noticed.

Genuine encouragement of woman and her worth demands that her maternal and familial role is clearly recognized. Her deepest and most authentic achievement remains the family. The question is not one of "emancipating" husband and wife, parents and children from each other. The reverse rather is true. The couple must become aware of the enormous dignity of their relationship, which reflects the union of Christ with the Church.[71] The Church and woman have corresponding roles to fulfill, by willingly yielding to Christ the Head, or, respectively, to the husband.[72] Man and woman find fulfillment in their union if both submit to each other unreservedly. As a result they complete each other positively according to their mutual characteristics.

Christian mothers strive to make their families the place of encounter with God. Due to their selfless and hidden work, they have always borne witness to the universal priesthood by making their families those "small churches" of which the teaching authority of the Church speaks today.[73]

This does not imply that the place of woman is restricted to a narrow milieu. Although we respect the dignity of work within the home, we must not overlook the fact that intellectual capacities and talents—intuition and interpersonal relations on one side, objective and abstract thought on the other—are not the exclusive property of one sex or the other. They are rather to be joined within a common pool, with each sex following its mental inclinations. Fundamentally, both sexes are capable of any mental work. By equally sharing the burden of responsibility, woman's access to public life is fully assured. What is expected of man is a genuine recognition of her abilities. They do not diminish his own but enhance the worth of being human.

The unmarried woman also achieves self-realization in a marian way, for Mary is both virgin and mother. Although virginity is not a necessary condition of the unmarried, it nevertheless appears to be its natural

---

[71] Cf. Eph 5:22ff.

[72] Cf. Eph 5:33.

[73] Cf. Pope John Paul II, Apostolic Letter *Familiaris consortio*, Nov. 22, 1981, no. 49.

expression. Today this argument is avoided because one forgets that virginity is not only a condition but an independent value. It is a value religious in character if chosen in full awareness, from love of God and for the sake of the Kingdom of Heaven.[74]

While marriage is a sign of God's love for man, the woman as virgin testifies to this love. The *mysterium caritatis,* intimated in marriage, touches her directly and allows her to find fulfillment on a level higher than that of nature. The woman as virgin lives in a direct I–Thou relationship with Christ, exclusively surrendered to Him.

The teaching authority of the Church has repeatedly pointed out that freely chosen virginity "for the sake of the Kingdom of Heaven" surpasses even the dignity of motherhood.[75] For the worth of a love or enthusiasm depends on *whom* we love and *about whom* we are enthusiastic. In the case of Christian virginity God himself is the immediate goal of our aspirations.

Nobody can *earn* this vocation to unrestricted surrender; God alone can grant it. Nevertheless, every Christian woman—as well as every Christian man—should be ready to accept such a gift. And if one really perceives a special call, one should have the boldness to abandon one's secure place and, like Mary, leave oneself to the designs of divine providence.

The woman as virgin signifies the religious emphasis and affirmation of her value as a person in its final immediacy to God. It is understandable that the liturgy places her next to the martyrs, for they too affirm the absolute value of the soul by sacrificing their earthly life.

In the degree, however, in which a woman gives of herself in the worship of God, her personality is enriched and enlarged. In contrast, she who only cares about herself and her importance, becomes poorer, narrower, and increasingly desolate. It is not surprising, therefore, that we observe today an alarming number of depressions and breakdowns in women whose sense of identity is insecure. One forgets that the only way to transcend one's own narrowness lies in the confrontation with the personal God.

[74] Mt 19:12.
[75] Cf. Conc. Trid. *De Sacramento Matrimonii,* Ses. XXIV (11.11 1563), Can. 10, DS 980; Pope Pius XII, Enc. *Sacra Virginites,* 1954; Pope John Paul II, *Familiaris consortio . . . ,* no. 16.

Unfortunately, the feminist theofantasy attains neither the poetic heights nor the speculative depth of the great teachers of the Church who talk to us about the love of God. I am thinking here of Hildegard of Bingen, Mechtild of Magdeburg, Bridget of Sweden, Catherine of Siena, Teresa of Avila, and Edith Stein. Men, too, can learn a great deal about the love of God and of his Church from such women. By women like these, men are sustained and confirmed in their service to the Church.

It is of course not an easy task to be radically in earnest about the Christian vocation in all its consequences. It demands a total dedication to love truly. Mary's consent at the annunciation was a consent to Golgotha. The consent to marriage or to virginity must approach the attitude of the virginal mother of God. Only then can woman be man's strength in building a new creation.

16

HELMUT MOLL

"FEMINIST THEOLOGY"—A CHALLENGE

Translated by Sigrid Nowicki

For some time now, in the United States and Canada, a new movement has been gaining ground, a movement with divers strategies which can be combined under the collective heading of the so-called "feminist theology". Based in North America, its off-shoots have been growing up in Europe for some years now although with a difference in scope and influence. In the Catholic domain, it is especially Catharina J. M. Halkes who approvingly introduces this new movement to the public in her 128-page book entitled *God Does Not Only Have Strong Sons. Outline of a Feminist Theology*.[1] This book then primarily provides the basis for the following report on the current trend of the "feminist theology"; in addition, a booklet by C. J. M. Halkes and D. Buddingh *When Women Speak: The Voices of Feminist Theology*[2] and an article written by C. J. M. Halkes entitled "Feminist Theology, A Provisional Balance Sheet"[3] were also consulted. This report, however, does not stop with a description of the phenomena outlined there but combines them with a critical analysis as well as with questions from the realm of theological thought.

[1] *Gütersloher Diary,* Siebenstern, p 371, (Gütersloh, 1980); 1982.

[2] *Gelnhausen* (Berlin: Stein, 1979); (abbrev. *Women*).

[3] *Concilium* 16 (1980) pp 293–300; (abbrev. *Theology*). Cf: also *Feminist Theology-Praxis*. A workshop book publ. by S. Kahl, H. Langer, H. Leistner, and E. Moltmann-Wendel = *Work Aid* 3, (Bad Boll, 1981).

1. BIOGRAPHICAL INFORMATION

The author was born in the year 1920, belongs to the Roman Catholic Church (9, 13) and studied at the universities of Leiden, Utrecht, and Nijmegen, specializing in philosophy, literature, and theology. She is the mother of three children, to whom her booklet is dedicated (5). For approximately twenty years she occupied herself with the emancipation of the laity in the Church until the "breakthrough to feminism in the seventies" (10). In this respect she feels especially indebted "to the American feminists and above all to the following theologians: Rosemary Radford Ruether, Mary Daly, Letty Russell, Nelle Morton, Elisabeth Schuessler-Fiorenza, Nadine Foley, and many, many more" (11). She includes R. R. Ruether who became known through her work *New Women, New Earth: Sexist Ideologies and Human Liberation* (New York, 1975) as well as L. M. Russell with the publication *Human Liberation in a Feminist Perspective: A Theology* (Philadelphia, 1974) among the moderates, "who wish to remain in the Judeo-Christian tradition" (34); M. Daly, on the other hand, belongs to the radical group which does not seek answers from the prevailing theology and philosophy but rather from myths, symbols, and images" (35). It is significant that her major work *Beyond God the Father* (Boston, 1973) was published with a " 'post-christian' preface in a new edition" (35). Halkes is linked in friendship with Elisabeth Moltmann-Wendel who "performed pioneer work in Germany" (15). Her book outlining her program entitled *Women's Liberation Biblical and Theological Arguments,* (Munich and Mainz, 1978) has lately been succeeded by another one, entitled *Becoming Your Own Person: Women Associated with Jesus* (Gütersloh, 1982).

Since 1977 Halkes has been at the theological faculty of the University of Nijmegen and occupies herself with the question of women's liberation; she is listed as a "doctoral candidate" (*Theology,* 300) and according to the book cover is "Assistant Professor for Feminism and Christianity at the Theological Faculty at Nijmegen".

2. BASIC ASPIRATION OF FEMINISM AND FEMINIST THEOLOGY

Whoever introduces an unknown concept into theology must first explain what he means and how that concept is to be understood. Being fully aware of the fact that a complete outline of the phenomenon is impossible (32, 36), Halkes develops a paraphrase which turns into a protest: "She revolts against a theology based on a natural law which fixes the roles of man and woman according to the laws of creation and against a culture which forcefully perpetuates these fixed patterns" (*Theology*, 293). It is here a question of "culture review and counter culture" (*Theology*, 300, n. 21) for it is a matter of "reaction" and of "protest against an androcentric and therefore unilateral theology of several centuries' duration" (*Theology*, 293). "It is one of the characteristics of feminist theology that it is an iconoclastic theology which wishes to create space so that we can be uninhibited in discovering new images and symbols; symbols which reprove, surprise, summon" (*Women*, 16f.). As the most appropriate paraphrase describing feminist theology Halkes picks out the one "according to which it should be understood as a liberation theology which, as such, is not based on the distinguishing characteristics of women but rather on their experience in suffering, in physical and sexual oppression, in being treated like children, and in structural invisibility because of sexism in Church and society" (*Theology*, 294).

When it is a question of liberating women from existing restraint, the "anthropological, psychological sin" (*Theology*, 297) of the so-called sexism has to be overcome first. This, however, means

> that we repent of a masculine dualism which not only turns women into "the others" but which degrades them by projecting on them all those traits which men don't dare to cultivate in themselves. . . . In this degradation and . . . the definition of the female sex in terms of the masculine norm is contained a subservience, an objectivism (. . .) which stands in the way of a true mutual relationship" (*Theology*, 297f., cf. 13, 76).

When asked from which intellectual-historical source this women's liberation movement receives its nourishment, they answer without hesitation, socialism and Marxism; because it is a fact that each needs the other, "feminism (as a counter movement against patriarchy) and socialism (as a counter movement against capitalism), if we are ever going to achieve a new human freedom" (*Theology*, 295). Both currents depend on each other and supplement each other because "reality and history teach us that feminism needs socialism, but that socialism does not have any less need of feminism" (117). Halkes goes one step further when she transcends socialism and, influenced by Herbert Marcus' book *Chronological Dimensions*, describes feminism and Marxism as analogous and having a mutual impetus (29f). This being so, then feminism "can contribute to a new realistic doctrine and in this way the women's liberation movement can assume the revolutionary function of the feminine in the formation of a new society" (29).

This new society which is supposed to be created and which is even given the exalted name of a "New Birth" (39), is supposed to eradicate the old image of the woman lock, stock, and barrel and supplant it with a new image which might be as follows: "This is the way I see the profound significance of the women's liberation movement (says Halkes), it is feminism in the best sense of the word, the desire and consciousness of women who finally become the subject of their lives. Not in hate against men, not that we alone should have power, but rather with the object of sharing power and opportunities" (117).

As a possible audience yes, even more as possible followers of this new movement, Halkes focuses on "women who have been extremely disappointed and frustrated and who have already left the churches in great numbers." To allow these women to "hear and see signals and signs" (13) is her noblest task, especially since the matter formulated here vastly transcends any one church since the feminist movement as a matter of course "from its very beginning has always been ecumenical and remains so" (14).

3. THE IMAGE OF GOD

If you interiorly affirm the basic goals as presented by feminist theology, and especially if you emphasize the attributes of liberation, you will also be able to see even in God "a source of unrest and creative chaos", a challenge "to reconstruction of what exists" (*Theology*, 296). Such a serious transposition of the image of God can be explained by the fact that feminist theology tries its hardest to look at Holy Scripture without prejudice and without seeing the dichotomous polarity of man and woman. "The masculine, patriarchal image of God bodes evil for women" (87). For that reason, they protest against such a God, yes, they rise up against him, because he is the "unchanging, exclusively transcendent God", "who is all knowing and all powerful, the total other" (*Theology*, 296). Halkes attempts to construct a contrast between this image and "God as the creative dialogue of love" (*Theology*, 296), although these two descriptions actually don't contradict each other. Behind the adjectives "all powerful", "all knowing", "present everywhere", she senses danger especially for black people because these adjectives have been used "by the oppressor up until the present time in order to keep the blacks down" (87).

In view of the manifestation of Yahweh in the thorn bush (Ex 3) she prefers to describe God as a reality which expresses "liberation, justice and totality of life" (87).

Since the male image of God is overwhelming, especially in the Old Testament, Halkes deliberately attempts to work out some female characteristics in order to break the superior power of the masculine (69; cf. *Theology*, 296). Even if this way can be justified and makes sense, there is still the danger that it conveys competition between the male and the female, which, as we have been told, is exactly what was supposed to have been eradicated and overcome.

4. CHRISTOLOGY

According to the basic beliefs of feminist theology, Jesus Christ is classified as a figure whom Holy Scripture describes as appearing on the scene as a "destroyer of prototypes, who breaks taboos, and who adheres to his tradition as long as it proves to be beneficial but who declares it irrelevant when it robs people of their freedom" (*Women*, 27). That is especially true in his unaffected social contacts with Jewish and Samarian women, indeed, with all who live at the margin of human existence, Jesus of Nazareth demonstrates clearly that his loving attention for all people knows no bounds.

In view of the declared position of K. Rahner according to which the masculinity of Jesus in the revelation of God should not be concealed (41), Halkes frankly admits to this point of view also, is even willing to declare as "important" the "significance of the masculinity of Jesus for the economy of salvation for women . . . and for the whole history of the Church as such" (40). This statement having been accepted and affirmed, Halkes again colors the image of Jesus considerably to make it correspond to her ideas by introducing the Son of God made Man as an exemplary hermaphrodite: "In Jesus of Nazareth, God's wholeness approaches us in an androgenous humanity, which does not want to hide Jesus' masculinity but makes visible the thrilling harmony of both coexisting components" (87). This view of Halkes finds confirmation in a book written by the former pastor Hanna Wolff, entitled *Jesus the Man,* which claims that "Jesus of Nazareth was an integral, androgenous person" (40).

Feminist theology resolutely opposes "the Church's teaching that God's revelation became final with the life, death, and resurrection of Jesus Christ and thereby ended once and for all" (*Theology,* 297). "It is because we humans have an incomplete and cloudy understanding of the Bible that I live in the experience of an ongoing development of revelation which necessitates the interaction of God and men if it is to be unlocked" (60). Halkes who shares that opinion works also for a new exegesis as well as for an increased exchange of experiences with respect to insight into biblical revelation in general. Should she, however, upon deeper penetration into the message of salvation as contained in revelation, be of the opinion that revelation as such did not come to an end with the work of Jesus and the death of the last apostle, she would then deny the unique and unsurpassable mediator Jesus Christ. This would be tantamount to promoting a relativism of the Christian message and would in fact considerably diminish the image of Christ.

5. PNEUMATOLOGY

The reason that the teaching about the person of Jesus Christ is being proclaimed in such a limited and contrived version, has its origin in a teaching method which revises the interpretation of the person of the Holy Spirit. According to Halkes, feminist theology is "above all a pneumatologic theology . . . , which tries to make visible the movement of God's action and spirit" (*Theology*, 297). She is correct in warning of an evident lack of appreciation for the revealed teaching on the Holy Spirit, a lack which now will have to be vigorously amended and rectified. Her reminder that the Holy Spirit is embedded in the entire teaching about the Triune God also has some merit.

This declared preference for the proclamation of the Holy Spirit again is not without a feminist weakness: "We know that formerly, in semitic languages, the word 'spirit' was described by a word of the feminine gender, *Ruach*" (*Theology*, 297); according to the prophecy of Joel about the end of time, sons and daughters will speak wisdom; indeed they will even be called prophets (cf. Acts 2:17–21). Not without some pride, Halkes reports on the participation of women who were present at Pentecost: "Pentecost is the feast day of God's community reaching its age of majority: the Holy Spirit descends upon the apostles, upon Mary, upon the other women present in the upper room. The Spirit breathes new life into them, the potential of the Kingdom of God is waiting to be turned into reality" (87).

6. FEMINISM AND HOLY SCRIPTURE

The manner in which feminist theology explains and understands God the Father, God the Son, and God the Holy Spirit, must unavoidably lead to the question of what meaning Holy Scripture actually holds for it and which exegetical criteria and methods are used in interpretation.

"For 'rebellious' women, the Bible becomes a very difficult book. All the books of Holy Scripture bear the traces of the patriarchal culture in which they were created" (54). Moreover, "these two main trends: the patriarchal culture and the fight for monotheism, turn the Bible into a nasty book for women who have finally come to the realization that they as subjects have hardly made an appearance either in the history of salvation or in the history of the Church" (55). Since in "this masculine book" (61) the images of God are masculine and are imprinted by a masculine culture, there remains little room for the development of women; but Halkes knows that God surmounts everything because he is spirit and therefore cannot adequately be expressed in images (61). The fight for monotheism which feminists mention and to which they object, they explain by the fact that all female images of God have been removed and eradicated by the old nation of Israel, much to the sorrow of women.

Holy Scripture, therefore, has become a battleground for feuding parties fighting for power which they must acquire for themselves. However in looking at revelation only through feminist glasses, she not only obstructs access to it, but will never penetrate into the heart of the message of salvation but rather remain at the level of mere words describing environment, exterior presentation, and historically conditioned expressions.

This troubled relationship of feminists with Holy Scripture, therefore, cannot remain without consequences. Some groups of women act in such a way that they "let the Bible remain what it is: a patriarchal book where women who read it, find themselves as in a foreign land" (59). Despite these serious reservations, however, Halkes does not want to belong to those who "because of 'this impossible Bible' (64) abandon it" (64) and turn their backs on Holy Scripture once and for all. She engages in self criticism when she continues: " . . . I appreciate the scepticism of those who warn us feminist theologians, especially the exegetes among us, of the danger of projecting our own concerns into our interpretations and of turning into a non-existing direction. Maybe twenty-five years or more from now we will come to realize that the Bible is indeed an androcentric book and that Jesus of Nazareth indeed freely interacted with women and his words transport us into a new dimension, but that nevertheless we will have little reason for joy" (64; cf. *Theology,* 298).

7. ECCLESIOLOGY

The platform of feminist theology also makes its appearance in ecclesiology because "they want an inclusive ecclesiastical community, a people of God on pilgrimage to the discovery of our common freedom and humanity" (86).

It logically follows that the place of the church of brotherhood must now be occupied by the church of sisterhood, this concept being introduced, however, as a challenging new vector:

> Sisterhood is church, in other words, "a place, a holy place" separate from and wrested from the sexist church, where women can become themselves and can fulfill themselves. She looks at sisterhood as a charismatic community in which women become whole and rise up prophetically against all dehumanizing structures. . . . Through all this, sisterhood acts as a critical tribunal against the institutional Church which is thereby reminded of its eschatological [end time] dimension (45).

They also declare war against that community structured according to the will of Jesus and the order of the early Church because this "voracious institution" (74) leaves no rightful place for women.

Looking at this divisive concept of the Church which is exclusive rather than inclusive, the word "Rome" becomes an irritant (67, 75, 76, 93). "Here it dawns on us that radical feminists hardly experience a desire to occupy themselves with the question of women in official positions. They would not even want to occupy those positions the way they are ecclesiastically structured at the present time. Church, for them, has become a different reality and they do not value a rigid ecclesiastical order" (45). In this statement Halkes manages to contradict herself because in other parts of her book, she takes a definite position in favor of a takeover of ecclesiastical positions; do these groups then represent moderate feminists who are rather inclined to "break into" the male-oriented church or are there so many and ideologically differing movements within the feminist theology that they ultimately do not even know themselves what they want? (cf. especially 45; 68, and 71f.).[4]

---

[4] Comp. here also H. Moll, " 'Faithful to Her Lord's Example': On the Meaning of the Male Priesthood in the Catholic Church", pp. 161–76, above.

Even the examination of Church history becomes an inquiry brushed against the grain and stereotyped in the familiar male-female pattern:

> A further study of the heretical movements and the apocryphal gospels (those not incorporated into the New Testament) presents us with the question: If the role and importance of women therein is greater and more vital than in the official Church and in the canonical writings, doesn't that present the reason or at least one reason why they have been rejected? (42).

At this point at last the insufficiency of a single cause explanation of all phenomena becomes evident.

8. MARIOLOGY

Pages 92 to 118 are of special interest since they deal with the expected position of the Mother of God in the economy of salvation as viewed through the eyes of feminist theology. The authoress evidently comes from a Catholic family of deep faith where the veneration of Mary was taken for granted. In this context she is conscious of the unique position of the Mother of God when she declares: "In Mary . . . the believing heart also experiences compassion: in all her vulnerability she is not an image of submissiveness but rather of receptive awareness of a salvation which is announced to her and which she by her attitude allows to become a reality" (94). He who lives in a Church closely linked to Mary, finds it painful, as is the case with Halkes, that the years after the Second Vatican Council have witnessed a lack of feeling for and the absence of Mary in the liturgy, in the petitions for intercession and in the scripture readings (95). Halkes is determined to change all that: "Mary has since then experienced a comeback thanks to my lectures on Christianity and feminism and a seminar at the theological faculty dealing with the personality of Mary!" (95). This renaissance of mariological thinking, however, follows the pattern of feminist logic: since it is evident that Mary was misused by the Church to keep women in their place (105), in other words, that Mary appears as the occasion for repression, the Mother of God can no longer serve as a role model for the woman of today and tomorrow; on the contrary: "Nobody will ever hear from me that Mary has any attraction as an ideal for feminism" (118). The old image of Mary is finished as far as Halkes is concerned, and the new image is beginning to assume aspects which need further study. As much as Halkes is fascinated by these different aspects in which Mary can be interpreted in a new and better way, she much rather wants to concentrate on the "expression of the prophetic life" (110).

Like the sons and daughters who according to the prophet Joel will become prophets in the end time, this especially becomes true for the Mother of God in her praise in the Magnificat in the presence of Elizabeth. However, this undergoes a fundamental change through the collection of different quotations. The verse "He has put down the mighty from their thrones and has exalted the humble. He has filled the hungry with good things; and the rich he has sent empty away" (Lk 1:52–53) is put into the center of the whole prayer so that it now becomes a "freedom song" (57) in conjunction with the liberation theology of Gutierrez, a theologian from Peru, a "battle hymn against the injustice of the world" (102).

> It is a song full of thanks and praise but at the same time a critical, prophetic song—a biblical protest song. Mary continues the sharp social criticism of the prophetic revelation and combines the political criticism with a messianic vision of social justice and a new sisterly and brotherly relationship between peoples. The Magnificat is a radical support for the poor, those deprived of their rights, the voiceless, the confined and oppressed (113).

This prophetic aspect, without a doubt, is to be looked at as an enrichment; however, it leads to one-sidedness if it is exaggerated and the essential truths of biblical and ecclesiastical proclamation are covered up.

9. THE SEARCH FOR THE NEW FEMALE IMAGE

The preceding section dealing with the attitude of feminist theology toward mariology made it clear how little the Mother of God is taken as a role model here since there exists a mutual incompatibility. That is to say, according to the words of the author, a dependency developed in the Church, "in which the woman has to be like Mary, but not like Eve and even less like a virago" (83). The distortions of reality begin to sound ominous as the rhetoric escalates. "Women are the negroes of Western culture" (81).

Thus shaking off the existing role model, one demands a new mental image to aim for that can better withstand criticism and is more worthy of the feminist ideal. At the present time, one can say this much:

> Feminists are those women who after their emancipation process have come to the conclusion that they have reached a decisive crossroads and, since their uncomfortable feeling about existing structures is still very much in evidence, are now making it their business to examine critically the previously-named rights and obligations, structures, values, and standards and to examine those with a view to their validity and humanity (19).

Over and above this presently existing condition, they strive after a "Liberation for Independence" (20), a view of a totality of things which has so far been obstructed by the male predominance (*Theology,* 295; *Questions,* 18), equality in view of their present powerlessness (84), and finally a "nuturing ground for the development of androgynous people" (85). They admit that they are only at the beginning of their quest for these goals (32).

All these futuristic perspectives plan to break the predominence of men but also culminate in the question of whether man and woman are to live opposed to each other or with each other; "I do not believe any more that man and woman complement each other and much less that woman is a useful and necessary complementary part of the man. Both sexes contain the capacity to be integrated and in this way to become independent, complete and androgynous (male-female), developing persons . . . every human being—man or woman—can develop without being dependent on the other sex for completion" (26). These explicit formulas cast a dubious light on marriage and family since here the deeper sense of a lasting and profound interrelation has been rejected emphatically. The newly designed human genus is self-sufficient, becomes "finally a subject" (117) of himself and is no longer in need of the other for his realization. Whoever lives as animus as well as self anima and translates it into reality, does not need a partner since the man-woman principle is now fulfilled.

10. AN EVALUATION

Whoever attempts to evaluate the different currents of feminist theology should suspend judgment for the time being, for this new movement is still in a state of development and at the present time presents anything but a uniform structure. Consequently, apodictic as well as conclusive evaluations are premature.

In the abundance of existing fundamental trends, the justified concern of feminist theology cannot be denied: under discussion here is a well-defined rejection of male-alienating influence which is being resisted, since up to this present time it has not yet been sufficiently overcome. To dismantle this influence step by step and to restore to woman the dignity to which she is entitled, according to the biblical revelation of redemption, is one of the noblest tasks of Christian anthropology. Catharina Halkes puts sufficient material at our disposal to show how this can be accomplished. The author honestly admits that the value of her studies is limited: "What I have to offer in this booklet is still not very impressive, not methodical, not the fruit of empirical inquiry, not thoroughly researched, not a brilliant and well rounded product, but rather the result of a laboriously struggling and questioning process" (12). She is conscious of bearing the responsibility "for all" deficiencies (15). She is not above self criticism and restraining or rejecting the voices from her own party. In the long run, she is concerned with giving this movement a "quality of 'being' and not only of 'having'.... We need a greater amount of tolerance for those who do not share our thinking if we want to develop this quality of being and to make ourselves free of any degree of dogmatism" (30f.). Indeed, she gets even more explicit when she warns women from her own ranks: "Whoever joins a struggle, even one for a good cause, runs the danger of becoming obsessed and blind to any positive developments that undoubtedly always exist" (50). Only the future will show what is to be, "since in the long run, just as with all critical theology, feminist theology will also have to be pronounced true or false" (*Theology*, 299).

The sources for this new variation of feminist theology come for the most part from outside the theological field; on one hand, they are derived from socialism and Marxism; on the other hand, they arise from the liberation pathos which has brought under its banner the radical emancipation of women. The theological forays are, to a great degree, often lacking in sustaining substance; much embarrassment is caused by its abbreviated form, much appears fragmentary and unbalanced, or some distorted and deficient. The valuable impressions are for the most part of an individual-subjective nature and therefore remain without a coherent general validity and objectivity in their demands. Furthermore, the individual viewpoint expressed has not really or not yet been discovered in each case. The state in which these struggling women find themselves is symptomatic of the lack of an intellectual position in this movement: "Women in a foreign land in search of a new self image" (64).

It is also regrettable that the author is unable to bridge the gap between feminism and Christianity in her book since she is of the opinion "that between those two, not even a confrontation is possible because they avoid each other, do not take each other seriously, have only preconceived notions and stereotypical conceptions of each other" (11). The attempted encounter to understand the other partner cannot take cover behind rejection and accusation if the dialogue is to succeed in solidifying and widening the horizon of understanding.

Therefore, one can only underline the statement according to which "feminist theology has the task of concentrating on theological reflection without losing sight of the larger context" (50). In other words, in the revelation of Holy Scripture are hidden all the treasures containing the reason for the existence of humanity, which while taking into account the earlier and the present cultural relationships, is then to be raised on high and illuminated. If this were to happen or at least if the attempt were made to let this happen, then many of those self-imposed chains, "which . . . were carried by hundreds of participants in their march through the city" (33) in order to symbolize a bondage, would fall off by themselves.

We therefore agree with the German theology professor Elisabeth

Gössmann, teaching in Tokyo, who sums it all up when she writes in her publication *"The Fighting Sisters. What Does Feminist Theology Hope to Accomplish?"* that the feminist theology—"despite the long-term, necessary criticism of society—is working toward the final end of making itself obsolete."[5]

[5] E. Gössmann, *The Fighting Sisters. What Does Feminist Theology Hope to Accomplish?*, Herder library 879 (Freiburg, Basel, and Vienna, 1981). Cf. also the chapter "Characteristics of Feminist Theology" by Manfred Hauke in *Women in the Priesthood? A Systematic Analysis in the Light of the Order of Creation and Redemption* (San Francisco: Ignatius Press, 1988), pp. 65–72, as well as the verdict of the Affirmation Movement "No Other Gospel" by Ingeborg Hauschildt, *Feminist Theology: A New Heresy* (Info. doc. no. 94, October 1982), pp. 5–13.

ACKNOWLEDGMENTS

Ignatius Press is grateful to these sources for permission to reprint articles in this Compendium.

Chapter 1: English edition originally published in the German edition of *Communio* (July 1982) and published in English in *Communio—International Catholic Review*, vol. X, no. 3 (1983), pp. 219–39.

Chapter 2: Originally published under the title "Gibt es einen objektiven Typus der Frau?" in *Jesus-Frau-Kirche* (Vallendar-Schönstatt: Patris Verlag, 1983), pp. 29–46.

Chapter 3: Originally published under the title "Die Stellung der Frau als Problem der theologischen Anthropologie: Lebendiges Zeugnis", vol. 2 (Paderborn: Bonifatius-Verlag, 1980), pp. 5–16.

Chapter 4: Originally published under the title "Erwagungen zur Stellung von Mariologie und Marienfrömmigkeit im Ganzen von Glaube und Theologie". Pastoral of the German Bishops, April 30, 1979.

Chapter 5: Originally published under the title "Maria als Exponent katholischen Glaubens" in *Katholische Glaubenswelt: Wahrheit und Gestalt,* 2nd edition (Aschaffenburg: Paul Pattloch Verlag, 1973), pp. 266–91.

Chapter 6: Originally published under the title "Würde und Aufgabe der Frau in Kirche und Gesellschaft", by Jutta Burggraf.

Chapter 7: Originally published under the title "Uberlegungen zum Weihediakonat der Frau" in *Theologie und Glaube,* vol. 77 (January 1987), (Paderborn: Verlag Ferdinand Schöningh), pp. 108–27.

Chapter 8: Originally published under the title "Zur Geschichte der Diakonissne: Ein bibliographischer Hinweis" in *Liturgisches Jahrbuch* vol. 34 (1984), (Munster: Verlag Aschendorff), 58–64.

Chapter 9: Originally published under the title "Welches Gewicht hat die ununterbrochene Tradition der Kirche bezuglich der Zuordnung des Priesterrung 'Inter insigniores' der Kongregation fur die Glaubenslehre mit Kommentar und theologischen Studien." Published in the German edition of *Osservatore Romano*, (Kevelaer: Verlag Butzon & Bercker, 1978), pp. 54–57.

Chapter 10: Originally published under the title "Aus Treue zum Vorbild ihres Herrn: vom Sinn des männlichen Priestertums in der katholischen Kirche: Pastoral blatt fur die Diözesen Aachen, Berlin, Essen, Köln, Osnabrück", vol. 35 (Köln: Verlag J. P. Bachem, 1983), pp. 6–14.

Chapter 12: Originally published under the title "Zum Thema: Priestertum der Frau" in *Vom Dienst der Frau in der Kirche: Aktuelle Fragen un biblisch-spirituelle Grundlegung"* (Vallendar-Schönstatt: Patris Verlag, 1980), 7–38.

Chapter 13: Originally given as a lecture to the Annual Conference of the Canon Law Society of Great Britain and Ireland on May 21, 1986, at Emmaus Retreat Centre, Swords, Ireland, and published in *L'Osservatore Romano*, English edition (March 7, 1988), p. 6.

Chapter 14: Originally published under the title "Uberlegungen im Anschluss and eine theologische Neuerscheinung uber das Frauenpriestertum: Pastoralblatt für die Diözesen Aachen, Berlin, Essen, Köln, Osnabruck) 35 (Köln: Verlag J. P. Bachem, 1983), pp. 93–95.

Chapter 15: Originally published under the title "Die Mutter der Kirche und die Frau in der Kirche: Korrektur der Irrwege feministischer Theologie: Arbeitstagung der Arbeitsgemeinschaft Marianischere Vereinigungen in Deutschland 9. bis 12. November 1985 im Johannes-Haw-Heim Leutesdorf am Rhein. Dokumentation. (Leutesdorf am Rhein: Arbetisgemeinschaft Marianischere Vereinigungen, 1986), pp. 57–72.

Chapter 16: Originally published under the title "Feministische Theologie: eine Herausforderung" in *Munichener Theologische Zeitschrift* vol. 34 (1983), (Aschaffenburg: Verlag Paul Pattlock), pp. 118–28.

ABBREVIATIONS

AAS	*Acta Apostolicae Sedis* (Acts of the Holy See)
DS	H. Denzinger and A. Schönmetzer. *Enchiridion symbolorum definitionum and declarationum de rebus fidei et morum.* Barcelona-Freiburg-Rome, 1979.
FAZ	*Frankfurter Allgemeine Zeitung*
HThK	*Herders Theologischer Kommentar zum Neuen Testament*
Ii	*Inter insigniores.* Sacred Congregation for the Doctrine of the Faith, 1977.
IKZ	*Internationale Katholische Zeitschrift "Communio"*
KNA	Katholische Nachrichten-Agentur: Ökumene
LThK	*Lexikon für Theologie und Kirche*
OrChrp	*Orientalia Christiana Periodica*
PG	J. G. Minge. *Patrologia Cursus Completus,* Series Graeca.
PL	J. G. Minge. *Patrologia Cursus Completus,* Series Latina.
RAC	*Reallexikon für Antike und Christentum*
RGG	*Religion in Geschichte und Gegenwart*
RQ	*Romische Quartalschrift für Christliche Altertums Kunde und für Kirchengeschichte*
RTL	*Revue Theologique de Louvain*
StL	*Studia Linguistica*